Scarecrow Film Score Guides
Series Editor: Kate Daubney

Alex North's
A Streetcar Named Desire

A Film Score Guide

Annette Davison

Scarecrow Film Score Guides, No. 8

The Scarecrow Press, Inc.
Lanham, Maryland • Toronto • Plymouth, UK
2009

SCARECROW PRESS, INC.

Published in the United States of America
by Scarecrow Press, Inc.
A wholly owned subsidary of
The Rowman & Littlefield Publishing Group, Inc.
4501 Forbes Boulevard, Suite 200, Lanham, Maryland 20706
www.scarecrowpress.com

Estover Road
Plymouth PL6 7PY
United Kingdom

British Library Cataloguing in Publication Information Available

Library of Congress Cataloging-in-Publication Data
Davison, Annette, 1971–
    Alex North's A streetcar named Desire : a film score guide / Annette Davison.
        p. cm. — (Scarecrow film score guides ; no. 8)
    Includes bibliographical references and index.
    ISBN-13: 978-0-8108-6393-4 (pbk. : alk. paper)
    ISBN-10: 0-8108-6393-6 (pbk. : alk. paper)
    1. North, Alex. Streetcar named Desire. I. Title.
    ML410.N6745D38 2009
    781.5'42–dc22   2008042911

For Colin and Georgia

CONTENTS

ILLUSTRATIONS

Examples

Tables

EDITOR'S FOREWORD

Since I established the concept of the film score guides in 1999 and wrote the first volume on Max Steiner's *Now, Voyager* score (in the series' initial incarnation with Greenwood Press), film musicology has continued to undergo rapid expansion and change. While ten years ago, the notion of score-focused scholarship seemed an obvious way to consolidate just one area in a rapidly diverging field, such is the diversity of film music composition practice now that the focus on the score as original text is at times anachronistic and outdated, as perhaps is the implication that techniques of film scoring are distinct from techniques used for composing soundscapes for other multimedia forms, such as computer games and other web-based creativity. The prevalence of the temp track, the influence of computer and electronic composition techniques, and the trend towards director's cuts in DVD release will all need to be reflected in the way this series evolves and the high level of analysis and reading its authors bring to bear on the music they reveal to us. These are the challenges for any academic discipline, to chart and understand the dynamic leading edge of a field while ensuring that its foundations have been soundly explored. Film musicology has, in most respects, managed to achieve this balance very well through the appearance of new journals, a significant increase in conference activity, and a broader recognition by mainstream musicology and film studies of areas of mutual interest. However, in one area the field still suffers as much as it did a decade ago, and that is in its relationship with the holders of copyright of film scores.

The idea of "fair use" in quotation from textual sources is commonplace and universally accepted in all other areas of academic research and publication, but scholars of film music continually find themselves obstructed by an archaic view that original manuscript film scores are somehow different from other textual sources. Despite the incredible expansion in interest in film music both inside and outside

academia in the last ten years and the concomitant increase in revenue
in DVD and soundtrack sales this must have generated, copyright holders still seem unprepared for applications for copyright permission;
they seem suspicious of authors' reasons for requesting such permission, with some charging outrageously high fees for small numbers of
quotations that do not represent in any accurate way a potential threat
to their revenue. The score extracts that are reproduced in these and
other scholarly contexts are so short and frequently analytically dis-
sected as to provide no useful resources for the unscrupulous and illegal
reproduction of sheet music. This renders the currently severe restric-
tions on reproduction of score extracts utterly out of proportion to the
threat. The time has therefore come for a consensus accord across the
industry to establish protocols for fair use and to make it easier for
scholars to access and reproduce extracts from original manuscript
scores and orchestral parts in legitimate academic publications. Such
consensus should also include publishers, with a common agreement
among them to apply and uphold the principles of fair use across all
areas of musical—and textual—quotation and protect authors who are
using those principles in a defensible and reasonable manner.

The Scarecrow series of Film Score Guides is dedicated to drawing
together the variety of analytical practices and ideological approaches
in film musicology for the purpose of studying individual scores. Much
value has been drawn from case studies of film scoring practice in other
film music texts, but these guides offer a substantial, wide-ranging, and
comprehensive study of a single score. Subjects are chosen for the series on the basis that they have become and are widely recognized as a
benchmark for the way in which film music is composed and experienced, or because they represent a significant stage in the compositional development of an individual film composer. A guide explores
the context of a score's composition through its place in the career of
the composer and its relationship to the techniques of the composer.
The context of the score in narrative and production terms is also considered, and readings of the film as a whole are discussed in order to
situate in their filmic context the musical analyses which conclude the
guide. Furthermore, although these guides focus on the score as written
text, bringing forward often previously unknown details about the
process of composition as they are manifested in the manuscript, analysis also includes exploration of the music as an aural text, for this is the
first and, for most audiences, the only way in which they will experience the music of the film.

Although the score for *A Streetcar Named Desire* is now almost sixty years old, the issues surrounding the producers' censorship of the original score in order to satisfy the Legion of Decency reflect some of the complexities which face film musicology at the present time. Scholar and audience are offered two filmic texts which are almost identical. The changes made were most notable in one key scene where, in combination with Kim Hunter's portrayal of Stella, and the framing and editing of her performance, Alex North's music was considered too provocative. Discussion of these changes provides an opportunity to consider the subtle varieties in reception which are unusual in traditional filmic contexts, but increasingly common in the multidimensional multimedia context of today's entertainment experiences. In this volume, Annette Davison has explored how the release of the restored version with North's original scoring generates a second version of the film, whose structure and emphases are substantially and significantly altered from the 1951 release by this single musical cue. Such reconstructions of meaning are more usually initiated by a director's re-editing of the visual text, so it is fascinating to consider the impact of the score as such a mechanism. Furthermore, Dr. Davison's transcription of aspects of the film's soundscape via Vivien Leigh's voice brings a new perspective to our understanding of musicality in the score. As in other Scarecrow Film Score Guides, the identity of the soundscape has been challenged and shaped by the analysis of it, and Dr. Davison's approach here is a fascinating example of how traditional approaches to understanding film music can be fused with new perspectives on what constitutes that music. However, just as North infiltrated the prevailing orchestral idiom with jazz instrumentation and harmony to create a sound of New Orleans that is evocative and powerful, so the reader—whatever his or her level of musical knowledge—will find much in this volume that will illuminate enjoyment of this striking and memorable film.

Dr. Kate Daubney
Series Editor

ACKNOWLEDGMENTS

I wish to thank the following for their willingness to allow me to reproduce excerpts from the film scores listed below. In all cases, music is by Alex North.

A Streetcar Named Desire: "Belle Reve" (Main Title), "Stan" (Reel 2: Part 3), "Stan Meets Blanche" (Reel 3: Part 1), "Blanche and Mitch" (Reel 4: Part 1b), "Stan and Stella" (Reel 5: Part 3), "Stan" (Reel 6: Part 1), "Soliloquy" (Reel 7: Part 1), "Blanche and Mitch" (Reel 8: Part 2), "Birthday Party" (Reel 9: Part 2), "Birthday Party" (Reel 10: Part 1a), "Birthday Party" (Reel 10: Part 2), "Blanche's Solitude" (Reel 10: Part 3), "Revelation" (Reel 11: Part 1), "Seduction" (Reel 13: Part 1), "Doctor" (Reel 14: Part 1), "Affirmation" (Reel 14: Part 2), "Stanley and Stella" (*New Version*, Reel 5: Part 3).
Viva Zapata! "Innocente's Death" and "Gathering Forces."
The Bad Seed: "My Baby" and "No More Children."
Cleopatra: "Bacchus" and "Caesar's Assassination."
Who's Afraid of Virginia Woolf? "Prelude" and "Colloquy."

Used by permission of Warner/Chappell North America Ltd., USA, and EMI United Partnership Ltd./Alfred Publishing Co., USA. Reproduced by permission of Faber Music Ltd. All Rights Reserved.

"Varinia's Theme" and "Vesuvius Camp" (from *Spartacus*).
Music by Alex North
© Copyright 2005 USI A Music Publishing.
Universal/MCA Music Limited.
Used by permission of Music Sales Limited.
All Rights Reserved. International Copyright Secured.

Excerpts from Tennessee Williams, *A Streetcar Named Desire*. Copyright © 1947 by The University of the South. Reprinted by permission of New Directions Publishing Corp. and Methuen Publishing Ltd.

Excerpts from *A Streetcar Named Desire* (Warner Bros. Pictures Inc. and Charles K. Feldman Group Productions, 1951). Reprinted by permission of the Motion Picture and Television Fund, Woodland Hills, California.

Edward Albee and Warner Bros. generously granted me permission to reproduce an excerpt from Albee's *Who's Afraid of Virginia Woolf?* (Warner Bros. Pictures, 1966). George Burt and Northeastern University Press kindly gave permission for the reproduction of the setting of North's "Prelude" (*Who's Afraid of Virginia Woolf?*) from Burt, *The Art of Film Music* (1994), 34.

With special thanks also to Dylan and Abby North, and to Kate Edelman Johnson.

Many individuals and organizations have assisted in the preparation of this book. First I would like to thank Peter Nelson, Music, and the School of Arts, Cultures and Environment at the University of Edinburgh for granting me sabbatical leave. I am also indebted to the Arts and Humanities Research Council who awarded me with matching sabbatical leave. Susan McClary and Robert Walser generously supported the preliminary stages of this research and thus kick-started the project. I was offered a warm welcome by their colleagues at UCLA, and also by Jim Buhler and David Neumeyer during my visit to Austin. David Cooper at the University of Leeds provided encouragement in the early stages. Further research trips were supported by a Small Grant in the Performing Arts, for which I thank the British Academy.

Much of the archival research was carried out in North America where I was assisted by excellent and attentive curators. Chief among these were: Haden Guest, Randi Hockett, and, more recently, Sandra Lee at the Warner Bros. Archives, School of Cinematic Arts, University of Southern California (Los Angeles); Barbara Hall and Warren Sherk at Special Collections, Margaret Herrick Library (The Academy of Motion Picture Arts and Sciences, Los Angeles); Tim Edwards and Frank Garvey of Music Special Collections, University of California at Los Angeles; Joan Miller of the Wesleyan Cinema Archives, Wesleyan University; Richard Workman of the Harry Ransom Center, University of Texas at Austin; Suzanne Eggleston Lovejoy of Special Collections,

Irving S. Gilmore Music Library, Yale University; J. C. Johnson of the Howard Gotlieb Archival Research Center, Boston University. Archive staff in the Music Divisions of the Library of Congress and the British Library helped me to locate copies of North's early published scores, as did Victoria Small and Liz Keller-Tripp of G. Schirmer Inc. I was able to view a number of otherwise unavailable films scored by North at the British Film Institute, the Library of Congress, and in the Music and Drama Library, Manchester University. I viewed and listened to unique materials relating to *A Streetcar Named Desire* and Anna Sokolow at the New York Public Library of the Performing Arts. I would also like to thank Sanya Henderson for her assistance on this project, and for writing the first book about Alex North and his film scores: it is an excellent resource.

Locating the copyright holders of various film music scores can be an arduous task. On this project I was fortunate to have the support of a number of individuals and publishers. First, Dave Olsen made it possible for me to view a copy of North's score for *Streetcar* in the U.K., for which I am very grateful. More recently, James Grupenhoff (Alfred Publishing) and Matt Smith and Zaid Ahmad (Faber Music) steered me through the process of copyright clearance for almost all of the music extracts. I am also grateful to Matt Greiner (Shapiro, Bernstein and Co., Ltd.) and Caroline Walker (Music Sales Ltd.) for their assistance. For the rights to plays and screenplays, Rachel McGhee of William Morris Agency, Shannon Fifer of Warner Bros., N. Tummons of Methuen Publishing Ltd., Sharon Siefert of the Motion Picture Television Fund, and Jeff Clapper of New Directions were extremely helpful.

Special thanks must go to Kate Daubney, the series' truly supportive and generous editor. I am very grateful to Kate for her incisive editorial skills and unstinting encouragement. Friends, family, and colleagues have, as always, formed an interesting and interested audience. I particularly appreciated the dialogue that followed research seminars at the Research Forum, ICSM, Newcastle University, and the School of Music, University of Liverpool. Mervyn Cooke read drafts of some of the chapters and made excellent comments and useful suggestions. Many different voices helped to shape this final version of the text, but the errors remain mine alone.

Finally, my most sincere thanks go to my long-suffering husband, Colin, who kindly forgot that I'd asked him to stop me if I ever decided to write another book. It was one of three fairly major projects that all shared the same date for completion. Georgia won that race, and was born in March 2007. Colin took the helm at home on countless occasions as the book was written. Both Colin and Georgia provide me with much needed perspective, belly laughs, and bags under my eyes. Colin continues to suffer . . .

INTRODUCTION

Elia Kazan's adaptation of Tennessee Williams's *A Streetcar Named Desire* (1951) is fascinating for a range of reasons. Based on a complex and critically lauded play, the film was nominated for twelve Academy Awards. This included nominations for each of the principal actors, for Kazan for direction, Williams for the adapted screenplay, for best picture, and Alex North for his score. The film won four: one for Art Direction and three for acting, though Marlon Brando lost out to Humphrey Bogart.[1] That Brando did not win for his groundbreaking portrayal of Stanley Kowalski is felt keenly in retrospect: the film is considered among the first, if not *the* first, to bring Method acting to a mainstream film audience. Nevertheless, the film made it possible for a mass audience to experience Williams's play, and to retain these landmark performances for posterity: all four of the principals first realized their roles in debut stage productions of the play.

The film is also infamous for its censorship or, to be precise, the producers' self-censorship of the film. *Streetcar* had already previewed well and gained the seal of the Office of the Production Code when the producers re-edited it to pacify the Catholic Legion of Decency, which threatened to condemn the film. The cuts were made without Kazan's knowledge. Alex North's "lustful and carnal scoring" for the film's staircase scene was a primary casualty. But in 1993, Warner Bros. restored the trims—including North's original cue for the staircase scene—and released the "Original Director's Version" of the film.

In producing a film score guide to Alex North's music for *Streetcar*, I was thus faced with a question: which score? On the one hand, North's original score best reflects the intentions of the film's creative team, given that compromises had already been made to gain the seal of the Production Code. On the other hand, the re-edited version won the awards, and was the only version of the film seen for forty years. By comparison with the original cue North composed for the staircase scene, its replacement sounds romantic and sentimental in the extreme. Yet, when viewed within the context of the score as a whole, it retains the score's integrity. I conclude my analysis with a comparison of the two versions of the film and score: I explore the role played by the staircase scene and its impact on the film's ending, for each version says something different. North's music for *Streetcar* problematizes the idea that a score guides a film's audience to a particular interpretation. While a score may be used to simplify the "message" of a film which explores a complicated narrative and/or moral issue, a score may itself be complex, even contradictory, and thereby encourage the audience to judge the film from a position of relative neutrality. Of course, taste and preferences differ, and readers may or may not agree with my interpretation, but in chapters 4 and 5 I argue that in these scores North achieved the same balance—or, ambivalence—that Williams emphasized to Kazan in the realization of the play: "[you must not] take sides or try to present a moral." The result is both highly integrated, as one might expect of a Hollywood score composed in the early 1950s, yet it is also fragmented and ambivalent in terms of its musical identity.

Williams's play indicated a variety of music: blue piano and hot or muted trumpet, ghostly dance music heard only by Blanche (the "Varsouviana"), the flower seller's chant, and popular songs of the day. In its transformation into a film, other pieces of light music and popular songs were added, along with North's dramatic score. In one sense, the score *itself* presents a fragmentary musical identity, combining music that portrays the nostalgic romanticism of the Varsouviana and the forlorn aspirations for protection that Blanche clings to, with jazz-soaked cues that depict and appear to bolster Stanley's physicality, his relationship with Stella, and the urban world of the French Quarter, so alien to Blanche. Yet, North also complicates these associations, using music to characterize Stanley as compassionate, while abrasive chromatic glissandi and funereal dirges underscore Blanche's revelations about the reality of her life at Belle Reve.

The film's music builds on techniques presented first in Williams's play, and intensified in Kazan's Broadway production. Musical elements are superimposed generating jarring clashes in places, but integrating layers of texture accumulatively in others; sound effects and the delivery of dialogue also form part of this fusion in places. North elided the distinction between jazz elements heard as source music and as underscore, creating ambiguity in terms of the level of narration at which they operate and thus also in terms of interpretation or commentary. The film retained Blanche's subjective "memory" music—the insistent and reverberant interjections of the Varsouviana, halted by a gunshot—but North developed it further through juxtaposition with the score, in places integrating the theme into the score.

The film industry continues to categorize the use of music primarily in relation to the image ("source," "score," and "scource"—"source music acting as score,"), while film music analysts tend to categorize music in relation to the narrative, through the roughly analogous term *diegesis*: diegetic music is part of the film's fictional world, and may thus also potentially be heard by characters in the film, while non-diegetic (or extra-diegetic) music is sourced beyond or outside of the film's fictional world, and thus cannot usually be heard by a film's characters. In practice, sliding unnoticed between different narrative levels is one of film music's defining characteristics. The limitations of the theoretical categories or boundaries we impose on film music in our attempts to explain how it functions become clear in analyzing a score such as *Streetcar*. Although these categories allow for basic distinctions to be made, the richness of North's score is founded on ambiguity and ambivalence.

As with the other books in this series, the first chapter outlines the composer's musical background prior to the score in question, and the second explores some of the salient features of North's approach to film scoring. Here I focus particularly on scores composed in the first two decades of his career in Hollywood. One of the most interesting features of North's music is its chameleon-like character: rather than impose generic conventions on the film scores he composed, North appeared to re-invent his scoring style with each score in his intention to write music specific to the film. This approach was supported by his eclectic taste in musical style, extended musical training, and a thirst for knowledge of other musical cultures, which he indulged in his research for scores such as *Cleopatra* (1963) and *The Agony and the Ecstasy* (1965). In the third chapter I explore the history and context of Kazan's film adaptation of *Streetcar*: I examine its relationship with the play and the film's well-known censorship issues, paying specific attention to the role of music. North's score and the film's overall soundscape form the focus of the fourth and fifth chapters. Here I consider the role of the Varsouviana, and North's decision to combine jazz-styling with a late Romantic, even Modernist approach to musical language. This is followed by a detailed analysis of the score, and its role in the interpretation of the film.

On Chord Labels and Bar Numbers

The score's complex harmony makes it necessary to indicate how harmonic descriptions and abbreviations are used here. Chords with minor sevenths above the triad are indicated conventionally (i.e., A^7). Triads with major sevenths above are indicated thus: A^Δ. In the case of further extensions, such as ninth or eleventh chords, readers should assume that sevenths are present in ninth chords, and sevenths and ninths in eleventh chords, and so on. Where this is *not* the case, I indicate this via the term "add." Thus "Am^{add9}" includes a triad of A minor plus a ninth; "$Am^{\Delta\#11}$" indicates an A minor chord with a major seventh, a ninth, and a sharpened eleventh. I represent chord juxtapositions or bitonality thus: "C/D" (a chord of C over a chord of D). Chords with a different root are labeled so that "C/D bass" indicates a chord of C with a D beneath in the bass. Triads without a third are described as "open," thus "C/D open" indicates a C chord over the tonic and fifth of D (D and A).

In terms of bar numbers, where these are correct in relation to the 1993 restoration of the film I refer to the conductor score or North's sketches for the cues in question. Since I am using the score as it is heard in the director's version of the film as my primary resource, I also note where differences exist between this and the conductor score or sketches.

1

ALEX NORTH'S
MUSICAL BACKGROUND

Alex North's first year in Hollywood was impressive by any standards: he received three Academy Award nominations.[1] Yet, the composer continued to think of himself as a visitor to the West Coast.[2] After a musical training in New York and Moscow, North began his composing career in New York City. There he produced forms of functional music—music for dance, theater, and documentary films—alongside music for the concert hall, hoping eventually to make a living from his concert music.[3] Undoubtedly his knowledge of, and eclectic interest in, a wide variety of musical languages and forms provided him with invaluable technical skills in composition and contributed to his success as a film composer in Hollywood, where his abilities as both a craftsman and innovator were recognized. The expertise North acquired through years composing for dance, documentaries, and the stage equipped him with many of the practical skills required of a successful film composer: he gained a solid grounding in working to tight time constraints and budgets, producing effective scoring from a relatively small group of musicians, for example. North's favored musical language was more dissonant than was the norm in the studio music departments in the early 1950s, much to the delight of some of his colleagues, but it was also tempered with an abundant facility for simple and effective lyrical melodies, as exhibited in the song "Unchained Melody" (with lyrics by Hy Zaret) for the Warner Bros. prison film *Unchained* (1955).

    In order to explore some of the key aspects of North's musical development which culminated in his score for *A Streetcar Named Desire* (hereafter, *Streetcar*), the following chapter is organized in terms of the media categories in which he worked from the 1930s through to the

1950s: dance, documentary, concert music, theater, and finally, feature film. Arranging the chapter in this way complicates the chronology of North's career somewhat, but has the benefit of allowing an assessment of the contribution of the various skills he developed working in each medium.

Childhood and Early Musical Training

Alex North was born Isadore Soifer in Chester, Pennsylvania, in the winter of 1910, the third of four sons born to Russian Jewish immigrants, Jesse and Baila Soifer.[4] His mother was widowed tragically young, and the family was not wealthy, but music flourished in the house. North took his first piano lessons from his eldest brother.[5] He continued to study the piano locally with teachers in Chester until the age of 12 and then began studying piano, theory, and sight-singing at the Settlement Music School in nearby Philadelphia. There he took piano lessons with George Boyle, later studying with him privately and at the Curtis Institute in Philadelphia (1928–29).

As a teenager North took trips to Atlantic City to hear the bands of Coon Sanders, Paul Whiteman, and Ted Weems.[6] He was drawn to jazz and swing, but also developed his knowledge of a variety of other forms and styles of music, making weekly trips to concerts at the prestigious Academy of Music in Philadelphia. North decided that the best way to continue his musical studies would require his learning a skill from which he could earn money: telegraphy. At the urging of George Boyle, North then auditioned for the Juilliard School of Music in New York, where Boyle also taught. He was awarded a 4-year scholarship which assisted with the cost of tuition. For several years he juggled his work as a telegraphist at night with classes at Juilliard during the day. Over time, however, North found his health diminished and he decided against pursuing a performing career.[7]

Dance (and Russian Interlude)

During his time at Juilliard he met Anna Sokolow, with whom he began a relationship. She was a member of Martha Graham's dance company but also performed her own choreographies, often inspired by social issues of the time. North began to accompany Sokolow's dance group, later composing for them. North and Sokolow were artists with a shared heritage and a passion for social protest and fighting social in-justice.[8] Their performances were given at various workers' organiza-tions with their first major collaboration being the *Anti-War Trilogy* (later *Anti-War Cycle*) in 1933. North said of this period, "All of us felt that we were trying to do our part to improve the domestic situation during the Depression. We wanted to give some hope. By reflecting the period in our work, we were trying to do positive things, lifting the spirit of the so-called 'masses.'"[9]

But North also wanted to further his musical training: he "wanted to go somewhere where my musical education could be subsidized. I was attracted to the idea of studying in Russia, partly because I idolized Prokofiev."[10] At the time the Soviet Union was looking for skilled pro-fessionals to assist with the development of industry there, all expenses paid. In late 1932 North successfully applied to the Soviet agency in New York to work in the Soviet Union as a telegraphist. In Russian, however, the term describes a "telegraph engineer," a role that requires significantly more training.

North left for the Soviet Union early in 1934. Soon after his arri-val, the authorities realized that he did not have the skills they needed. A friend, Grisha Schneerson of the International Bureau of Music, in-tervened and interpreted for North, explaining that North's motive had been to come to study music. An audition was arranged at the Moscow Conservatory and he won a scholarship. North spent two years there studying composition with Aleksandr Veprik and Victor Bielyi.[11] While in Moscow, North enjoyed a rich musical and cultural life of concerts, opera, and theater; he praised Borodin's *Prince Igor* and Shostakovich's *Lady Macbeth of the Mtsensk District*, along with the theatrical work of Meyerhold.[12] He was disappointed at the state of dance, however, noting that prior to the Revolution it had been the most progressive of the arts in Russia.[13]

North was greatly impressed by the Soviet system for students which ensured that food and accommodation were affordable and en-abled those from proletarian backgrounds to study music. It was the first time he was able to focus on his musical studies full-time.[14] He was commissioned to write a set of piano variations and two choruses by the newly formed Union of Soviet Composers.[15] Yet, although North spoke highly of the training he received at the Moscow Conser-vatory, he felt he was "writing in a style that was not myself."[16] North told an oft-quoted story of his motivation for returning to America: at a party he heard a recording of Duke Ellington's "Mood Indigo" at which he "got very morose and sad and tearful, and said 'What am I doing here?'"[17] The experience reminded him of listening to jazz bands on the

Steel Pier in Atlantic City, and of Ellington particularly, his all-time favorite jazz composer. He decided that "getting back to [his] Roots" was not for him, or rather, he discovered that his roots were in America, not the Soviet Union.[18]

On his return to New York North continued to work with Sokolow, and also began to work with a number of the other leading dance groups and choreographers, such as Martha Graham, Hanya Holm, Agnes de Mille, Marthe Krueger, and Doris Humphrey.[19] North was also involved in the Federal Theatre Project (1935–39).[20] During the same period he began to score documentaries and also gave lectures on functional music at a number of colleges locally.[21]

Dance performances often took place in an auditorium at the YMHA (Young Men's Hebrew Association) on 92nd Street in New York City, where they are still held. On 5 April 1936, Anna Sokolow presented the first full evening of her own work there. North composed the music for two of her dances, one of which—*Ballad in a Popular Style*—became something of a trademark for Sokolow, described as "a wistful, lyrical excursion into jazz, danced to piano and whistled obbligato."[22] Her choreography for North's *Excerpts from a War Poem*, based on the poem *War Is Beautiful* by the Italian Futurist Marinetti, was also popular at the time. The music was described by Elie Siegmeister as using "all the resources of contemporary music to deliver a savage attack on Fascist barbarism."[23] North was being noticed. In a review of Sokolow's work as recipient of a Bennington Fellowship in the summer of 1937, *New York Times* critic John Martin stated that the dancer was "very fortunate, incidentally, in having Alex North as composer of her music."[24] In his review of her Broadway debut in November of the same year, Martin described North as her "invaluable collaborator": "His music has vitality and imagination and that rarest of attributes, a feeling for movement."[25] This latter characteristic was to become key in North's film scores.

In 1939 Sokolow's dance group was invited to perform in Mexico. While there North became friends with the composer Silvestre Revueltas: he attended his composition classes and spent a good deal of time discussing music with him.[26] North grew to love Mexican folk music during this trip. Although Sokolow and North ended their personal relationship during the Mexican tour, they continued to collaborate professionally for several years via shared recitals. Frequently such programs comprised a first half of dance, and a second half of concert music by North.[27] His composition for dance continued with works for Hanya Holm, Marthe Krueger, and Truda Kaschmann in 1941–42.

Later, North recognized that his growing interest and involvement with functional music was a development of his composition for dance, in particular, the significant period of collaboration with Sokolow, which had provided an invaluable training for a career in film music. Through Sokolow he met people working in theater, and subsequently in films. Furthermore, there were similarities between composing for modern dance and for film: "The dancer does the dance first. The film is shot first. You have to tailor the music to the dance as music is tailored to a film. This skill I first learned working with Anna."[28] In a more detailed exposition of the working practice involved in modern dance, North noted that having worked out the dance, the dancer

> would give you the counts, and one bar would be a 3/8 bar, and the next would be a 5/8, and the next would be a 2/4. That in a sense was good training in attempting to make a formal piece of music with all these mixed bar meters so that after eight or nine years of that kind of training, I was more or less prepared, plus the documentary experience, to step into the Hollywood scene.[29]

Shifting meters can be found in cues in many of North's film scores, as demonstrated in the following chapters.

Documentary Films

After a brief spell writing for theater in the mid-1930s—North composed a score for a group workshop that featured W. H. Auden's *Dog Beneath the Skin* in 1936—North scored his first documentary film, *China Strikes Back* (1937). The film was produced by the Frontier Films collective, as was the next documentary he scored, *Heart of Spain* (1937), a pro-Loyalist documentary directed by Herbert Kline.[30] For the latter North created a score that used Spanish motifs and native bagpipes, a use of folk materials that was praised by Elizabeth Noble in *New Masses*. Sokolow choreographed a dance inspired by the film, with music also composed by North: *Slaughter of the Innocents* (1937).

In the same year, North scored *The People of the Cumberland*, directed by Sidney Meyers and Jay Leyda.[31] This film documented the struggle of those living in the Appalachian region of Tennessee and emphasized the advantages of labor unions.[32] During production, North first met the young Group Theatre actor and budding director, Elia Kazan, though only casually; Kazan was working as an assistant on the film. Elie Siegmeister conducted the music and praised North for

[his] uncanny sense of musical timing, derived from his dance experience. Two aspects of the composer's talent found free play: his sense of jazz rhythms and his unusual melodic invention. He is not specifically a jazz composer. But the tempo and the quality of popular rhythm and melody are in his bones; they come out naturally in the midst of any American subject he touches.[33]

North's score for *The People of the Cumberland* anchored both the tone and the temporality of the film, ranging from stillness on guitar chords to underscore the plight of the Cumberlanders, through to upbeat instrumental music that signifies their "new spirit" when the union is created. Bright, fanfare-like tonal music for trumpet and piano is used to indicate the catalytic role of the teachers who organize the Highlander Folk School and is gradually enlarged to encompass a small band of brass, wind, and piano. A harmonica is added as the community is taught about the benefits of labor unions. Simple arrangements of traditional tunes of the South underscore sequences of the community as it comes together for the hog-calling competition or the rejuvenation of traditional dances from the past, for example.

The film has a dialectical structure with a central section that breaks with the documentary frame. At this point mobs are sent to break up the unions and the organizer is murdered. During this climactic sequence there is a brief shift to first-person narrative and what might be described as dramatic reconstruction. North scored the sequence with emphatic dissonance that verges on bitonality, but also demonstrated restraint by using only percussion to underscore the organizer's murder. The attempt to disrupt unionization having failed, there is a return to documentary-style footage underscored by joyful marching music.[34]

Other documentaries North scored included *Venezuela* and *Recreation* (1939) for the Department of Agriculture, *Rural Nurse* for Willard Pictures in 1940, and a State Department film, *City Pastorale*. While in the army, he also scored a number of documentary films for the Office of War Information, including two directed by Alexander Hackenschmied in 1945: *The Library of Congress* and *A Better Tomorrow*. Some sources indicate that through the 1930s and '40s North scored a huge number of documentaries, though a complete list of this work has yet to be confirmed. Given his interest in social justice and his political ideals, his scores for documentaries enabled him to work with subjects toward which he likely felt some sympathy, in some cases at least. Although most of these films were short, the norm for documentary filmmaking was for continuous scoring. Thus North also developed his skills in writing music of significant length for these films, by contrast to the shorter cues he was later to write for the theater and feature films. He also began to hone his ability in objective scoring in these short films; the opposite of the "subjective" writing he later preferred and which he associated with the small, intimate dramas he scored for stage and screen in which interpersonal relationships were the central focus.[35] The distinction is explored in chapter 2.

Concert Music

On his return from the Soviet Union North continued to study composition, working first with Aaron Copland (1936–37) and then Ernst Toch (1938–40). He wrote several works for the concert hall including a Woodwind Trio (1939), a Suite for flute, clarinet, and bassoon (1938), a String Quartet (1939), and a Suite for chamber orchestra, *Quest* (1938). Sanya Shoilevska Henderson notes that already in these works North had developed the lyrical approach to melody that defines so much of his work.[36] He also recounted being told by Copland, in response to a romantic piece he had composed, "Alex, we're living in a different age."[37] Nonetheless, both he and Samuel Barber (with whom he had been friends since childhood) continued to put their faith in a lyrical approach.

In the 1940s North turned to vocal music. In 1940 he wrote a cantata to the text of a poem by Langston Hughes, *Negro Mother* (1931). There were also patriotic choral ballads (1941–42). North was also involved in musical shows, revues, and various theater projects, the most popular being his musical for children, based on a book and lyrics by Jerome Gury: *The Hither and Thither of Danny Dither* (1941).[38] During preparations for one of these revues in the summer of 1939—'*Tis of Thee*—North met a young entertainer called Sherle Hartt. They married in late 1941, and North became a father for the first time in 1942.[39]

The Hughes poem on which North based *Negro Mother* tells of the three-hundred-year struggle for civil rights for blacks through the words of a fictional "mother" to her children, her people, a subject that resonated with North given his interest in social injustice.[40] Siegmeister writes of the cantata that

> [North] evolved a style in which popular and serious elements are so completely fused that there is no longer any question of "how to bring jazz and classical music together." Here they are in one single

American music.... *Mother*, with its direct, effortless melodic and its structural simplicity—a simplicity enriched by all the resources of modern harmony when needed—is definitely a music of the American people.[41]

Some of the same characteristics were noted by Martin McCall following one of North and Sokolow's joint recitals in 1940. McCall found North's dance music "concise, eloquent and vivid," matching the impetus provided by Sokolow's choreography, which "has a minimum of superfluous or irrelevant material."[42] McCall went on to note that much the same could be said about his music for documentaries. The second half of the program comprised works by North for the "Concert, Theatre, and Musical Review." In his review, McCall stressed that "[a] gift for melodic creation, such as North possesses, is uncommon. The frank interest in rhythmic exploration, on the other hand, makes for brilliant melodies, and resurrects, so to speak, the long obscure expression, 'con brio.'"[43] These early appraisals of North's compositions acknowledge and commend several of the key elements that featured throughout his career: the synthesis of jazz and concert music, the directness and simplicity of melody and structure enhanced by dissonance, and a fascination with rhythm. This list functions equally well as a description of the essential characteristics of North's feature film scoring.

For a significant part of the 1940s North was in the army, during which time he rose through the ranks from private to captain. He continued his involvement with music, but primarily in terms of his service; he was music director of the Army's 23rd Regiment Chorus, for example. Later he was placed in charge of the rehabilitation of traumatized soldiers through forms of "self-entertainment." Working with the influential psychiatrist Dr. Karl Menninger, North developed forms of music therapy that were then called "psycho-dramas." The techniques he devised were later taken up and used to assist in group therapy for the mentally ill more generally.[44]

After his discharge from the army in 1946, North was commissioned by the *New York Herald Tribune* to write a cantata for the annual *Herald Tribune* Forum, on the recommendation of Virgil Thomson. The Forum's theme that year was "The Struggle for Justice as a World Force." For this North wrote *Morning Star*, based on the Nuremberg trials, though the work appears to have been less successful than *Negro Mother*.[45] The same year North also received a commission from the jazz clarinetist Benny Goodman, who was then looking for works for a program with the New York City Symphony Orchestra to be conducted by Leonard Bernstein. At its premiere on 18 November

1946, North's *Revue* for clarinet and orchestra received a standing ovation and was well reviewed by the press. The composer described the work's three movements as follows: "1. Colloquy—here the clarinet and accompaniment engage in lively conversation 2. Lyric—a quiet blues treatment sets the mood 3. Speciality—a syncopated, brisk finale."[46] The *New York Times*'s critic praised North's "felicitous" writing for clarinet, with orchestral timbre "neatly emphasizing and contrasting [with the] solo clarinet," and his skill in assimilating "jazz idiom … in a style that is flexible and quietly assured."[47] This stylistic synthesis was to become a focus of his score for *Streetcar*.

The desire to integrate jazz with other musical languages was clearly important to North. Shortly before the premiere of *Danny Dither* in Hartford in 1943, North told the *Hartford Times*, "We, songwriters, should make use of our own culture, particularly folk music and jazz. We must lose our highbrow attitude toward jazz, take what is good in it and put it to work writing American music as vital, democratic and dynamic as our land."[48] North's attitude to jazz and folk may well have been influenced by Copland who echoed this vision for a distinctly American voice in music that drew on these sources: via jazz in the 1920s, then later with pan-American folk resources in scores such as *El salón México* (1932–36), *Our Town* (1940) and *Appalachian Spring* (1943–44). Copland said he felt the need to reach a wider public in his compositions, to "say what [he] had to say in the simplest possible terms."[49] The works Copland listed as exemplary of this "imposed simplicity" often drew on folk music, both borrowed and imitated.[50] Copland also stressed the importance of functionality in the works he composed under this banner, which included a commission for radio, an opera for schoolchildren, a ballet, and film scores.[51] As Elizabeth Crist emphasizes, this notion of "imposed simplicity" is thus multifaceted, signifying both an "aesthetic orientation" and "a compositional attitude that focused on accessibility and conceived of the musical work as a functional as well as artistic creation."[52] Such a conception of music was common within composers' circles in the period (the Great Depression into the Second World War), and was underpinned by the Popular Front's social movement, as were North's own interests in functional music, accessibility, and a democratic voice that spoke to and for America.

North wrote two pieces for chamber orchestra in the latter half of the 1940s: *Holiday Set* in 1945 and Three Pieces for Chamber Orchestra (premiered 23 January 1950). A cycle of jazz-influenced and highly chromatic preludes for piano were also published: Twelve Dance Preludes (1948). There are no key signatures in this collection, which features copious accidentals throughout. There is much syncopation and play with meter: several of the preludes involve almost constant changes of time signature (II *Allegretto* and III *Andantino*), while others feature off-kilter meters such as 5/8 and 7/8 throughout (VIII *Allegro misterioso* and XI *Allegretto*). Seven of the preludes were performed together under the title Little Dance Preludes in September 1947. Of this performance, one reviewer noted their "somewhat dissonant, intense flow,"[53] while another highlighted their "pleasant melodies and interesting sonorities."[54]

North also continued to write for children. Works from this period included *The Yank and Christopher Columbus* (1943) and *Little Indian Drum* (premiered 18 October 1947 at a concert for the under-9s). The critic of the *New York Herald Tribune* described the latter as "a quaint pictorial work, replete with all sorts of virtuoso orchestral effects, yet constructed along the simplest rhythmic and melodic lines."[55]

Theater

Most of North's work for theater began in the late 1940s. Early in 1947 he composed scores for plays produced by the Experimental Theatre of the American National Theatre and Academy: *O'Daniel* by Swarthout and Savacool, and *The Great Campaign* by Arnold Sundgaard, which featured music and dance numbers and gained better reviews than *O'Daniel*. The same year, North received a Guggenheim Fellowship of $2500 to enable him to write his first symphony. To get away from the fast pace of his lifestyle in New York City he moved his young family to a house in the San Fernando Valley in California for this work. After only three months away he was called back to New York by the Broadway producer Kermit Bloomgarden to work on a musical, entitled *Queen of Sheba*, with Molly Day Thacher, then wife of Elia Kazan.

It was during this period that North got to know Kazan well; he often stayed at the couple's home in Sandy Hook, Connecticut. Kazan heard and liked North's music. When the director was working on the debut stage production of Arthur Miller's *Death of a Salesman* the following summer, he suggested that North compose the music. Miller's play appealed to North on a personal level because he identified with the characters.[56] The salesman at the center of Miller's humanist play is Willy Loman, a hardworking man who has spent his life in pursuit of the success of the American dream, only to find that it fails him as he nears the end of his career. At his first joint meeting with Miller and

Kazan after he had read the script, North played a number of thematic ideas to Miller on the piano. Miller later said, "I don't think we changed very much of what he first initiated."[57]

North's score for *Death of a Salesman* was written for four musicians—flute doubling alto flute, cello, trumpet, and clarinet doubling bass clarinet—and it ran to twenty-two and a half minutes.[58] The musicians performed to a microphone in an off-stage room, as the four-piece jazz band for the debut stage production of *A Streetcar Named Desire* had some fourteen months earlier. In the case of *Salesman*, however, the decision was due to the lack of a pit at the Morosco Theatre rather than for aesthetic reasons.[59] The music was organized around a handful of primary themes associated with different characters: the melancholic solo alto-flute line for Willy; a more forthright theme for his brother, Ben; a lullaby for his wife, Linda (with a sleazy jazz version of the same theme for Willy's memory of his mistress in Boston); and a more sprightly optimistic theme for his sons in their youth. The placement of most of the cues was used to indicate the transition from reality into Willy's reminiscences of, and hallucinations with, these characters. Willy's suicide was not shown on stage, but was represented by North's climactic cue, "Willy's Deathride." This was followed by the final cue, "Requiem," which provided a painful and melancholic commentary on Willy's funeral and life. The play opened on Broadway in February 1949. In their reviews several commentators highlighted the holistic character of the production, noting the role of North's music in the integration of the various elements, in particular.[60]

North's next Broadway score was for William Archibald's *The Innocents*, an adaptation of the Henry James novella, *The Turn of the Screw*, which ran at the Playhouse Theatre from 1 February 1950 to 3 June 1950. Very little happens during this tale of a governess who arrives at an isolated English country manor to teach two young children, the wards of a largely absent guardian. Ghostly occurrences lead the governess to fear for the safety of the children, while she also begins to suspect them of playing a role in her haunting. The play is built on ambiguity and confusion over the boundary between reality and imagination. As such it must have been a fascinating project for North whose score was again much praised. He was particularly pleased by the review of the *New York Times*'s theater critic, Brooks Atkinson, and intended to begin his autobiography (should he ever have written one) with an extract from the review: "And Alex North ... has composed a witches' chorus that is pithy, practical and terrifying. Give Mr. North a theme, and he goes straight to the heart of it without any musical pretensions."[61] Henderson states that the score was written for Novachord,

English horn, oboe, flute, bassoon, and a number of percussion instruments.[62] The critic Barbara Strong wrote of the score:

> Mr. North feels that in *The Innocents* it is advisable to reflect, not the mood or tension of the actor at a particular moment. He wants, instead, to portray their basic traits of character. Thus the theme of the governess, the major character in the play, is a simple musical study of the line between normal and abnormal and an endeavor to show the only slight margin between the two.[63]

In this, the last theater score he composed before turning to write for feature films, North thus engaged with some of the issues that would feature in his score for *Streetcar*, notably the idea that two elements which are seemingly opposed—here normality and abnormality—may be more closely related than their appearance suggests.

Despite his self-confessed "yen" to focus on concert music, North recognized that his gifts—to the extent that the modest composer was willing to acknowledge them at all—were focused on "the function of theatre."

> Adding that other dimension to the film or to a play or to a dance that isn't there visually, in a sense, just enhances the drama of a film, establishes the character or goes beneath the character, and that's not easy to do. The audience may not grasp it, but you, as the creator or composer, you know yourself what you are saying.[64]

North's experience as a composer of music for a wide variety of media through the 1930s and 1940s enabled him to develop the skills that were fundamental in his subsequent scoring of feature films. His collaboration with modern dancers was crucial in this, particularly in terms of composing music for changing metres and durations. Similarly, his work for theater included writing cues which could be expanded or condensed as required to fit the actors' timing and other variables of live performance.[65] Of course, the final cut of a film's edited image is fixed with the score timed accurately to fractions of a second, but the rhythmic and metrical interest in North's film scores suggests that the methods he developed for the adaptability of duration of music for dance and for theater also proved useful in composing music for film.

Stylistically, North's passion for jazz and folk music of various kinds was interwoven into his use of musical language, into which he integrated dissonance and the simple lyrical melodies for which he was noted. The sparse, direct quality of his music—the elimination of the unnecessary—was highlighted by those who reviewed his music for

dance, theater, and documentaries, while his interest in unusual orchestration flourished in the works he wrote for children, in which melodic
and rhythmic simplicity were also a feature. North's adaptability in
terms of writing for a variety of media and audiences, along with his
eclectic musical interests, prepared him well for the next stage of his
career: Hollywood.

Feature Films

Kazan offered North two film scoring projects on the strength of his
score for *Death of a Salesman*. The first was expected to be *Viva Zapata!* for Twentieth Century-Fox, but *Streetcar* went into production at
Warner Bros. first. North deferred making a permanent move to California. His career seemed more assured in New York where he was
relatively well known; he felt that Hollywood would be a "closed
shop," difficult for an outsider to enter. However, in Kazan North had a
sponsor who was fast becoming hot property as a film director after a
string of successes on Broadway, though even he had a difficult time
convincing the producers that North was the man to score his films.[66]
North was asked to supply examples of his documentary scores. These
were sent to the heads of the Music Departments: Alfred Newman at
Fox and Ray Heindorf at Warner Bros. Once they had seen the scores,
however, both supported Kazan's choice.

For five years North commuted between the East and West Coast,
renting a house in California when commissioned to score a film but
returning to the apartment in New York and the family's Connecticut
retreat after each score. Over this peripatetic period he became good
friends with Heindorf and with Hugo Friedhofer, who was also on the
staff at Warner Bros. Friedhofer was forthright in his pleasure at
North's arrival, telling him "now we can do perhaps some of the things
we've been wanting to do for a long time."[67] North's first year in Hollywood was a particularly busy one with the following scores in production: *The 13th Letter* (1951), directed by Otto Preminger, produced
by Fox; *Streetcar* directed by Kazan for Charles Feldman and Warner
Bros.; *Viva Zapata!*, again with Kazan but for Fox; and an adaptation
and reorchestration of his score for *Death of a Salesman* for a film adaptation of the play, directed by Laslo Benedek for Stanley Kramer's
independent production company.[68] As highlighted by Warren Sherk,
in the same year North also began work scoring *Distant Drums* (1951)

for United States Pictures though his contract was terminated by the film's producer and a score by Max Steiner substituted.[69] *The 13th Letter* may well have functioned as a formative experience for North in terms of scoring for the Hollywood studios. He later said that his discussions with Alfred Newman about the score led to the only occasion he could remember of having to rewrite a cue.[70] North had initially decided to ridicule the film's manipulative mayor by scoring him satirically in a scene in which he made an exploitative speech at a funeral. Newman stopped him: a funeral was a funeral. North realized that his original idea for the scene

> was not important [or] in keeping with the whole story. And that is a part of film scoring, getting to the roots of the story, the basic conflict that is in the picture, and not scoring a scene because it happened to appeal to *me* to do it in that manner.[71]

The year 1951 was auspicious for North as the start of his career in feature film scoring. It was also the year that his daughter Elissa was born. With the exception of only one or two quieter periods, he was kept very busy with film score commissions throughout the 1950s. A significant proportion of his first scores were adaptations of stage plays. In addition to *Streetcar* and *Salesman*: Carson McCullers's *The Member of the Wedding* (1953), which starred Julie Harris as the young tomboy making an uncomfortable transition into adolescence; Tennessee Williams's *The Rose Tattoo* (1955), which featured Anna Magnani and Burt Lancaster; Maxwell Anderson's adaptation of William March's novel *The Bad Seed* (1956), about a psychopathic child; and N. Richard Nash's heartwarming *The Rainmaker* (1956), which starred Katharine Hepburn and Burt Lancaster. North went on to score two important play adaptations in the 1960s, a period of his work more usually associated with high-profile, big-budget epics: Lillian Hellman's *The Children's Hour* (1961), which starred Audrey Hepburn and Shirley MacLaine as teachers suspected of lesbianism due to a child's callous lie[72]; and Edward J. Albee's award-winning *Who's Afraid of Virginia Woolf?* (1966), which starred Elizabeth Taylor and Richard Burton and was Mike Nichols's directorial debut. North also scored adaptations of novels by key figures in American and European literature: *Viva Zapata!*, after a novel by John Steinbeck, which allowed North to indulge his fascination for Mexican folk music[73]; Victor Hugo's epic nineteenth-century novel about a man's search for social justice and redemption, *Les Miserables* (1952); Faulkner's *The Sound and the Fury* (1959), one of several North scores that create a sultry sound for Southern states[74]; and later, Malcolm Lowry's *Under the Volcano* (1984), and James Joyce's *The Dubliners* as *The Dead* (1986), with a score built around a selection of Irish tunes. During the 1950s North also produced a small number of ballet scores. These included an adaptation of his *Streetcar* score (premiered in 1952), and music for the tripartite ballet sequence in the Fox film, *Daddy Long Legs* (1955), which starred Leslie Caron and Fred Astaire.

Through the 1960s North became better known for his scores for "high production value" epics. Indeed, *Spartacus* (1960) can be read as a departure from the more intimate dramas of the 1950s. North considered the score to indicate the return to a more objective approach to scoring, one that he had used on *Zapata*. Both *Spartacus* and *Cleopatra* were set in the first century BCE, and North took the opportunity of lengthy production schedules to research the little that is known about Roman, Italian, and Egyptian music of the period. Later he studied the sacred music of sixteenth-century Italy, particularly that of Giovanni Gabrieli, in preparation for his score for the dramatization of the life of Michelangelo, *The Agony and the Ecstasy* (1965). Yet even in his scores for historical epics, North balanced an objective approach to the large-scale scoring of set-pieces such as ceremonial sequences, battles, battle training, celebrations, and so on, with solo or chamber cues of intense lyricism to underscore the personal conflicts and sacrifices of individual characters and their relationships. North privileged unusual woodwind and percussion textures over lush string sounds. His choice of musical styles was eclectic. Dissonance, quirky asymmetrical meters, and unusual timbres were just as likely to feature whether the score was built upon traditional functional harmony or drew upon jazz, folk, ancient musical styles, or nursery rhymes. Yet each score was also highly unified due primarily to North's skill in thematic construction, which enabled the creation of a web of interrelationships across otherwise disparate cues. This is heard most clearly in the scores that use variation technique or a number of recognizable leitmotifs. It is important to note that such coherence was the norm for Hollywood scoring of the period. Within this context of coherence, though, a balance of familiarity and innovation was ensured through North's stylistic eclecticism, his interest in unusual orchestral timbres, in writing treatments of related thematic material for radically different groups of instruments, and in rhythmic and metrical vitality.

Such characteristics made North an inspired choice to compose music for a four-hour documentary about Africa for the American television network ABC in the late 1960s. The commission was unusual though. North was asked to compose a symphony, parts of which would then be used to score the footage once it had been edited together.[75] Along with viewing much of the unedited footage North again took the opportunity to engage in research about the music of another culture, particularly in terms of African rhythms and the sound of African instruments. He composed a four-part *Africa Suite*, and a second symphony, *Symphony to a New Continent* as a result of the *Africa* commission. During the recording of these works in Germany, North met Annemarie Hoellger, who was to become his second wife, and mother to his third child, Daniel.[76]

North successfully scored films in a huge variety of genres, from comedies to Westerns, and horror to historical epics, but he was deeply upset by the rejection of his score for Stanley Kubrick's sci-fi epic, *2001: A Space Odyssey* (1968), and disappointed by the difficulties he experienced on the fantasy epic *Dragonslayer* (1981).[77] North continued to receive commissions into the late 1980s, albeit less frequently than in his first two decades in Hollywood. He had always refused to score films that he found distasteful and in these latter years, after the demise of the Production Code, he found himself turning down more and more films as a result of their depiction of sex or violence.[78] Most of his work in these latter years signaled a return to smaller, more character-driven films. This was the type of work he had always preferred.

Despite bring written at the very beginning of his lengthy career in Hollywood, North's score for *Streetcar* is an excellent demonstration of his skills as a film composer. It was also a harbinger of changes in the style, process, and production of Hollywood film scoring. North avoided signing lengthy contracts with individual studios and thus ultimately scored only a fraction of the films that a composer under contract to a studio might have done. Although it made his position in Hollywood more precarious, it gave him greater freedom to choose the projects on which, or individuals with whom, he wished to work. He collaborated with the director John Huston on five films over twenty-five years, for example, and worked repeatedly with Daniel Mann over a similar period of time.[79] Initially, however, North's freelance status was also due to a desire to stay in New York, to continue the thriving portfolio career he developed there through the 1930s and 1940s. North's arrival in Hollywood coincided with a period that the studios perceived as at best difficult and, at worst, potentially calamitous. In the years that followed, working as a freelance composer became more the norm than the exception, where previously this independence had been characteristic of a much smaller group of composers, such as Bernard Herrmann and Erich Wolfgang Korngold.

Between 1951 and 1984, fourteen of North's film scores were nominated for Academy Awards: *A Streetcar Named Desire* (1951), *Death of a Salesman* (1951), *Viva Zapata!* (1952), *The Rose Tattoo* (1955), *The Rainmaker* (1956), *Spartacus* (1960), *Cleopatra* (1963), *The Agony and the Ecstasy* (1965), *Who's Afraid of Virginia Woolf?* (1966), *The Shoes of the Fisherman* (1968), *Shanks* (1974), *Bite the Bullet* (1975), *Dragonslayer* (1981), and *Under the Volcano* (1984), in addition to the song "Unchained Melody" (with lyrics by Hy Zaret) from *Unchained* (1955). Sadly, he never won. However, at the 1985 (58th) Awards, he was honored with a Lifetime Achievement Award by the Academy: "in recognition of his brilliant artistry in the creation of memorable music for a host of distinguished motion pictures." This was the first time an Honorary Award was given for film music and demonstrates the high regard in which his work is held by his colleagues.[80] North died in 1991, having composed some of the twentieth century's most remarkable film scores.

2

NORTH'S TECHNIQUE OF
FILM SCORING

North believed that "each picture calls for its own solution," and succeeded in achieving this individuality in characterization.[1] As Norman Lloyd wrote in the journal *Film Music* in 1955, "North has the gift of seeming to write in a new style for each picture, and yet each measure of his music is typically his own."[2] For this reason, and because he scored such a wide variety of films over his career, a survey of North's *typical* approach to film scoring inevitably falls short. Rather than conceiving North's scoring technique in terms of a particular *style*, it is better in the first instance to understand his approach as guided by intention, purpose, and interpretation.

North found it "practically impossible" to write music for films that failed to move him emotionally.[3] His preference was for "projects involving personal conflicts as the theme,"[4] such as Miller's *Death of a Salesman*, which North described as a story "full of inner conflicts, undersurface tensions and frustrations."[5] His score for *Salesman* focuses on expressing the subtext rather than the surface action, resulting in music that frequently "[runs] counter to what's going on on screen."[6] Not surprisingly, North's scores for more small-scale, intimate, character-driven films express this tendency most clearly. Indeed, North distinguished between subjective scoring and objective scoring, where the former allowed him to "say something that has something to do with myself personally and mould it, so it fits the content of the film. I write best when I can empathize."[7] By contrast, he defined objective scoring as concerned primarily with atmosphere or spectacle, having "nothing to do with the personalities involved."[8] The lengthy historical epics of the 1960s offered plenty of opportunity for objective scoring: the training, traveling, battle, and celebration scenes in *Spartacus*, the battle and entertainment scenes in *Cleopatra*, particularly Cleopatra's arrival in Rome, and the sacred ceremonies of *The Agony and the Ecstasy*, for example. North's interest in scoring some of these films was driven by the subject matter: "the struggle for freedom and human dignity" in the case of *Spartacus*, and the challenge of finding a musical solution to an idea that he considered to be "every bit as relevant in today's world as it was then."[9] Nonetheless, even where films clearly demanded an "objective" style of scoring, North would "try to personalize the films as much as possible, to concentrate on the character relationships."[10] This approach was supported by the Hollywood star system, and the growing power of actors in the post-divorcement era. For example, a significant proportion of the vast score for *Cleopatra* is built from the development of three primary themes which represent the interpersonal relationships of the key protagonists and identify Cleopatra as the motivating force for the clash of Roman and Egyptian cultures: the principal theme represents Cleopatra's ambition, Cleopatra and Caesar's relationship is depicted via a gentle melancholy love theme, and a third theme represents the love between Cleopatra and Anthony, but also demonstrates partial derivation from the Cleopatra/Caesar theme, thus highlighting the complicated nature of these interrelationships.

North's Practice of Film Scoring

For North, scoring usually took place during post-production, after a rough cut of the film had been produced. Nonetheless, he preferred to look to a film's script rather than its rough cut for inspiration. This is perhaps not surprising, given North's experience of composing music for theatrical productions prior to his move to Hollywood. Also, as many of the films he scored were adaptations of plays or novels this sometimes afforded him a kind of production practice rarely experienced by composers working in Hollywood at that time. North's music for the 1951 film adaptation of *Death of a Salesman* was primarily a development of his incidental music for the play, much of which had been composed in response to the script, and in discussion with Kazan and Miller prior to the play's production. In the case of *Streetcar*, North's friendship with Kazan afforded him ample opportunity to discuss his ideas for the film score ahead of the film's production.[11] With *Spartacus*, North stated that he studied the script "for several months and ran the completed film many times before setting a note down on paper."[12] For *Who's Afraid of Virginia Woolf?*, the director Mike Nichols required that North sit in on three weeks of rehearsals and conferences prior to the shoot.[13] Only exceptionally was North asked to provide music for scenes *before* they were shot or edited, however. This prioritization of music can only occur when pre-existent music is used, or a composer is contracted into the production process early. North found himself in this fortunate position on both *Spartacus* and *Cleopatra*: he worked on the scores for over a year in each case, though very few cues were composed prior to production.[14] North visited the set of *Cleopatra* in Rome during production, watched some of the material that had been assembled, conceived how the music for Cleopatra and Caesar's relationship might be distinguished from that for Cleopatra and Anthony, and wrote cues for scenes in which musical instruments could be seen, all in advance of the completed film.[15] For *Spartacus*, he provided a temporary scaled-down version recorded to a click-track for the final large-scale battle scene (a "temp" track for two pianos and percussion), to which the scene was subsequently edited. He also provided a "lead sheet of chords" for the recitation of Antoninus's song.[16]

As a freelance film composer North enjoyed a degree of choice in the projects he worked on, which allowed him to focus on those that suited his interests best. His freelance status did not necessarily allow him to negotiate on the length of time he would be given to compose a score, however. Nor did it protect him from problems if the director or producer decided that the score did not benefit the film. In practice, film scores are substituted fairly regularly in Hollywood: a film's score is often the cheapest and easiest element to replace entirely if the film is deemed to have difficulties, whether or not the problems lie with the film's music.[17] North was introduced to the practice of the "throwing out" of scores early in his career. Between 9 July 1951 and 5 August 1951—that is, after *The 13th Letter* and *Streetcar*, but before scoring *Zapata* and the film version of *Salesman*—North was contracted by United States Pictures to score *Distant Drums* (1951). Warner Bros. was again the releasing studio and Maurice de Packh was to orchestrate the score. Shortly after the recording sessions for North's cues began, Max Steiner, then a composer in the music department at Warner Bros., was asked to write a replacement score.[18] North's contract was terminated by Milton Sperling, the film's producer, who apparently found North's music too contemporary. In instances where a score is replaced, the composer usually retains his or her fee but sacrifices ownership of the score. However, as Warren Sherk explains, North had a "quitclaim and release" drawn up between himself and the producer. With agreement from US Pictures, North paid back the fee he had received for writing the score in return for ownership and copyright of

the music. This enabled him to re-use the music as he saw fit.[19] North's
contract for *Streetcar* was also amended to include provision for quitclaim release.[20]

The replacement of a North score was a relatively rare occurrence,
however. While there were instances of producers insisting on a particular musical treatment which ran counter to North's own views,[21]
rather more frequent were cases of unconditional support from influential directors such as Elia Kazan and John Huston, studio music department heads, including Alfred Newman at Twentieth Century-Fox
and Ray Heindorf at Warner Bros., and producers such as Jack Warner.[22]

The Scores

As was common for the period, North composed reel by reel rather than
in terms of scenes. Within reels, cues would be distinguished by part
number: Reel 8: Part 2, for example. Segues or overlaps (from one reel
to the next, or from one cue to the next on the same reel) are usually
started on the next clean page and signaled via annotation.[23]

Many of North's film score sketches survive in holograph and take
the form of short scores of four staves, with four bars across each series
of staves.[24] Scoring is usually in pencil, with annotations in blue or red
colored pencil for emphasis, changes, some accidentals, dialogue cues
and timing, and bar numbering.[25] The use of more staves—most often,
six—is generally reserved for complicated cues, which might involve
the use of a great number of overlapping lines, or detailed instructional
information for unusual percussion instruments, as with part of the
"Snails and Oysters" cue (9A) from *Spartacus*, for example.[26] These
slightly expanded short scores are most often used in cues for North's
epic scores—such as *Spartacus* and *Cleopatra*—which employ greater
forces and a wider range of instrumentation than the chamber ensembles of the more intimate scores, such as *Who's Afraid of Virginia
Woolf?*

North's orchestrators worked from these detailed sketches. They
are written at concert pitch. Key signatures are used for cues that are
clearly tonal and modulate little, though in most other cases no key
signature is given and accidentals are used throughout. North's short
scores include clear indications of instrumentation, dynamics, registration, expression, phrasing, timing, and sometimes also bowing. Action
and/or dialogue "hit-points" are signaled when required (that is, points

of synchronization with action in the image, or editing). Annotations for the orchestrator tend to increase with the complexity of the musical material, or where bars have been reworked leading to problems of decipherability. Where corrections to individual parts are required they are typically written onto additional pages.

It is not unusual to see frequent time signature changes in North's scores. As discussed in later chapters, there are also instances of separate instrumental lines written in different time signatures concurrently (cf. Reel 8: Part 2 in *Streetcar*). Pitch space across the short scores is more or less analogous to the space of the four (or six) staves, though specific instrumental cues may appear wherever there is space. The top two staves are usually in the treble clef, the lowest in the bass clef, with the second stave from the bottom used more flexibly, depending on the material. Instruments are not generally assigned to individual staves, although exceptions occur where unusual instruments have been used to create particular textural effects, for example. Melody and counter-melody are most often located in the upper staves, with accompaniment figures and bass beneath. Where the melody is pitched lower than the accompaniment, this hierarchy is reversed. For example, at the opening of the cue "Peace" in *The Children's Hour* (Reel 14: Part 1), the clarinet solo is placed on the third stave down, followed by a bass clarinet solo on the lowest stave, while sustained chords in strings, piano and celeste are written onto the upper two staves.

Standardized Italian musical terms are used to indicate instructions regarding expression, dynamics, and so on. Occasionally other terminology has been chosen as being more appropriate. In the cue that leads to the rape in *Streetcar* (Reel 13: Part 1), for example, North indicates that certain trumpet entries should be "dirty" (e.g., bb. 26, 29, 42, 43). In addition, where the line splits (bar 29) the upper line is cued with the name of a particular trumpet player in the Warner Bros. orchestra: Sullivan (Larry). North's additional annotations to his orchestrators tend to be functional rather than personal: "chord as before," "arc strings sweetly not dramatically," "new pattern," "brass fig into perc," "not tied in saxs," "3 vlns, try tremelo, 3 more vlns."

Although North went on to conduct the recording of the majority of his film scores, including *The Misfits* (1961), *Cleopatra* (1963), and *Cheyenne Autumn* (1964), this was not the case with his first Hollywood scores.[27] In those instances he preferred to leave it to people with more experience of click-tracks and conducting to the image, such as Warner Bros.' department head, Ray Heindorf. This allowed North to sit in the control room and monitor the music's balance, making changes or suggestions if required.[28] Those conducting tended to use

copied-out versions of the composer's short scores—conductor
scores—since their flexible format holds a great deal of information in
fairly compact form.[29]

Example 2.1. Page one of Main Title, North's sketches for *A Streetcar
Named Desire*

Orchestration

North had always orchestrated his own work prior to his arrival in Hollywood and began the score for *Streetcar* expecting to do the same again. But after orchestrating cues for the first five or so of fourteen reels he found he was short of time. Maurice de Packh orchestrated the remaining cues.[30] North knew of de Packh from his screen credits and respected his work. Over the years, he worked with a variety of orchestrators, but repeatedly with de Packh, Henry Brant, and Edward Powell. North's sketch material for his film scores includes a high level of detail, which implies that his orchestrators were limited in the degree of creative contribution they were able to make. Indeed, North once stated that "in my case the orchestrator more or less executes my orchestration."[31] However, he was also keen to give credit where it was due and added that "very often, if the orchestrator is a creative man, naturally, if he has an idea and if it's a good idea, you give him the satisfaction of using it."[32]

In addition to *Streetcar*, de Packh's orchestrations for North included *The 13th Letter* (Fox, 1951), *Viva Zapata!* (Fox, 1952), *The Bad Seed* (Warner Bros., 1956), and *Spartacus* (for Bryna Productions and Universal, 1960).[33] Edward Powell's orchestrations also covered some of the early scores for Fox under Alfred Newman—*Pony Soldier* (Fox, 1952) and *Les Miserables* (Fox, 1952)—and, later, *The Children's Hour* (Mirisch World Wide Productions, 1961).[34] Brant's orchestrations for North came later, and included *Cleopatra* (Fox, 1963), *Cheyenne Autumn* (Warner Bros., 1964), *Carny* (Lorimar, 1980), and *Good Morning, Vietnam* (Touchstone, 1987). Brant and North shared a fascination with unusual timbres and stylistic eclecticism, but where in North's case this was heard primarily by audiences of the films he scored, Brant became better known for his concert music.[35] Both North and Brant received Guggenheim Fellowships in 1947, and lived and worked in New York during the 1930s and 1940s, composing and arranging music for dance, documentaries, and ballet. They also shared an interest in jazz, and both produced works for the clarinetist Benny Goodman. Many years before he worked as an orchestrator on North's film scores, Brant orchestrated Aaron Copland's score for the documentary, *The City* (1939).[36]

Salient Scoring Techniques:
North Scores of the 1950s and 1960s

While there is no specific North "sound," it is possible to highlight a number of salient scoring techniques in *Streetcar*, and the scores that followed. North made eclectic and extensive use of a wide range of harmonic languages from dissonance and chromaticism through to diatonicism and lyrical and structural simplicity, the latter particularly in themes that characterize love and/or women (as with "Varinia's theme" in *Spartacus*, for example). Jazz and the musical styles of other cultures and periods were "simulated" or "assimilated" by means of a synthesis with contemporary compositional techniques used in concert music (in *Streetcar*, *Zapata*, and *Cleopatra*, for example). Arrangements of familiar songs or themes were similarly integrated with North's compositional style in some scores (e.g., "Skip to My Lou" in *The Children's Hour*, "Au clair de la lune" in *The Bad Seed*).

Typically North's scores of the period are highly unified in terms of thematic construction and manipulation, and privilege variation technique or a form of the leitmotif principle. The emphasis on variation is expressed in forms that are predominantly episodic, or follow song-structure. The sequential distribution of thematic material between groups of instruments generates animation and contrast, with metrical asymmetry and syncopation used to generate vitality. For dance, North was required to compose music to fit the choreography and this frequently led to the use of a variety of time signatures in quick succession. In his film music, North went on to explore the "feeling for movement" he demonstrated in his music for dance.[37]

In the main North avoided lush string writing, emphasizing writing for wind, brass, and percussion instead. His scores for smaller films often rely on sparse, chamber-like orchestration, while those for epics typically involve enormous orchestral forces, particularly in terms of the range of percussion instruments used. Yet even with the extended resources available for these films, North often scored intimate scenes for a small number of musicians, much to the chagrin of some studio Music Department heads.

Most of North's film scores embody several of these traits. Thus, rather than discuss each characteristic in turn, in the following section I explore these features via reference to a small number of specific scores composed in the fifteen years that followed his work on *Streetcar*, beginning with *Zapata*, another Kazan-led project.

Viva Zapata! (1952)

Folk themes feature in many of North's scores: Mexican and American Indian music in *Viva Zapata!*, *Under the Volcano*,[38] *Cheyenne Autumn*; Sicilian music in *The Rose Tattoo*; American folk in *The Rainmaker*. The composer's approach to both folk and historical musical materials was more or less the same: he would research, absorb, and assimilate as much as possible of each type of music, then write original music wholly infused by what he had learned, but would also draw upon contemporary compositional techniques. He sometimes called this a process of "simulation."[39]

After *Streetcar*'s simulation of jazz, the next score in which he drew on the technique was Kazan's *Viva Zapata!*, which Hugo Friedhofer believed to be the "best film score by a North American in the Mexican idiom."[40] The film tells the history of the Mexican revolutionary Emiliano Zapata (1879–1919) and was scripted by John Steinbeck. North described the film as "epic and documentary in feeling," though, as with *Cleopatra* and *Spartacus*, North's score also assists in personalizing the key protagonists.[41] The film's narrative has a dual focus: Zapata and the people of Mexico. Their collective goal is land reform—that is, the recovery of land taken by the dictator Diaz. Ultimately, however, after experiencing the corrupting influence of power, Zapata urges the villagers to take charge of their own destiny and not look for leaders to command them. North's score provides a balance for this dual focus while also infusing almost all of the cues with the rhythms and melodies of rural Mexico. His interest in the country's music had been prompted by a tour he made there with Anna Sokolow's dance group in the late 1930s. During preproduction, North took the opportunity to revisit Mexico to research folk songs, after which he made suggestions to Kazan regarding the choice of the songs to be sung and played by the villagers as source music.[42] Much of North's score for *Zapata* is organized around the treatment of Mexican and American Indian folk tunes of the region, as with the melancholy solo flute line based on a Yaqui death chant in the cue "Innocente's Death" (Reel 3: Part 3).[43]

Example 2.2. *Viva Zapata!*, Innocente's Death, bb. 5–11

The score's extremely bright "Main Title" is structured episodi-
cally and begins with a mildly cacophonous fanfare sequence. A spir-
ited and heavily accented shrill trumpet motif is heard in octaves, with
interjections from strings, woodwind, and percussion (tambourine,
snare drum, and crash cymbals) that drive forward in figures of single
and double quavers, with accents that frequently fall on off-beats, presenting rhythmic clashes with quaver triplet figures in the brass. An
introductory passage signals the next section and sets up a more regular
meter only to upset it briefly soon after. Here a more extensive theme is
introduced by wind and upper brass. At the end of each phrase, strings
and brass interject with a response. After four phrases (in a variant of
an AA'BB' pattern), continuity is disturbed by the return of themes in
diminishing lengths, unsettling the meter further. A number of North's
other Mexican-influenced cues for the film also use irregular patterns
of notes and rests to create the metric instability that characterizes the
rural music of Mexico.[44]

Metric ambiguity to a lesser degree is generated in the most dramatically impressive cue of the film, "Gathering Forces" (Reel 4: Part
1), heard when Zapata is taken away by the Rurales (government
troops) to be hanged for his interference in the arrest of a peasant for
slipping into what used to be his own field at night to plant corn. The
villagers hold Zapata in high esteem for this stand against the Rurales.
When Zapata is dragged away with a rope around his neck, his brother
begins a primitive form of telegraph by knocking stones together in a
regular rhythm. The villagers join in and very slowly peasants working
the land begin to appear alongside Zapata as he is led through the coun-
tryside. The source sound of the rhythmic pattern is then taken up by
North's underscore.

The cue begins quietly with bongos and timbales. A side drum is
added with a triplet semiquaver figure heard as a drum roll. Although
the cue is written in 3/4, the percussion articulates a regular, accented
(compound) duple-meter pattern (6/8), adding to the sense of a controlled militarization (Ex. 2.3). This continues through to the end of the
cue. Flutes and guitar join quietly two bars later, and so begins the
gradual amassing of the peasant forces on screen and the orchestra on
the soundtrack. As the forces gather, the tempo accelerates generating
an overwhelming sense of impending action. In bar 23, cellos enter
with a simple and dignified Mexican song theme in A major articulated
clearly in 3/4, which unsettles the hitherto regular 6/8 meter generated
by the percussion track (Ex. 2.4).[45] The orchestration of the theme is
steadily augmented by the remainder of the orchestra, with major third
harmonies added along with counter-melodies and more substantial

accompaniment figures. The cue's theme is built from four, four-bar phrases (A) plus coda, which are then repeated in a slightly developed form (A'), followed by a bridge passage (B) built from fragments of the wind interjections heard in the first part of the cue, now more uncertain in terms of meter. This overall AA'B form is repeated, with the theme now pitched two octaves higher and led by the upper strings. The cue ends partway through the second bridge passage as Zapata's brother arrives on horseback with others to challenge the Rurales directly.

Example 2.3. *Viva Zapata!*, "Gathering Forces," bb. 1–8

Example 2.4. *Viva Zapata!*, "Gathering Forces," bb. 23–30

Along with "Caesar's Assassination" from *Cleopatra* (discussed below), North regularly cited "Gathering Forces" as one of his favorite cues. The fact that the scene contains no dialogue is key to its success. When it was dubbed, Kazan asked that the sound effects be cut to enable the music to "carry the scene."[46] Such opportunities are rarely experienced by film composers. Here North judged perfectly the escalation of the dramatic qualities in the scene, matching it with a theme of quiet dignity that is gradually transformed into one of triumph.

The Bad Seed (1956)

A thriller of sorts, and one of the earliest films with an evil child plotline, North's score for *The Bad Seed* abounds with classic tension-generating features: murmurings from bass clarinet and bassoon with or without lower strings; fragments of atonal melodies; clusters of high string pitches; brief flourishes and interjections at the extremes of register; dissonant harmony; ostinato figures that comprise circular chord sequences, rather than functional progressions. But the score also displays a high degree of thematic unity in its development of a pre-existent tune—the French children's song "Au clair de la lune"—and three interrelated original melodies that emphasize North's ability to write simple, memorable diatonic melodies. These themes are little altered through the score, though they are dramatically recontextualized in subsequent cues, most often by means of a dissonant accompaniment, counterbalancing their diatonicism. Cues that feature these melodies are usually formed from song structures.

From the outset of the film, "Au clair de la lune" is associated with the child Rhoda Penmark; she plays the tune on the piano on three separate occasions, and hums it on a fourth.[47] Its melody is extremely simple, as befits a child's song: melodic motion is largely step-wise, the harmonic language basic (tonic and dominant), and it is structured in AABA form. The tune also frames the film's narrative: it forms the central melodic material of the Main Title credits and the final cue: "The final bang."[48]

Example 2.5. "Au clair de la lune," bb. 1–2

The main title is characteristically episodic, with contained musical units passed between groups of instruments animated by syncopated interjections. The delivery of frenzied lines competing for attention generates cacophony. In fact there is little substance or real progression in this stormy scherzo, rather a sense of boisterousness or flighty childish excitement, which thus succinctly sets the tone for the film's narrative.

Thunder ‖ Intro ‖ A ‖ Intro ‖ A' ‖ A" ‖ Thunder ‖ Coda
          (fanfare)   (fanfare)

Table 2.1. *The Bad Seed*, **Main Title, Episodic structure**

The cue begins with a crack of thunder followed by a bright and deliberate descending figure in brass and wind, given momentum by emphasis on the last quaver of each 4/4 bar. This is followed by a hurried rendition of the first four lines of "Au clair de la lune" on tuned percussion with a sequential counter-melody in lower brass and forceful interjections at quirky and off-kilter points in the bar from brass and wind (A). The fanfare-like opening descent returns, followed by another rapid version of the melody on percussion, interrupted after two lines by a much slower, stodgier version of the theme in low brass. Above this strings dart about in the middle register in a *moto perpetuo* figuration later taken up by upper wind and strings (A').[49] "Au clair de la lune" appears again at the initial tempo, first in a high register, then a lower one, closing with a flourish (A"). A second crack of thunder is heard, followed by a short sinister coda with interjections from timpani, and low then upper wind as the camera turns its view away from the pier back towards the town, the setting for the film's action.

During the film, the same theme functions in the underscore as a leitmotif for Rhoda; she is usually either present or in the thoughts of another character when it is heard. As arranged by North, the melody lacks expressive manipulation, and is subject to no more than rudimentary variation—shifts in register, instrumentation, tempo, or augmentation of duration, for example—though its accompaniment is frequently dissonant. This unemotional presentation of the melody in the context of a disquieting background serves as a musical analogue to Rhoda's pathological indifference, her failure to register even basic moral distinctions. Reference to "Au clair de la lune" ranges from fragments of the repeated pitches at the start of the melody, to an insistent repetition of the first phrase as Rhoda confesses to the boy's murder to her mother, through to expressions of the theme in full, as in the version for piano heard in increasingly dissonant contrary motion as Rhoda walks resolutely through the storm to the pier to recover the medal at the end of the film.

The expressive and melancholy thematic material that North generates in the three additional diatonic themes contrasts with the mechanical insistence and cold orchestration of "Au clair de la lune." One theme is simple and fluid with step-wise motion in triple-time answered by a more arpeggiated second phrase with slight syncopation (see below, Ex. 2.6). The second theme is a little more complicated, though it retains the fluid scalic motion of the opening of the previous one. Leaps of a fourth and fifth add emotional intensity and a more resolute quality (Ex. 2.7). Through the course of the film, both themes become associated with mother-daughter relationships: Christine's gradual realization that she is the daughter of Bessie Denker, an infamous serial killer; Christine's growing suspicions about her daughter, Rhoda; Rhoda's confessions of her crimes to her mother; Christine's attempt to murder her daughter with sleeping pills prior to attempting suicide. A third theme is heard on the two occasions when Mrs. Daigle visits Christine, expressing her grief at the loss of her only child (Ex. 2.8). The theme takes the form of a lullaby with a simple repeated accompaniment figure that continues throughout, inscribing an alternation between two chords. The melody begins with an emotive octave leap, followed by an elaborated descent back to the original pitch. While each of the themes is simple and constructed to indicate the naiveté of music associated with childhood and nursery rhymes, only this latter theme—given to the family of one of Rhoda's victims—is truly "innocent."

Example 2.6. *The Bad Seed*, My Baby (Reel 13: Part 1), bb. 60–67

Example 2.7. *The Bad Seed*, My Baby (Reel 13: Part 1), bb. 1–4

Example 2.8. *The Bad Seed*, **No More Children (Reel 6: Part 2), bb. 5–8 (vl II and vle)**

Spartacus (1960)

Despite North's notoriety as a composer of dissonant chromatic scores, some of the most memorable of his themes are simple, lyrical diatonic melodies, such as those mentioned above. In the main these are used as love themes or for female characters (cf. Blanche in *Streetcar*, Varinia in *Spartacus*, Linda in *Salesman*, Deborah in *Cheyenne Autumn*). In several cases, the referential qualities of these motifs widen to encompass more universal themes as the narrative develops. In *Salesman*, for example, Linda's theme can be understood to develop an association with redemption and forgiveness more generally. In *Spartacus*, Varinia's theme develops to include mutual respect through Spartacus and Varinia's love, through to hope for the next generation. This is experienced most powerfully at the end of the film when Varinia shows the crucified Spartacus their son. A key theme in *Streetcar*'s score offers a similar case of referential widening, as I explain in chapter 5.

In a number of North's film scores, including *Streetcar*, extended versions of these lyrical themes are heard in song-form. Structural repetition and simplicity adds to their familiarity and memorability. Examples include the lullaby in *The Bad Seed* (Ex. 2.8 above) and the theme that is generated gradually via accumulation in the "Gathering Forces" cue in *Viva Zapata!*, and "Varinia's theme" in the score for *Spartacus*. The theme is first heard when Varinia is delivered to Spartacus's cell, where he reveals to her that he has "never had a woman." His awe and respect for Varinia lead to taunts from Batiatus—watching from above with Marcellus—and to her removal from the cell.

Example 2.9. *Spartacus*, **Varinia's theme (a), bb. 1–4**

The repeated three-note figure at the opening of "Varinia's theme" is developed and expanded to generate the theme's continuation (bars three and four) (A). A number of North's themes develop in this way, and are thus highly unified within themselves in addition to relationships generated with other themes. The second four-bar phrase (A2) is an almost identical repeat of the first, with the pitch of the penultimate note raised by a tone. These opening phrases are mainly accompanied by an alternation between the chords of Em^{add9} and Am^7, which present a relatively stable tonic-subdominant relationship, albeit a melancholy one. The second phrase opens with a chord on the submediant—C— which lifts the mood slightly and prepares the listener for the brief shift to G (the relative major) in the third phrase (B). Here, North shifts into 4/4 for five bars, with the opening phrase in G and developed slightly. The shift to 4/4 incurs a slight lengthening of the sustained pitch (here, B), with the motif extended via ornamentation in bars 9 and 11:

Example 2.10. *Spartacus*, **Varinia's theme, bb. 7–12**

A rest bar is added at the end of the phrase. This functions as a deliberate pause before the return of the opening motif in 3/4. It does not return in full immediately, however. Instead, it is completed by modified versions of the figure, followed by an altered recapitulation of the opening theme and accompaniment, now in E major and incorporating the three-quaver figure from bars 9 and 11 of the B section. This phrase is subsequently repeated in a slightly modified form, but cut short at three bars.

Example 2.11. *Spartacus*, **Varinia's theme, bb. 18–21**

Batiatus and Marcellus's laughter and mockery of Spartacus follow. This is underscored by eight bars of an arpeggiation of a single dissonant chord of $B+^{{\flat}9{\flat}13}$ played by strings (*sul ponticello*), harp and four clarinets: an augmented major chord that incorporates a tritone. The sequence ends with a pause bar. As the focus returns to Spartacus and Varinia much of the cue is then recapitulated with only minor alterations to instrumentation and arrangement. The four bars of B—now heard in 3/4—are followed by a brief pause during which Spartacus asks Varinia's name, which she reveals as the theme reenters. The cue ends with four bars of the theme in E following Varinia's removal from the cell. The theme is played predominantly by solo wind instruments, notably oboe and oboe d'amore, supported by muted strings and horns, with delicate ornamentation from a variety of tuned percussion instruments.

3A							
Theme:	A	A2	B	A3	A4	A5	
bars: 2	4	4	5	4	4	3	‖ 8 ‖
Key:	Em		G [4/4]	Em	E		B+♭9♭13
3B							
Theme:	A	A2	B	A3'	A4'		
Bars: 2	4	4	4	4			
Key:	Em		G	Em	E		

Table 2.2. *Spartacus*, **Varinia's theme (3A and 3B), Structure**

This gentle and intimate scene is followed by loud, repetitive, agitated, quick tempo sequences of gladiator training which are intercut with much more placid scenes of the developing relationship between Spartacus and Varinia, largely unspoken but usually underscored by elements or arrangements of Varinia's theme. Fragments of the theme's opening figure are heard briefly during the cue "Painting" (4B), when Marcellus uses Spartacus's body to demonstrate the different levels of injury that may be inflicted upon an opponent in the arena, though this is actually generated from a minor key version of the Slavery theme. The opening motif is heard in the cue "Cell" (4C), played on solo violin, as Marcellus mocks Spartacus further by having Varinia enter his cell, only to pull her out and send her to another gladiator. It is repeated as Spartacus looks protectively at the wall that connects his cell to the next, where Varinia has been placed. Extended arrangements of the theme are heard in the two "Kitchen" cues (4D and 4F/5A), in which "no talking" is allowed. Once again, then, the theme does not have to compete with dialogue.[50]

The music for the gladiator training sequences demonstrates well the "feeling for movement" in North's music. In these sequences North creates an energetic and agitated, yet utterly relentless atmosphere that does much to suggest that the gladiators are still enslaved. Musically this is achieved through a combination of fanfare-like motifs, insistent *moto perpetuo* string figures, unsettling and slippery ostinatos, and persistent accented interjections—both regular and irregular—played on brass, wind, and percussion and which undermine metrical stability. A more relaxed sense of metric instability combined with a sense of martial discipline is heard in the cue "Vesuvius Camp" (12B), which accompanies scenes in which the gladiators begin to train the slave army and reflects well their newfound freedom (see Ex. 2.12 below). It is a bright, upbeat cue, its theme heard first played by horns, lending impetus with an accented note at the end of the 3/4 bar (later replaced by cymbal crashes). Further lines are added, first by the trumpets, later in strings and winds. The cue retains a folky, playful quality throughout, not least due to the 5/8 meter, but it also displays a driving sense of purpose and energy through the gradual buildup of additional lines and orchestral forces. By contrast, the brief but sharply drawn cue heard a little later and associated with the march of Glabrus and his soldiers towards battle with the slave army—"Glabrus March #2" (14A)—is dissonant, shrill, repetitive, and rigid in a four-square 2/4 meter. It includes tropes and instrumentation associated with military marches. Musically speaking, North's music for the slave army is far more vibrant and engaging than that which he uses to represent the expertly drilled but utterly inflexible might of the Roman legions, however imposing.

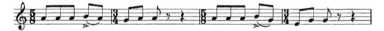

Example 2.12. *Spartacus*, **Vesuvius Camp, horn theme**

A similar distinction can be heard in the rhythmic features of the music used to represent the recreation of the slaves in contrast with that of the Roman nobles. For the slaves, North synthesized folk and other secular materials of the region and period. Typically such cues involve large instrumental ensembles that express emphatic, repeated rhythmic figurations, often in dance rhythms, with accents that alternately confirm the metric pulse and then deviate from it. Such cues capture well the sense of the slave army as a collective, experiencing liberation for the first time. By contrast, as Henderson points out, "The music of the Roman nobles mainly has continuous rhythmic and melodic flow, longer note values, light, not rhythmically determined percussion fillings."[51] This more "rarefied" music depicts the nobles' own view of their culture as superior, sophisticated, and deserving of respect. Yet, while the slaves' recreational music is more obviously rooted in the body and its celebration, it is the music of the Romans that is imbued with decadence through exoticism. This is most explicit in the cue "Snails and Oysters" (9A Source), initially a bath scene in which Crassus makes a thinly veiled reference to bisexuality and attempts to seduce Antoninus. The scene was cut from the film prior to release to satisfy the Production Code but has recently been restored.[52] The cue— in the Phrygian mode[53]—is characterized by a slow melodic line in a high register played in unison by instruments that include a Novachord and crotales, punctuated and supported by delicate interjections on guitar and harp, and glissandi performed on a Chinese bell tree.[54] The timbre is unusual and exotic and is similar to that heard in other scenes where source music provides a background to the conversations of Roman nobles: the conversations between Batiatus and the visiting nobles at the gladiator training school in Capua, scenes at the Roman baths (in which a sistrum and kithara are seen on screen), and Crassus's attempts to win Varinia's heart.

Cleopatra (1963)

North further developed his experimentation with orchestral timbres in *Cleopatra*, noting that certain of his cues for the film were "even more way-out" than those for *Spartacus*.[55] In one scene, North's score includes sistrum, crotales and small dinner-bells, gamelan, tuned cowbells, five suspended cymbals, triangles, and small gongs. In another cue he used all seven members of the saxophone family—sopranino, soprano, alto, tenor, baritone, bass, and contrabass—noting that they make "a great sound when played without any vibrato."[56] The first of the "African Dancer" cues (Reel 11: Part 3), which accompany Cleopatra's ceremonial entrance into Rome, features steel drum, boo-bams, timbales, conga drums, timpani played by wooden mallets near the rim, log drums, tambourine, and bass marimba. The second (Reel 11: Part 4) also includes tuned cowbells and tuned temple blocks, with hard mallets or sticks stipulated for most of the percussion.

North used modal writing, particularly in the Phrygian mode, to indicate the period and region of the action, as when the banquet is set before Cleopatra's other guests on the golden barge in the cue "Food" (Reel 18: Part 5). The relative simplicity of the cue—a plain and rhythmically austere melody on flutes and piccolos in triple time, which is accompanied by regular interjections of more florid wind ornamentation and a modest collection of exotic percussion—contrasts with the more exhilarating, sumptuous, and rhythmically intricate music for the entertainment: a celebration to honor Bacchus, the god of wine and intoxication. A larger ensemble is used and formed into groups, each of which articulates and repeats a pithy rhythmic pattern in rapid compound duple meter, later modified or replaced by a new pattern. Much of the first section is performed in upper registers. Towards the end, piccolos play patterns built from fragments of the theme "Cleopatra's Ambition." The second section appears to set a quicker tempo (in duple meter), but slower thematic material plays in a lower register, with sleigh-bells, tambourine, and Chinese bell tree heard more prominently. This section accompanies Anthony's drunken attempts to reach Cleopatra's double, featured in the dance. As he kisses the double he sees the real Cleopatra depart. Visual effects reveal the extent of his inebriation.

Suddenly, an additional cue—labeled variously "Insert [or Sweetner (sic)] (Reel 19: Part 2A)"—begins, layered atop the entertainment music which has now been faded a little lower in the mix; it enters shortly before the return to 6/8 in the entertainment music beneath (see below, Ex. 2.13). The insert is performed primarily by strings and flutes and is marked "Very Intense." The cue depicts the strength of Anthony's anguish caused by the depth of his feeling for the Egyptian Queen combined with his drunken state as he tries to escape the dancers to reach her. The layering of this haunting music over the continuation of the frivolous entertainment enhances our perception of Anthony's powerful emotions and his confusion. Playing high in their register, the string sound is both harsh and potent. The chords slide from one to another—often chromatically—with a trace of *portamento*. Most of these chords are triads which include both major and minor thirds (major triads with added sharp ninths). This generates intervals of crunchy minor seconds and a confusion of major/minor functionality which remains unresolved through a series of chords of the same type.[57] This layering of two different pieces—most often with at least one organized into a clear rhythmic pattern—can be heard elsewhere in North's oeuvre to indicate mental confusion or an interpolation of memories, as happens in *Streetcar*, for example.

The synthesis of archaic and regional styles and instrumentation with contemporary scoring techniques can be heard in another cue from *Cleopatra*: "Caesar's Assassination" (Reel 14: Part 1A).[58] The cue accompanies the scene in which Cleopatra appears to watch Caesar's murder in the flames of a ritual fire with the assistance of her High Priestess. As elsewhere in North's scores, the music builds to a climax when several separately developed elements begin to function collectively.

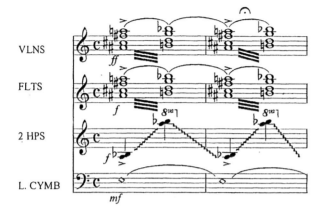

Example 2.13. *Cleopatra*, Bacchūs, Section 2, Insert, bb. 1–2

The cue begins with *divisi* bassoons and contra bassoons articulating a simple accompaniment figure low in their registers, with subtle atmospheric support from percussion (gongs, bass drum, and timpani). Harp and celeste enter with arpeggiated figures as violins perform a glissando between a dissonant cluster chord (B F A B♭ C♯ D) and a chord of D$^{\Delta\sharp11}$. Clarinets mimic the bassoon entries at a brief delay. Alto and bass flutes enter at bar twelve with a serpent-like figure that embellishes the pitches of C and G♯ (see below, Ex. 2.14). Simultaneously, celli enter with a line that is to become the central unifying feature of the cue. Each of these elements continues with gradually modified figures and additional instruments added throughout. But the slow and deliberate unison cello line progressively takes center stage with its microtonal pitch adjustments, insistent short-lived *crescendi* from *fortepiano*, combined with an alternation of pitches warmed by vibrato and those labeled "Cold. No Vibrato." Through the cue, the line steadily ascends almost two octaves from its starting point, D above the bass staff. Pressure for the ascent seems to come from within, with sustained pitches regularly nudged sharp by a quarter tone. Intensity increases with the rising pitch and the addition of further strings: third violins at bar 29, seconds at bar 35, and the remaining violins at bar 39. These additional string voices are needed for the line to be heard above the growing clamor of other instruments—particularly percussion—that continue beneath. Caesar is stabbed as the pitch finally reaches A above the treble staff (the dominant), expanding the frame of the D–G♯ interval first heard in violin chords at the start of the cue (bb. 5–8). High brass join, with horns adding a motif that indicates Caesar's inevitable fall. The strings and trumpets continue their rise as Caesar stumbles toward Brutus, ending at C above the treble staff as he is stabbed by Brutus.

Example 2.14. *Cleopatra,* **Assassination (R19: P1A), bb. 12–15**

Who's Afraid of Virginia Woolf? (1966)

Although North had already produced scores for a number of play adaptations by the mid-1960s, he found it hard to find an approach that was suitable for Edward Albee's *Who's Afraid of Virginia Woolf?* He described it as "Probably the most difficult assignment that I've ever had in my whole career [...]. [...] what do you do with all this dialogue? With all this tension that's there in front of you?"[59] North's answer, ultimately, was to "try and establish a sort of musical statement that was partly melancholy—simple and sort of. quasi-baroque."[60] In this way the tragic, turbulent relationship between Martha and George is reconciled with the depth of feeling they have for one another.

The film begins with a short cue—"Moon"—heard as the couple leave a campus party by moonlight, which quickly segues into the next—"Prelude (Main Title)"—after we overhear a little of the couple's conversation. Here, as George Burt notes, "North highlights two dramatic factors. One is on the surface—the lazy quality of a casual walk home. The other is a deeper, more ethereal quality associated with a quiet, moonlit environment."[61] In "Moon," these different elements are underscored by alternating timbres and harmonies. First, woodwinds and trombones play a chord Ebm^9 over an Ab bass (or Ab^{11}, no third). Then, strings and harp trill over a sustained cluster of the pitches of a diatonic C major cluster chord over G, high in their registers. Essentially this presents an alternation between the black and white notes on a keyboard with no clear sense whether the first (largely wind) chord is major or minor. A three-note celeste motif is heard over the wind chords and acts as a timbral bridge linking the wind chords to string and harp clusters. It also connects with the melodic figures of the guitar and harp of the "Prelude (Main Title)."

After the hazy atmospherics of "Moon," the unambiguous diatonic simplicity of the "Prelude (Main Title)," with its lyrical surface dialogue between guitar and harp, presents a more peaceful and stable character. The guitar and harp figures and elements of their accompaniment recur during the film, adding a background of calm against the much noisier foreground in which Martha and George engage in verbal abuse, histrionics, and psychological aggression. Yet, ultimately, both the play and the film suggest a strong bond of love at the heart of their marriage. It is this deeper-level truth that so much of North's film music underscores.

Like "Varinia's Theme" in *Spartacus*, the structure of "Prelude (Main Title)" is simple: a basic AA'BA form in 4/4, in which A' varies from A only slightly. More unusually, the A sections are in units of ten bars in G, while the B section is in G minor and is eleven bars long. Despite the surface motion and the functionality of the harmony, the cue feels held back or tardy. This may be the result of the unusual phrase lengths or the relatively slow meter emphasized by the plodding crotchet motion of the bass-line (crotchet = 52). This lack of dynamism assists in presenting an atmosphere of calm and resignation.

Example 2.15. *Who's Afraid of Virginia Woolf?* **Prelude (Main Title), bb. 1–10**

Many of the play adaptations that North scored employ a great deal of dialogue, monologues, and sometimes soliloquy. North underscores some of these sequences in his film scores, though the same sequences were probably not scored in their original stage productions. Burt argues that the dynamic relationship that can develop between an actor and his or her audience members in a live setting through a simultaneity of time and space negates the need to underscore the dialogue: "An aura of collective involvement in what is being said spreads throughout the audience."[62] With cinema, of course, the action in the film projected on screen does not take place live before the spectators, however: it is performed and recorded, often out of chronological sequence, and only then edited together. Along with continuity editing, music can play an important role in generating engagement between the spectator, the film, and its characters similar to that experienced between the actor and spectator in live theater. In his discussion of part of the dialogue-laden "Bergin" scene in *Who's Afraid of Virginia Woolf?*, Burt argues that the "need for music originates, in part, with the necessity for a coalescence of these images into a directed pattern. A rhythmic frame of reference or sense of pulse can contribute to this process."[63] North was particularly good at providing apt and appropriate musical "frames" for key scenes in which dialogue (or monologue) forms the dramatic focus. North scored such scenes highly selectively, however, thereby emphasizing their significance. Several of these sequences are exceptional in their holistic integration of music, dialogue, acting and choreography, sound, camerawork, and editing.

As many film composers have stated, it is extremely difficult to underscore dialogue in such a way that the semantics of language and its performed delivery are enhanced, but not detracted from. This was even more difficult in the earliest years of synchronized sound due to the limitations of the microphones used for recording and the playback equipment in cinemas. Putting technological constraints to one side, the composer must also remain mindful of the physiological, psychological, and cognitive constraints that may be experienced by a spectator when presented with an overload of auditory information, particularly when different sources use the same or similar frequencies. In successful sequences of dialogue underscoring, composers choose instrumentation and register carefully to avoid conflict between the frequencies of the music and those of the actors' voices. For such scenes, North stated that he avoided "anything that's thick texturewise and all doubling, and I try for a more-or-less transparent score, depending on the scene."[64]

North's score for *Streetcar* includes one of the most extraordinary examples of such sequences, as I explore in chapter 5. The scene in which Blanche reveals the truth of her life in Oriel to Mitch—underscored by North's "Revelation" cue (Reel 11: Part 1)—is truly operatic in its conception, and in the extent to which the dynamic of the drama is structured and emphasized by North's music. A scene in *The Member of the Wedding* approximates a similar sense of integration, though to a lesser degree.

An adaptation of a novel by Carson McCullers, *The Member of the Wedding* follows a young girl from a Southern family, Frankie, through an awkward adjustment to adolescence when her older brother marries. With her mother long dead, Frankie (Julie Harris) is tended to by the family's housekeeper, Berenice (Ethel Waters). In a particularly affecting scene, Berenice tells Frankie and her playmate of the night that her true love died: "Bernie's Philosophy" (6B). North emphasized that in this cue he aimed to complement Ethel Waters's performance of the scene: "I was very much taken with her performance. As you recall, it was very, very unusual. So touching and poignant, and I wrote this piece which is—well, it's an accompaniment to what she was saying, rather than a duplication of what she was trying to recall of her one and only romance."[65]

Dramatic pauses in the delivery of the dialogue are gently pulsed and pressed forward by the continuing flow of the music. Specific spoken phrases are emphasized by musical phrasing, where the melodic line and its rhythms resonate with the pitch and rhythm of significant words spoken by Berenice. The effect is of a powerful amalgamation of music and dialogue, with music supporting Berenice's heightened and dramatic speech. On the one hand, the effect might be considered similar to operatic recitative, where vocal writing is used to mimic dramatic speech in sung form. However, given North's use of song-forms in the structure of extended cues such as this, alongside the dramatic power of the dialogue and its delivery, it is plausible to suggest that such sequences are analogous to operatic arias rather than to recitative.

Burt provides an excellent and detailed analysis of an equally dramatic scene in *Who's Afraid of Virginia Woolf?*: George's poignant monologue underscored by North's "Bergin" cue (Reel 6: Part 1).[66] In a subtly different vein, below I provide an extract from North's cue, "Colloquy" (Reel 5: Part 1), which precedes the Bergin sequence, assisting in its preparation. In its Latin roots, the cue's title may be interpreted as "conversation," but, unlike the Bergin monologue, here the dialogue is low-key: it appears to be a humdrum exchange between a couple of drunken men—George (Richard Burton) and Nick (George Segal)—in which they talk of their wives. But this seemingly banal and confused conversation culminates in the revelation of intimate secrets.

North's cue creates a gentle but regular pace as Nick leaves Martha (Elizabeth Taylor), to tend to his vomiting wife, Honey (Sandy Dennis). The extract below is from a section that begins as Nick joins George, Martha's husband, in the garden. The thematic integration of the score is also demonstrated here: the cue's melodic material is clearly developed from "Prelude (Main Title)" (see Ex. 2.15 above). The familiarity and simplicity of the cue's thematic material supports the audience's focus on the dialogue, which I have added at its approximate placement in relation to the cue, with Nick's lines above those of George (see below, Ex. 2.16).

As can be seen, here North frequently emphasizes dialogue via melodic entries and movement, as with "drink," "yum-yum," "she gets sick." Elsewhere, words are emphasized by their occurrence on strong beats, as with "slim-hipped" and "Martha?" The section is built around a development of the score's guitar theme with slight rhythmic variations, presenting a smoother version of the theme in terms of dynamic motion. The extract outlines a slow build to a registral peak, which is followed by direct reference to the guitar/harp figures in their original dotted crotchet rhythm. The pitch climax is heard as George tells Nick that Martha has spent time in a rest home. This is also the longest continuous segment of dialogue. By sustaining a chord, North keeps the music out of the way of the line, but through its prominence as the (prolonged) registral highpoint, North also suggests that George is "performing" for his guest, since soon after George reveals that Martha has not visited a rest home, though, quietly, he adds that *he* would like to. The cue ends with George's next line: "It gets a little bouncy around here sometimes."

Example 2.16. *Who's Afraid of Virginia Woolf!*, **Colloquy, bb. 52–79**[67]

    The types of approaches taken by North in the examples discussed above have been selected as representative of some of the principal techniques the composer used in his film scores of the 1950s and 1960s. More specifically, elements from each of these practices can be found in the score for *Streetcar*, as explored in chapters 4 and 5.

3

THE HISTORICAL AND CRITICAL
CONTEXT OF *STREETCAR*

Tennessee Williams's play *A Streetcar Named Desire* debuted on Broadway in December 1947 after out-of-town tryouts in New Haven, Boston, and Philadelphia. It was produced by Irene M. Selznick,[1] and at Williams's request it was directed by the young Elia Kazan, who went on to direct the film adaptation three years later. The play won critical acclaim and several awards: the Pulitzer Prize for Drama, the New York Critics' Circle, and the Donaldson Award. It ran for almost two years at the Ethel Barrymore Theatre in New York, and road companies were also established. The play was also something of a *cause célèbre*, particularly in its interrogation of sexuality, and this goes some way towards explaining the initial reticence of Hollywood to adapt it into a film.

Williams adapted the screenplay himself, with the assistance of Oscar Saul. It follows the play's script relatively closely, though changes were made to placate the Production Code Administration (hereafter, PCA) and gain its seal. With the exception of a small number of scenes filmed outside the apartment, Kazan changed little in terms of his direction of the action. He briefly considered opening out the play thoroughly to include sequences depicting Blanche's life in Laurel, but in the final analysis decided to "[film] the play as it was because there was nothing to change. ... *Streetcar* is a perfect play."[2]

In their collaboration on *Streetcar*, Kazan and Williams demonstrated great respect for one another's work.[3] Kazan influenced the shaping of the play significantly in its progression from preproduction into rehearsals and tryouts, as did the play's first cast and crew. As he later stated: "Williams's play ... now had to be transformed into a living thing, and I had the responsibility of supervising the metamorphosis."[4] Although the playscript was complete before Kazan was contracted, Williams's presence at rehearsals enabled both the playwright and the director to effect changes to the script. As discussed in chapter 4, Kazan also made significant changes to Williams's instructions for music, and this had implications for the characterization of Blanche, in particular. In the main these changes were retained and developed in the transformation of the play into a film.

Given the similarity between the film and the play, and the continued collaboration of director and playwright in the development of the film, I begin this chapter with a short synopsis of the play's action. This is followed by a brief contextualization of Williams's and Kazan's aesthetic approaches during the period. Each brought a distinct style to the play's production, though ultimately their ideas were complementary, resulting in a concept usefully encapsulated by Brenda Murphy as "subjective realism." In Kazan's direction of both the play and film this is demonstrated most clearly in the finely wrought balance between Blanche and Stanley.

Synopsis

> BLANCHE: "They told me to take a street-car named Desire, and then transfer to one called Cemeteries and ride six blocks and get off at—Elysian Fields."[5]

The setting for the play is a rented two-room apartment in New Orleans, next to the L&N rail tracks. A long-widowed sister arrives for an extended stay with her younger sibling, Stella, who is married to Stanley Kowalski—a second-generation Polish immigrant. Stella is pregnant with their first child. The sisters are of aristocratic Southern stock fallen on hard times. While Stella left the ancestral home—Belle Reve ("beautiful dream")—to pursue a life of her own, Blanche, a high school teacher of English, stayed on and nursed the older-generation family members until their deaths. Her early marriage to the young, beautiful, and sensitive Allan Grey was cut short by his suicide, for which she blames herself. Unseen, she saw him in bed with a male friend. Later the same evening while dancing the Varsouviana with her husband at the Moon Lake Casino she revealed what she had seen and told him that he disgusted her. He pulled away from her, ran outside and shot himself. Blanche later realized that he had turned to her for help, but that she had not understood. She treasures the poems and love letters that he wrote to her, and is haunted by the music they danced to that night and the sound of the shot that follows. Her sudden arrival in New Orleans is due to a leave of absence from her teaching post, apparently caused by shattered nerves. Belle Reve has been lost to debtors.

Blanche's presence has an unsettling effect on the relationship between Stella and Stanley. Blanche is affronted by Stanley's rough manners and lack of refinement. She is also disturbed by the physical basis of Stella's love for him ("brutal desire"[6]), and her sister's apparent acceptance of a social situation far beneath that for which they were groomed by their upbringing. Stanley is irritated by Blanche, and is highly suspicious of her. He is angered by her patronizing yet flirtatious manner, her constant bathing, and her collection of seemingly fine clothing and jewelry. Her arrival drives a wedge between the couple, leaving Stella caught between Blanche and Stanley at the center of a tug-of-war for affection and loyalty.

Raised as a wealthy debutante but now a poor and lonely widow in her thirties, Blanche is wholly reliant on her looks, charm, and breeding to find the protection she seeks. She is vulnerable and sensitive about her age, all too aware that her beauty is fading. When she meets Stanley's friend, Mitch, she sees in him a final hope of security. As she says of Stanley, "Maybe he's what we need to mix with our blood now that we've lost Belle Reve."[7] Mitch is fascinated by Blanche and the world of magic and illusion that she creates; for her, it is a refuge from harsh reality. Terrified that Mitch will lose interest in her, she gently resists his advances in the hope of securing a proposal of marriage. While she awaits Mitch's arrival early one evening, a boy comes collecting for a local newspaper and for the first time we see Blanche's desire for young men: we watch as she charms a kiss from the stranger's lips just moments before Mitch appears.

Keen to get rid of his sister-in-law, Stanley uses his connections to investigate Blanche's story. He discovers that after the loss of Belle Reve she moved to the Hotel Flamingo, a residence known for turning a blind eye to its guests' behavior. But her conduct was so outrageous that she was asked to leave. She had been trying the same act on every man that came along. She was fired from the school when an affair with a 17-year-old boy was discovered. Out of loyalty to his friend, Stanley tells all this to Mitch, who then also checks up on the facts.

Blanche realizes something is wrong when Mitch fails to turn up for her birthday tea. After setting the sisters straight on who runs the household, Stanley gives Blanche a bus ticket back to her hometown. Stella is horrified by his cruelty, but soon afterwards has to ask him to take her to the hospital; she is in labor.

Blanche is left alone in the apartment. Mitch arrives, drunk and angry. He pushes her face into the glare of a bare lightbulb to assess her age; he has realized she has only ever agreed to meet him in the dark, or in dimly lit places. He feels that her lies have made a fool of him, but she tells him that she never lied in her heart. He mentions the Flamingo, and finally she tells him the reality of her life in Laurel. After Allan's death, she had sought out protection anywhere she could find it. She is interrupted when a blind Mexican woman knocks at the door, selling "flowers for the dead." Blanche sends her away, but continues the monologue, explaining to Mitch how death had invaded her life. She even sought escape in the arms of the young soldiers from the nearby barracks. At this Mitch pulls her close: he wants to claim "what I been missing all summer."[8] But as she begs him one last time to marry her, he tells her that she is not clean enough to enter his mother's house. After pushing him away she chases him from the apartment screaming "Fire."

Blanche is no longer able to distinguish between imagination and reality. Stanley returns from the hospital in high spirits to find her dressed in an evening gown and tiara, packing for a cruise to the Caribbean with an old beau, Shep Huntleigh, who wired earlier that evening. In his happy and slightly drunken state, Stanley offers Blanche an olive branch, but she responds by patronizing him which angers him once more. Blanche tells him that after she expelled Mitch for his accusations, he returned to beg forgiveness asking to be given another chance, only for Blanche to realize that their differences were too great to overcome. At this Stanley realizes that there has been no wire. Blanche's comforting illusions are just more lies to Stanley. He flies into a rage. As Blanche unravels further and begins to fear for her safety, Stanley enjoys the physical power he holds over her. She smashes a beer bottle to protect herself, but he sees it as an invitation for some "roughhouse." He overpowers her and carries her to the bed, telling her, "We've had this date with each other from the beginning!"[9]

The final scene takes place after Stella returns home with the baby. Blanche told Stella that Stanley raped her, but Stella refuses to believe her, explaining to her neighbor that she couldn't if she were to continue living with Stanley. Blanche is to be taken into an asylum, though in her confusion she believes that Shep Huntleigh is to visit and take her on a trip. When the doctor arrives, and Blanche realizes that it is not her beau who is taking her away, she tries to escape. A matron struggles with her in an attempt to pacify her, leaving Stella and Mitch overcome at the horror of the scene. After conceding defeat, the doctor gently invites Blanche to take his arm. She thanks him: "Whoever you are—I have always depended on the kindness of strangers."[10] Stella cries out after her sister, while Stanley coos over her, trying to calm her.

Streetcar and Subjective Realism: Characterizing Blanche and Stanley

The more I work on Blanche ... the less insane she seems. She is caught in a fatal inner contradiction, but in another society, she *would* work. In Stanley's society, no![11]

Elia Kazan

One of the play's key strengths is the complexity and ambivalence with which Williams depicts the opposing forces of Blanche and Stanley. In a letter that was to become the "key to the production" for Kazan, Williams attempted to clarify his intentions regarding the play[12]:

There are no "good" or "bad" people. Some are a little better or a little worse but all are activated more by misunderstanding than malice. A blindness to what is going on in each other's hearts. Stanley sees Blanche not as a desperate, driven creature backed into a last corner to make a last desperate stand—but as a calculating bitch with "round heels.".... Nobody sees anybody truly but all through the flaws of their own egos. That is the way we all see each other in life. Vanity, fear, desire, competition—all such distortions within our own egos— condition our vision of those in relation to us. Add to those distortions in our *own* egos, the corresponding distortions in the egos of *others*, and you see how cloudy the glass must become through which we look at each other. […]

I remember you asked me what should an audience feel for Blanche. Certainly pity. It is a tragedy with the classic aim of producing a catharsis of pity and terror and in order to do that, Blanche must finally have the understanding and compassion of the audience. This without creating a black-dyed villain in Stanley. It is a thing (Misunderstanding) not a person (Stanley) that destroys her in the end. In the end you should feel—"If only they all had known about each other."[13]

Williams wanted audience members to be left to make up their own minds about Blanche and Stanley, and this required ensuring that neither was portrayed as essentially evil, nor without flaws. Finding the right balance in bringing this aspect of the play to performance was difficult. Ultimately, the sense of equilibrium that was achieved was also dependent upon other collaborators: notably, Jo Mielziner—the play's production and lighting designer—and the acting of Marlon Brando (Stanley) and Jessica Tandy (Blanche).

In his most successful plays of the 1940s, Williams sought to fuse the expressionism of the experimental theater—the style in which his earlier plays had been written—with the realism associated with Broadway theater. In *Streetcar* he combined realistic storytelling with an expressionist use of language. As Arthur Miller noted, "One knew it had been *written* rather than having been overheard in somebody's kitchen; its lines were fluent and idiomatic but at the same time rhythmically composed."[14] This musical quality in Williams's writing was also to have an impact on North's scoring for the film in at least one key scene, as discussed in chapter 5. In a manifesto that Williams wrote into the production notes for *The Glass Menagerie*—his previous play and his first hit on Broadway—he stated clearly his aesthetic stance:

> Expressionism and all other unconventional techniques in drama have only one valid aim, and that is a closer approach to truth. When a play employs unconventional techniques, it is not, or certainly shouldn't be, trying to escape its responsibility of dealing with reality, or interpreting experience, but is actually or should be attempting to find a closer approach, a more penetrating and vivid expression of things as they are.[15]

In the play script for *Menagerie*, Williams's use of expressionism incorporated slides, scrims, and an important symbolic role for music.[16] The character of Tom frames the play and recounts "what happened." In doing so his subjective memory of events infuses and intertwines with the audience's acceptance of the past presented before them as objective reality. As Brenda Murphy explains, in this way "Williams's drama exploded conventional notions of truth by exposing the inadequacy of the language used to convey them, and did so [...] by exposing the 'hidden secret selves' of its characters at the same time as it maintained the illusion of objective reality regarding events happening in the present of the stage action."[17] Subjective realism also plays an important role in *Streetcar*, most obviously in Williams's characterization of Blanche.[18]

Elia Kazan trained as an actor with the Group Theatre in a technique heavily influenced by the Method developed by Constantin Stanislavski in Moscow. Here "action" as opposed to "acting" took center stage in an approach that was focused on generating a naturalistic manner of performance. Actions formed the "spine" of the play, and of the characters. In addition, actors were encouraged to draw upon their own experiences and memories to recreate the emotional state of the character: emotional memory. As a director, Kazan co-founded the Actors Studio in New York in 1947 where he developed a version of the Method which combined its more cerebral approach with an interest in the body and expressive movement. In this he was influenced by a younger generation of Russian directors such as Evgeny Vakhtangov and Vsevlod Meyerhold, who at least partially rejected the Stanislavskian focus on the naturalistic expression of realism.[19] While retaining the notion of the spine and the importance of improvisation in his work with actors, Kazan's direction focused on "an expressive use of the visual elements of a play—space, movement, gesture, props, set, costumes—to externalize the psychic life of the characters, to objectify the subjective."[20] For Kazan, a character's actions and behaviors reflect the social reality they have experienced, albeit as constructed by the playwright.[21] Indeed, as he later observed of his own directing technique, he "choreographed scenes more than purely psychological directors do."[22]

These elements are evident in the detailed and insightful notes Kazan made in his "director's notebook" regarding *Streetcar* and its key protagonists. A summarized account of some of these notes follows, since they also formed the basis of his preparation for the film. Importantly, Kazan believed that a "stylized production" was necessary because "a subjective factor—Blanche's memories, inner life, emotions, are a real factor. We cannot really understand her behavior unless we see the effect of her past on her present behavior."[23] To this end, the play's props, production style, and characters' behaviors should assist in establishing the characters as social types. Blanche is an "emblem of a dying civilization, making its last curlicued and romantic exit," thus she should be "played, [...] dressed, should move like a stylized figure."[24] By contrast, Stanley is overtly focused on self-gratification:

"Get what's coming to you! Don't waste a day! Eat, drink, get yours!"[25] Kazan believed it was vital to objectify Stanley's hedonism, emphasizing his self-absorbed preoccupation with satisfying his physical needs, even when others try to engage him. Stanley's objects must be "sensuous and sensual—the shirt, the cigar, the beer (how it's poured and nursed, etc.)."[26]

Blanche's spine is defined as "find Protection: the tradition of the old South says that it must be through another person."[27] However, Kazan also argued that in order for the audience to feel pity for her and to recognize her doomed situation as tragic, the negative effect she has on Stella and on her relationship with Stanley must be foregrounded initially: at the start of the play she must be a "heavy."[28] As a social "type," Blanche is headed for "extinction," but "[on] the other hand she is a heightened version, an artistic intensification of all women. [...] Blanche's special relation to all women is that she is at that critical point where the one thing above all else that she is dependent on: her attraction to men, is beginning to go."[29] It is her isolation—caused most conspicuously by the demise of her role as a woman of the grand old Southern tradition—that drives her to seek warmth elsewhere when it can no longer be found within the tradition, and which forces her to seek it on the terms of others. This same isolation alienates her further through her superiority. So intense is the loneliness that this generates that only "a destruction of all her standards, a desperate violent ride on the Streetcar Named Desire can break through the walls of her tradition. [This] tragic flaw creates the circumstances, inevitably, that destroy her."[30] She cannot accept her "physical or sensual side," but by calling it "brutal desire," she is able to separate it from her real self, her "cultured self."[31] As a destructive force that comes between Stanley and Stella, its flames fanned by Blanche's condescension towards him and distaste for him, Stanley seeks out the means to destroy her. Ultimately, this destruction is of her own making.[32]

Stanley's spine is "keep things his way (Blanche the antagonist)."[33] Kazan saw Stanley as a simple character, driven by hedonism: a "hoodlum aristocrat."[34] It is in his contradictions that he becomes interesting: his soft and tender moments, his crying over Stella, the moments when he almost makes up with Blanche. Although he doesn't show it often, Stanley is proud of his wife. He "means no harm. He wants to knock no one down. He only doesn't want to be taken advantage of."[35] If he is able to satiate his desire for physical pleasure he is happy, if not "then his bitterness comes forth and he tears down the pretender," venting stored-up frustration and violence.[36] Stella submitted to his domination willingly, but Blanche's belief in her superiority provokes him. Kazan envisioned the rape through Stanley's eyes as the last possible means open to him of bringing Blanche "down to his level."[37]

Stella is the pivotal character. Kazan saw her as the apex of the play's triangle.[38] Her spine is to "hold onto Stanley (Blanche the antagonist)."[39] The arrival of Blanche leads to Stella's "re-subjugation" (as the younger sister), but her presence also reminds Stella that without Stanley she would be in the same position as Blanche. Thus, "Stella loves her, hates her, fears her, pities her. ... Finally rejects her for Stanley."[40] Kazan sees her living in a "sensual stupor," with Stanley as the sole focus of her life.[41] Blanche reminds Stella of what she gave up in her compromise and this changes her relationship with Stanley. Stella previously blinded herself to Stanley's imperfections. Although Blanche cannot persuade Stella to leave him, her eyes have been opened.

Mitch's spine is to "get away from his mother (Blanche the lever)." The character's doting relationship with his mother means that no woman can live up to Mitch's expectations, with the possible exception of someone like Blanche, raised in the tradition. Although he is rough and burly, he is also fragile. But where his mother's love "keeps him eternally adolescent," Blanche allows him to be a man, albeit one that she dominates.[42] Mitch's rejection of Blanche also closes down his own last avenue of escape.

As the play's tryouts began, Kazan saw that he had not yet achieved the balance between Stanley and Blanche; preview audiences in New Haven empathized with Stanley rather more than with Blanche. Williams reminded the now anxious director that he must not "take sides or try to present a moral. When you begin to arrange the action to make a thematic point, the fidelity to life will suffer. Go on working as you are. Marlon is a genius, but she's a worker and she will get better. And better."[43] The leads were from radically different schools of acting. Marlon Brando was a young American who had trained in the Method with Kazan, as were most of the other cast members. Jessica Tandy was a highly successful and experienced British actress who was classically trained. During rehearsals Kazan realized that "[the] contrast in acting styles helped create the contrast between the cultured woman from Belle Reve and the New Orleans 'Quarter' redneck."[44] But it wasn't until partway through the Boston tryouts that Williams's instincts were proven correct, and the antagonistic clash between the primary characters that was so crucial to the playwright's vision was formed and held in balance. Three years later, this same conflict enabled the film to accomplish the same balancing act, though with Tandy replaced by the cast's only Hollywood star, the British stage actress Vivien Leigh. Leigh had played another infamous Southern belle—Scarlet O'Hara—more than a decade earlier in *Gone with the Wind* (1939).

Jo Mielziner's single set for the play captured well the growing sense of claustrophobia in the apartment. The exterior "walls" were created via layers of scrim and gauze. In combination with the designer's extensive and intricate design for the lighting, these fabric walls could be made solid or transparent in scenes in which it was necessary to see into the street beyond the apartment. For Brenda Murphy, the genius of Mielziner's design lay in "the juxtaposition of this impressionistic background with detailed realism in props and costumes."[45] The props, along with Lucinda Ballard's costumes, functioned as a means by which the characters expressed themselves as exemplars of Kazan's "social types." In addition, Blanche's increasing infringement of Stanley's space was demonstrated materially through her interior design for the place, as items from Blanche's world spill out from the tiny space she inhabits into the rest of the apartment.

Where expressionism offered Williams a means to communicate multiple views or positions within a framework of apparent reality, and thus explore the inability of language to express "truth," Kazan sought to rationalize characters' behaviors in terms of social and psychological causes, though he also sought to *objectify* their behavior—and their conflicts—via motion, action, and other visual elements. The complementarity of these approaches is expressed most clearly in the holistic character of the play's production, in which Kazan's vision for the play's music played an important role (see chapter 4).

The Context of the Film's Production

For some twenty years, the five largest studios in North America—the majors—had been vertically integrated; they had produced, distributed, and exhibited their films. However, as a result of antitrust cases initially brought against them more than a decade earlier, in 1948 the studios were served with papers demanding that they divest themselves of their theaters and end restrictive distribution practices such as "block booking." The late 1940s were an anxious time for the majors. Competition from independent production was on the rise although often reliant on studio co-financing or distribution. Stars and key directors were beginning to challenge their contractual arrangements with the studios; some set up their own independent production companies. At the same time, box office figures began to fall sharply. The decline was due to a number of related causes, which included the "baby boom" of the immediate postwar period; increased prosperity and availability of material goods; the shift towards suburban living and interest in other forms of leisure activity, including those focused on the immediate domestic environment such as television. Having sold off their theaters, the studios no longer needed to maintain the same volume of new films. In the twenty-plus years prior to this, studios had been managed in terms of economies of scale to enable them to produce a constant stream of films for their theaters. They employed rosters of expensive contract players, and a large salaried staff organized into highly compartmentalized units of specialized labor to ensure a continuous flow of films in preparation, in production, and on release. All the equipment they needed to achieve this was kept on expensive studio lots. Production had already been pulled back once, at the point at which the United States had joined the Second World War, but ironically the studios' profits had soared during these years. In the late 1940s production slowed again, in some cases almost totally, albeit briefly. The majors began to look much more carefully at how their money was spent, where it could be saved, and which pictures would offer the greatest profit for the lowest risk.[46]

The adaptation of material originally written for the stage was popular in Hollywood since the film could trade on a play's reputation and achievements in its promotional material. As a successful play that won a number of prestigious awards, in some respects *Streetcar* presented film producers with less financial risk than an original screenplay, though the cost of the rights to adapt and produce the play as a film were steep as a result. While cost implications may have played a role, it was essentially *Streetcar*'s notoriety and the censorship problems it was expected to cause that led to Hollywood's hesitation.

Co-production

Warner Bros. Pictures was on the cusp of monumental change in terms of its mode of production in the late 1940s, though there are signs that the shift began much earlier. Through the 1930s, Warner Bros. had developed perhaps the most formulaic approach to filmmaking of any of the studios, which resulted in a highly efficient production system matched by an equally efficient mode of storytelling.[47] Darryl F. Zanuck—Warner Bros.' highly successful centralized-producer during the late 1920s and early 1930s—was instrumental in its development. When Zanuck left, Warner Bros. decentralized some of its management and production operations, and so began the shift towards unit-production.[48] In 1940, along with the other four majors, Warner Bros. signed an initial three-year consent decree, a requirement of the anti-trust case made against them. As a result they could no longer require that exhibitors buy their B-pictures as part of the package for their A-pictures. Like most of the other studios, Warner Bros. cut back its B-picture schedule dramatically to focus on a smaller number of more prestigious projects in an attempt to beat the competition in the cinemas. As Thomas Schatz points out, this shift prepared the studios perfectly for the moment when the U.S. joined the Second World War. In many ways these were boom years for the majors. Relatedly, tax hikes affecting high earners were brought in to fund the war effort. Stars and highly paid studio directors and officials looked to profit-sharing deals as a way to avoid tax on their salaries. In this way, though perhaps somewhat inadvertently, the swing towards independent production had already begun at Warner Bros., RKO, and Universal.[49] When the anti-trust case was renewed after the war the studios were threatened with the loss both of their theaters and their special arrangements with other theater circuits. At the same time, studio talent enjoyed newfound independence after successfully challenging restrictive contracts. Alongside the unfavorable market conditions of the postwar era, such adjustments required that Hollywood change its mode of production.

The film version of *Streetcar* was co-produced by Warner Bros. Pictures and the independent producer Charles K. Feldman. Feldman had trained as a lawyer and previously headed the Famous Artists agency in Los Angeles. He had begun producing films in the 1940s, with credits that included Howard Hawks's *Red River* (1948) and an adaptation of Tennessee Williams's previous Broadway hit, *The Glass Menagerie* (1950), directed by Irving Rapper.

Bidding for the screen rights to *Streetcar* opened in April 1949. Williams required director approval, though he was willing to agree to Huston, Litvak, Wyler, Cukor, and Kazan with no further discussion necessary. Interested parties included Sam Goldwyn of Metro Goldwyn Mayer, Paramount with William Wyler directing, and Feldman. Discussions with the Production Code Administration began in earnest to identify just what would have to be changed in order for the screenplay to gain the Code's seal. Feldman finally secured the screen rights for $350,000 in the autumn of 1949.[50] Williams was very keen for Kazan to direct, but Kazan was not interested in directing the film if a seal was required.[51] Feldman and Williams then both tried to sign up the unwilling director: a difficult task now that his career was at an unprecedented high (both on Broadway and in Hollywood) and because, as he told Williams, it would be like marrying the same woman twice: "I don't think I can get it up for *Streetcar* again."[52] Williams persisted, however, and Kazan finally agreed to direct for a fee of $175,000.[53] With the play and its director on board, Feldman then sold the package to Warner Bros. Pictures in December 1949 in an arrangement that was to become the norm across the studios in the years that followed. Warner Bros. financed fifty percent of the production's costs, which included the cost of leasing the studio's facilities, in return for distribution rights and profit-share. Warner Bros. required that the film gain the Production Code seal. They also changed the name of Blanche's home town to Oriel to avoid offending the residents of Laurel.

Kazan wanted the film adaptation to include a transfer of all of his key players from the original stage production, including Jessica Tandy, but Feldman and Warners insisted that the film feature at least one star. Early casting ideas included a loan-out of Bette Davis or Olivia de Havilland as Blanche, with Burt Lancaster or Brando as Stanley, and Joan Fontaine as Stella.[54] Vivien Leigh was Feldman's choice, not Kazan's, and the director objected.[55] Leigh had played Blanche on stage in London under the direction of her husband, Laurence Olivier. But with Leigh in place, Kazan was able to cast the rest of the principal actors from the Broadway production, none of whom were contract players at Warner Bros. Neither were most of the key figures in the crew.

Like Jessica Tandy, Leigh was a classically trained British actress and thus also distanced from Kazan's favored Method. In the early weeks on set, Kazan was irritated by Leigh repeatedly deferring to her husband's direction of the play. Kazan reminded her that she was under his directorship now, not Olivier's. As Linda Costanzo Cahir and other commentators highlight, "Vivien Leigh was to the cast and set of the film what Blanche DuBois was to the Kowalskis and New Orleans,"[56] just as Tandy had been in the Broadway production. In both the film and the debut stage production, the primary opposition between Blanche and Stanley—the fragility of imagination and illusion vs. earthy, visceral physicality—was intensified by the actors' stylistic differences. Kazan judged Leigh to be weakest in the scenes shot in the first weeks, in which she appears "most artificial" and "most strained."[57] Yet this fits perfectly with Williams's characterization of Blanche. Leigh's performance emphasizes Blanche as consummate performer, as she tries on numerous masks in an attempt to find one that will please her audience.[58] Only much later in the film, in the scene in which she tells Mitch about her "real" life in Oriel, does she dispense with masks, as I explore in chapter 5.

Adaptation of the play into a film allowed Kazan to stress some of the play's elements further. For example, facial expressions were identified and emphasized for dramatic impact via close-ups. By building the set of the apartment in sections, the walls "could be removed, so making the set grow smaller as time passed, more constricting and more threatening to Blanche."[59] The film's costume designer, Lucinda Ballard, made Blanche's dress for the prelude to the rape scene from a "light, diaphanous material" the same color as the curtains where she is cornered by Stanley.[60] This enabled Kazan to capture Williams's image of "a moth beating its wings against a wall, literally."[61]

Shooting began on schedule on 14 August 1950 and closed on 17 October 1950, nineteen days behind schedule. This included a couple of days shooting exterior scenes on location in New Orleans later in October. Re-takes were shot on 3 November 1950. The preliminary budget put the costs at around a million and a half dollars ($1,570,014): an unremarkable figure for a prestige production at Warner Bros. during this period. Ultimately, the grand total was almost three hundred thousand dollars more, primarily caused by the overrun most probably. The cost of the film's music was $54,839.14.[62] Again, not an excessive amount by comparison with other Warner Bros. productions of the period. The largest proportion of the music budget was spent on payroll for the performing musicians, most of whom were contracted to the Warner Bros. orchestra, though a small number of additional players—jazz players—were also brought in.[63] Just over $9,000 was spent on copyright costs for the use of pre-existent music, including Arlen, Harburg, and Rose's "It's Only a Paper Moon," sung on screen by Vivien Leigh. North's fee was $8,000.

Streetcar and (Self-)Censorship: Part 1

> For the first time we were confronted with a picture that was obviously not family entertainment. Before then we had considered *Anna Karenina* a big deal. *Streetcar* broke the barrier. Other studios had asked us for advisory opinions on *Streetcar* and we had said we did not know how it could be done. *Streetcar* made us think things through.
>
> Geoffrey Shurlock, PCA[64]

The film adaptation of *Streetcar* played a role in the gradual demise of the Production Code Administration, though the Code's seal was not replaced by classification until the late 1960s. The PCA was set up in 1934 by the Motion Picture Producers and Distributors of America (MPPDA, later MPAA[65]) to combat allegations of immorality against Hollywood by enforcing adherence to a set of guidelines for producers: The Production Code. Earlier incarnations of the industry's attempts at moral self-regulation had existed under the leadership of Will H. Hays, but the Association's Studio Relations office (or, the Hays Office) sometimes found its guidance difficult to impose, not least because Hollywood was then under significant financial strain and seemingly willing to risk a certain amount of censure to make and release films with "morally objectionable" content in order to gain success at the box office. A more effective method for the enforcement of self-regulation was needed to stem the escalating threat of federal censorship, the heavy-handed cutting of prints by local and regional censorship boards, and increasing pressure from the Catholic Church.[66] Along with the installation of Joseph I. Breen as head of the PCA, adjustments to the Code between 1931 and 1934 went some way towards increasing its power.[67] The MPPDA and the Motion Picture Producers' Association now also had to accept mandatory script approval before filming. Appeals would no longer go to a jury of Hollywood producers, but would be sent to the Association's New York Board of Directors. Members of the Association who flouted the Code would receive a heavy fine. Theaters owned or operated by Association members would bar films that did not carry a Production Code seal.

Ten days after the opening of *Streetcar* on Broadway in 1947, Russell Holman sent a seven-page report on the play to the Breen Office concerning its suitability for transfer to the big screen.[68] While recognizing the inherent difficulties in the adaptation of the play into a screenplay, Holman was incisive and upbeat: *Streetcar* was "one of the best plays of the current decade." He also noted that the play's script did not do justice to the merits of the play as an experience: "So much is contributed to the impact of the show by its direction, its acting, its incidental business and even the atmospheric music and scenery that you have to see the play in order to fully appreciate it."[69] He saw it as "full of censorship problems," though not insurmountable ones: "Some picture producer will devise a way of doing it without killing the merits of the play."[70] He believed that several of these "problems"—bad language, and such incidents as "Stanley going to bed with his wife after their violent quarrel"[71]—were easily modifiable. He suggested that Blanche's revelation of her young husband's homosexuality could be changed to a discovery of Allan with another woman. Blanche's past, which some critics described as "nymphomania," was a greater problem, as was the rape. Although Holman discredited sordid views of Blanche's character, seeing her instead as a "victim of birth, heredity and circumstances rather than a temptress," he accepted that her story would be difficult to tell without censorship problems, though he also noted that her suffering may offer some appeasement.[72] Alternative solutions to the rape were offered: its difficulties were not limited to censorship issues but also related to Stanley, "who should be in pictures a more sympathetic person than he is in the play."[73] Holman concluded by emphasizing that there was a constructive rather than a tragic heart to the play, and that this could be built on ("if it can be done without becoming corny") by Stanley comforting his wife with the explanation that "people like her can't take care of themselves in the world today, and they can't take care of the world. That's up to people like you and me, and that new kid of ours. We've got a job to do for him, ourselves and the world. ..."[74] Holman's suggested speech thus closed with a rather more positive ending, in that for all Stanley hated Blanche, she may have been a good influence on him: "Maybe she's made me a little less selfish and crude, and I'll be less of a beer-drinking mugg [sic] and treat you better, etc. I hope so."[75]

The discussions between and negotiations of the parties interested in adapting *Streetcar* are well documented and demonstrate that the issues raised by Holman remained the same for Breen and the PCA.[76]

Breen explained the view of the PCA in a letter to Irene Selznick: films have a broad appeal by comparison with stage plays, and the industry has a responsibility to protect its mass audience from material which may be unsuitable, though such material may have a perfectly legitimate place on the stage.[77] Compromises were made on both sides in order for the story to transfer from stage to screen with the seal of the Code, though disagreements continued through to November 1950, after filming was complete. In December 1950 the PCA issued Charles Feldman with a certificate of approval for *Streetcar*, subject to various terms and conditions including the right to void the certificate at a later date.

As Holman's original report intimated, the three main stumbling blocks during these negotiations were elements prohibited by the Code: Allan Grey's homosexuality (classed as sex perversion); Blanche's "nymphomania" and attraction to young boys (again, sex perversion); the rape, which appears justified since it goes unpunished. The first two were ultimately solved by changes to dialogue that responded to the PCA's prohibition on sex perversion by cutting all direct reference to it. The compromises suggested by Kazan and Williams still communicated some of the original meaning to sophisticated viewers, however.[78] Discussion of the rape continued up until the scene was shot. It included a threat from Kazan that he would withdraw from the film if the rape was removed, and an impassioned and eloquent letter from Williams in which he too pleaded that the rape be retained. Williams emphasized the play's morality, and the importance of the rape as a "pivotal, integral truth of the play ... which is ravishment of the tender, the sensitive, the delicate by the savage and brutal forces in modern society."[79] Kazan's solution—ultimately agreed to by the PCA—involved the omission of some dialogue, and a sensitive and indirect implication of rape in terms of the image ("done by suggestion and delicacy").[80] Crucially, though, Stella was to leave Stanley at the end of the play, running upstairs with the baby: "We're not going back in there [...] Never, never." In this way the rape would not go unpunished: Stanley would lose his wife and child. Yet viewers would already have seen Stella escape to Eunice's apartment after a drunken beating from Stanley at an emotional flashpoint earlier in the film, only to return of her own volition almost immediately. The more mature viewer would recognize that Stella would return to her husband; indeed, she would have little choice.

Streetcar and (Self-)Censorship: Part 2

In the following months, minor cuts were made to tighten up the film's pace after initial previews suggested the film was a little long.[81] Subsequent previews in May and June 1951 were judged extremely favorably. In a letter to Kazan, North reassured the director that "the minor cuts and changes didn't affect the overall impact and beauty of the film."[82] Ironically, given what was to happen to the film in the months to follow, North also noted that "[the] audience reaction was splendid and spontaneous with applause following the staircase [scene]."[83] He also mentioned the response of a friend, Jay Leyda, a colleague of Eisenstein's who "sat there stunned and told me he has rarely seen such a perfectly integrated and moving film, from every [respect]."[84]

Kazan thanked Breen for his "cooperation" on *Streetcar*, and even told Jack Warner and the press that he felt the PCA had let the film off relatively lightly in terms of the Production Code.[85] Then the situation began to change. It appeared that a price would be paid for the PCA's "cooperation," since the degree of self-censorship applied to the film satisfied neither the regional censor boards nor the Catholic Legion of Decency. Without Kazan's knowledge, the producers edited the film further to avoid a "C" rating from the Legion of Decency. These cuts also had an impact on the film's score. Indeed the score enjoys a certain notoriety as one of the few documented cases of musical censorship in Hollywood, albeit self-censorship.[86] North's cue for the staircase scene—in which Stella returns to Stanley from the apartment upstairs—was singled out by the Legion's reviewers.

In July 1951 Jack Vizzard of the PCA went to New York at the request of Warner Bros.' Ben Kalmenson, with regard to "trouble brewing" for the film. The Legion of Decency had not yet been given an opportunity to see the film. Given the number of published press reviews about the film, they wanted to know why. The film was screened for them and the prognosis was bad: most response cards apparently indicated a "C" rating.[87] If made official, the Legion would condemn the film as morally offensive, which would potentially harm the film's box office revenues.[88] Vizzard stayed in the background at first, liaising quietly with Mary Looram, head of the International Federation of Catholic Alumnae's Motion Picture Bureau and coordinator of the Legion's volunteer reviewers. Looram suggested that even if the Legion did give a "C" rating, she believed that they might withhold it if Warners were willing to "correct the problems."[89] A full list of the is-

sues, scenes, and lines that troubled her reviewers was passed to Vizzard, who concocted a backstory for his presence in New York in order
to avoid arousing the suspicion of the Legion.[90] Vizzard told the Legion's Father Masterson that while visiting on another matter he had
heard rumor of the Legion's difficulties with *Streetcar* and suggested a
meeting. Father Masterson agreed to discuss the matter once the Legion's official judgment had been made and passed to Warner Bros.[91]

The official line given to Warner Bros. Pictures soon after was that
the Legion "condemns the picture entirely and completely in its present
form, and does not seem to feel that any alteration that might be made
could change that rating."[92] Vizzard passed the letter on to Breen but
with annotations that suggest that he was rather more hopeful that a
compromise could be found. Warner Bros. appointed a mediator, Martin J. Quigley, the publisher of a film industry trade paper, a Catholic
layman, and an influential advisor to the Legion. Quigley was key in
writing the Production Code in 1930 and in setting up the Legion in
1934. Vizzard, himself previously a Jesuit priest, emphasized that he
found his first discussions with the Legion's priests and Quigley to be
promising, but after a further screening things looked bleak.[93] Nonetheless, a list of problem points was passed on which confirmed those
made by Looram's reviewers along with some additional difficulties.
Quigley told Vizzard that *Streetcar* was "the 'toughest' picture to put
into shape he had ever encountered in all his years in the business."[94]
Quigley's and Vizzard's combined solutions were passed to Warner
Bros. who were asked if they were "willing to go along the full way, or
whether they just wanted us to go home."[95] Vizzard emphasized to
Warner Bros. that the film was wholly theirs, as was the decision; he
did not wish to be blamed for having "yielded too much."[96] Jack War-
ner immediately dispatched the film's editor, Dave Weisbart, to New
York to produce a new edit.

Vizzard explained the specific difficulties in a letter to Breen.
Stella was the "key to fixing this picture": in their focus on Blanche and
Stanley, they (the PCA) had "completely missed what this bastard Kazan was doing with Stella."[97] In doing so, Vizzard emphasized the important role music can play in guiding an audience toward a particular
interpretation of a scene:

> I have never, since starting to work with you, seen an instance in
> which the music made such a difference. We saw it without final mu-
> sic. Only "leads" were sketched in. But the lustful and carnal scoring
> they introduced into the finished print, underscores and highlights

what were mere subtleties and suggestions in a way I never thought
possible. The result is to throw out into sharp relief in the finished
film the purely lustful relationship between Stella and Stanley, that
creates a totally different impression from the one we got when we
saw it.[98]

On arrival in New York, Weisbart requested a work print and various out-takes and trims from the West Coast.[99] However, to Vizzard's
surprise, Quigley asked for fewer cuts than he himself would have
done.[100] Vizzard believed that if Warner Bros. had not appointed Quigley, then Quigley would have assisted the Legion, which would likely
have resulted in a very different outcome for the film. Instead, Quigley
found himself in the position of defending the revised version of *Streetcar*. Vizzard also made reference to "a very good crack" about the music in the staircase scene: "[Quigley] said that it is jazz music, but in
that other sense in which that word is sometimes used."[101]

Vizzard listed and explained each of the eliminations in detail,
writing of the staircase scene, that,

> This has been changed into several long-shot angles, to get away
> from the very sexy "register" on the countenance of Stella as she re-
> turns to Stanley. We hope and believe that this will change the flavor
> of this scene, since this is essential to our plan. What we figure on
> creating here is the impression that this is more simply a devoted
> wife, who chooses her husband over her sister's protests, and goes
> back to him "to cook his hamburgers, mend his socks, or whatever
> you will."[102]

He also noted a lucky "break": the Legion reviewers would see only the
work print of the film, not the composite, and would thus not hear the
music track: "This will be a bit of a fast shuffle, but what the heck. It
may not work anyway."[103]

Alex North was living in Weisbart's home on the West Coast at the
time. When Jack Warner sent Weisbart to New York, North contacted
Kazan. When Kazan called Weisbart, it was clear to him that the editor
had been instructed to tell him nothing; only then did Kazan realize
something was happening to *Streetcar* in his absence. Kazan spoke to
Steve Trilling at Warner Bros. in New York and was told that having
seen the film, the Legion of Decency had asked for some minor cuts.
He asked what the cuts were; if they were minor he might agree to
them. At this point, the Legion requested a second screening, and this
was more of a concern. Kazan was told to wait and see what would

happen. The director's previous experience of the Legion prepared him for the outcome: cuts would be made in the hope of securing a "B" rating; that is, the film would be classed as "morally objectionable in part." Kazan believed that Warner Bros. had already demonstrated that they were "ready to do anything necessary to knuckle under to [the Legion],"[104] by sending Vizzard to New York. Kazan cared deeply about *Streetcar*: he thought it "the finest picture I ever made, bar none. ... I don't want it castrated."[105] He warned the studio that he would not keep quiet if he was unhappy with what was done to the film to appease the Legion.

Through Feldman, Kazan entered into a dialogue with Quigley in August 1951 in the hope of repairing the "artistic damage" done to the film and to his reputation as a director, as a result of the cuts made.[106] He stated that he had "the most violent possible objection to the recutting of the staircase scene." Previously the sequence had shown Stella's "moral conflict": between the "overwhelmingly powerful hold, largely one of sexual magnetism, which Stanley was able to exert over his wife and under the power of which she was helpless" and for which she "despises herself."[107] With the evidence of this turmoil removed, a different story was told: a *less* moral one in Kazan's view. In addition, he objected to the "cutting of the very fine music which accompanied this scene. Just how it could be morally damaging really escapes me."[108] Feldman agreed with Kazan completely about this sequence, and urged him to forgo restoration of all other cuts in favor of retaining this scene intact: "for to me it is one of [the] real highlights of film and elimination of the music really frightens me. If we have to substitute old score."[109]

Despite further correspondence, Kazan's appeals were not successful.[110] After the release of the roadshow print of the film in September 1951, discussion among those who had reviewed the film earlier in the year led to revelations that additional cuts had been made after the trade previews. The *New York Times* asked Kazan to make a statement.[111] In essence, Kazan's piece was well balanced, the director's anger no doubt tempered by his wish to avoid damaging the picture—or its prospects—any further. He stated that the cuts were minor and did "not hurt the total impact of the picture."[112] Kazan praised Feldman and Warner Bros. for their brave decision to adapt this "fine and unusual play," and for their generosity toward him throughout.[113] He then recounted what had happened over the summer: cuts were made to avoid the Legion's judgment on the film which had already gained the seal of the Production Code. The cuts were made with no input from or discussion with either the play's author or the film's director.

Although Kazan emphasized the minor character of the cuts, he added that as the film's director he saw the excised elements as "necessary." Of the staircase scene, he wrote:

> This scene was carefully worked out, in an alternation of close and medium shots, to show Stella's conflicting revulsion and attraction to her husband, and Miss Hunter played it beautifully. The censored version protects the audience from the close shots and substitutes a long shot of her descent. It also, by explicit instruction, omits a wonderful piece of music. It was explained to me that both the close shots and the music made the girl's relation to her husband "too carnal."[114]

North wrote a replacement cue for the scene, as his contract required. As he later recounted in an interview, "I had to redo it with a French horn and strings, and a mournful quality. In a sense it worked, but the other [...] the other was more consistent with the character of Stanley."[115] The replacement cue was written and rerecorded sometime between mid-July and the premiere of the film's roadshow release on 18 September 1951.[116] In the same interview, North added that he objected to the film's closing music "having this big swell [...], which I didn't think belonged, dramatically," though he understood that the reason for it was "retribution. Stanley had to be blamed at the end."[117]

Another of North's cues was removed much earlier in the filmmaking process: the cue entitled "New Orleans Street" (R1: P3). This music was to underscore Blanche's search for her sister's apartment soon after her arrival in New Orleans. It was written in such a way that it suggested that it might be source music spilling out from one of the clubs along the street. The cue was replaced by source music: Furber and Braham's "Limehouse Blues" performed by a small jazz combo.

Critical Reception

Streetcar is one of the most celebrated and discussed American plays of the twentieth century. As a successful adaptation, Kazan's 1951 film has also been the focus of a good deal of critical scrutiny and scholarly debate, though the play has garnered far more attention than the film.[118] Limited space permits only a brief review of these sources, beginning first with the play, then responses to the film as viewed on release in

1951, and then the restored version, released in 1993, with the cuts made in the summer of 1951 reinstated.

Initial reviews of the play were enthusiastic in the main, though not unanimously so.[119] Negative reviews tended to focus on the play's shocking content, Williams's pessimism, and the play's loose, episodic structure—the latter subsequently seen as one of the reasons for its successful adaptation into a film. John Chapman of the *New York Daily News* described the play as "throbbingly alive, compassionate, heart-wrenchingly human."[120] Richard Watts of the *New York Post* described it as "a feverish, squalid, tumultuous, painful, steadily arresting and oddly touching study of feminine decay along the lower Mississippi."[121] Irwin Shaw of *The New Republic* insightfully summarized *Streetcar* as "a despairing and lovely play, in which the author, in oblique parable form, says that beauty is shipwrecked on the rock of the world's vulgarity; that the most sensitive seekers after beauty are earliest and most bitterly broken and perverted. [...] "A Streetcar Named Desire" [...] tells us that Illusion is an armor, but one which is always pierced, and in the most mortal spots."[122]

Several critics highlighted similarities between *Streetcar* and *The Glass Menagerie*, but most saw *Streetcar* as more assured and mature, though bleaker. Despite writing careful and attentive reviews that emphasized that the play did not sensationalize its subject matter, many reviewers of the first production characterized Blanche as a nymphomaniac or prostitute. Williams's poetic language was praised, as was the use of heightened realism or naturalism. Indeed, the play, the design, and the performances were all endorsed with superlatives.

In terms of scholarly responses, a number of commentators focus on the play's genesis and evolution, and its context in relation to Williams's earlier one-act plays. Williams repeatedly re-drafted and revised his work. Vivienne Dickson highlights that with *Streetcar* the process led to the transformation of the play from a romance in the earliest drafts, to a tragedy in the final versions.[123] The play was also transformed in production, through Williams's collaboration with Kazan.[124] The writer's penchant for revision also found its way into the various published versions of the play: considerable differences exist between the acting and reading versions, and between British and American editions. The difficulty of fixing *Streetcar* in terms of authorial intention is mirrored in the seeming impossibility for critics and commentators to agree on a dominant reading of the play. Indeed, many of the surveys and collections that focus on interpreting *Streetcar* emphasize that a defining characteristic of the play—and its film adaptation—is its openness to, and perhaps demand for, interpretation. As Williams scholar Philip C. Kolin explains, "*Streetcar* is a highly contentious yet enchanting script that invites, yet defies, any one reading."[125]

Some authors focus on biographical readings, interpreting *Streetcar*'s plot and characterization in relation to Williams and his family, often identifying similarities between Blanche and Williams himself.[126] But where—crucially—Williams recognized the division of the "puritan" and "cavalier" within himself, Ruby Cohn points out that Blanche was kept in the dark about this division within her character.[127] Such accounts interpret the play as an externalization of this unacknowledged battle within Blanche, in some cases in Freudian terms. Others highlight Williams's (closeted) attraction to Stanley as expressed via Blanche as heterosexual female.[128]

The play's symbolism has also been addressed, with some critics exploring its relation to particular literary and dramatic traditions or influences, such as Strindberg, Chekhov, and Lawrence.[129] Others interpret the play in relation to philosophy, or as Williams's pessimistic commentary on, and reversal of, Darwinian natural selection.[130] For many, *Streetcar*'s morality—or the perceived lack of it—is the key issue, with Stanley and Blanche viewed as ciphers of specific views or types: the physical and the spiritual; the Old South and modern industrial society. Indeed, the vast majority of the play's critics focus their attention on the Stanley/Blanche dichotomy, though no general agreement has been reached over whether Williams valorized one or the other character: while some criticize Williams for his ambivalence about the two characters, others have argued that Williams was clearly biased towards one of them, though views vary as to whether this is good or bad, or which character is championed. The same is true of readings of productions: a number of critics suggest Kazan's debut production sided with Stanley, while Harold Clurman's touring production presented a more sympathetic characterization of Blanche (played by Uta Hagen). Many critics champion the play's polysemy, though some feminist critics warn against accepting Williams's apparently ambivalent stance towards Stanley and Blanche, given that Stanley rapes his sister-in-law and ousts her from his home.[131] I am sympathetic to such arguments, though I am not convinced that in accepting Williams's characterization as ambivalent we necessarily accept or condone Stanley's behavior.

Interpretations of *Streetcar* say as much about the interpreters as about the play. As Kolin adds, "[Criticism] of *Streetcar* reflects the shifts in our perceptions, assumptions, our awareness of awareness itself."[132] However, in contrast to the diverse range of approaches taken in relation to the play, much of the academic criticism that deals specifically with one and/or the other release of Kazan's film adaptation focuses on fidelity to the play and the film's censorship. For example, in "The Derailment of *A Streetcar Named Desire*"—written over a decade before the film's 1993 restoration—Ellen Dowling explores the extent to which Kazan was successful in transferring the play to the screen "faithfully," given the film's censorship. After the various excisions both Blanche and Stanley are changed characters, she argues: Stanley is more "brutal, unattractive, and villainous," and Blanche more virginal.[133] As a result, the film lost one of the play's most appealing features, "the ability of its central characters to elicit both sympathy and antipathy towards themselves—as people do in real life."[134] Despite these alterations and the resulting oversimplifications, Dowling argues that the film is still successful, and with this point I agree. Yet, while Blanche certainly appears *more* virginal than in the pages of the playscript as a result of the additional cuts made in the summer of 1951, I find Stanley's character only subtly changed, perhaps even *less* villainous than in the play. But, as reviews of the play in production emphasize, these roles accept a wide range of interpretations: no single, authorized version of *Streetcar* exists.

In her post-restoration essay, "The Artful Rerouting of *A Streetcar Named Desire*," Linda Costanzo Cahir begins from a position similar to that presented by Dowling in her conclusion, though in contrast, Cahir argues that "the success of the film, oddly, is due in part to the way in which Kazan and Williams turned the tables and made potentially destructive constraints work constructively in the movie."[135] For example, concerning the rape, she argues that Blanche is actually defiled three times in the film rather than just once. This occurs first via the close-up of her face as Mitch tears the Chinese lantern from the light turning the bare bulb to her face—a cruel act, which Cahir suggests "parallels Blanche's cruelty in symbolically shining the light on her young husband."[136] Second, her rape at Stanley's hands: her collapse and the oblique reference to the sexually violent act to follow achieves what Williams had hoped the play would depict in its "ravishment of the tender."[137] Third, the Matron's struggle with Blanche in which she is pinioned to the floor. In addition, Cahir sees the film's ending—in which we watch Stella run away from Stanley, up the stairs to Eunice's apartment—as an improvement on that of the play, since it both satisfied the censors, yet "[preserved] what is best in Williams: the tender ambivalence that does tortuous battle within his characters."[138] Maurice Yacowar is of a similar view, suggesting that the compromise of the film's ending is "richer in irony and in directorial inflection than the usual Hollywood ending. All in all, the film is as subtle and as powerful as the play."[139] I return to interpretations of the film's ending at the end of chapter 5 in light of the changes made elsewhere in the score.

Gene D. Phillips and Maurice Yacowar have both written books concerning film adaptations of Williams's plays, and are thus also concerned with specifically cinematic qualities. Phillips notes that although the camera is largely trapped within the confines of the building in *Streetcar*, "[Kazan] adroitly keeps moving it round the set so that the film does not become static or stagey."[140] Kazan stated that it was only on the film prior to *Streetcar—Panic in the Streets* (1950)—that he developed his skills as a *film* director, rather than as a director *per se*:

> I also learned, at last, that the camera is not only a recording device but a penetrating instrument. It looks *into* a face, not *at* a face. [...] A camera can even be a kind of microscope. Linger, enlarge, analyze, study. It is a very subtle instrument, can make any face heavier, leaner, drawn, flushed, pale, jolly, depraved, saintly. I was so late finding all this out. I'd always placed the camera at eye level—the equivalent of the stage view—instead of all the other places it could be. I'd not known there was a valuable choice in lenses. [...] The close-up underlines the emotional content.[141]

On the completion of shooting on the lot, Kazan suggested to Jack Warner that Dave Weisbart should be credited as "Associate Producer" rather than "Editor," given that the printed film was "chock full of his suggestions in the way of set-ups, business and everything else that generally comes under the heading of <u>Directing</u>."[142] It is thus also tempting to suggest that Kazan learned a great deal about the world of film from Weisbart on *Streetcar*.

Focusing on Kazan's "opening-out" of Blanche's arrival at the train station in New Orleans, Yacowar argues that viewers are immediately given an insight into Blanche's mental state through her discomfort with several key elements: the *heat* of the steam trains and her "buffeting" by the sweating crowds of other people in the station, the *noise* of the station's bustle, and *light*—Blanche moves into shadow as a passing train illuminates her. He interprets these elements as "projections of [Blanche's] mental state" which continue throughout the film in various guises.[143] She cannot escape the heat that so disturbs her: it is "emblematic both of her own sensuality and of the pressure of other people's presence upon her. [...] Fever pervades the film."[144] Yet Blanche also seeks escape from the stifling heat by repeatedly bathing in hot water. As well as the noises of the city, Blanche is also beleaguered by the tune that she danced to with Allan on the night of his suicide—the Varsouviana—which no one else hears. Her fear of strong light stems from sensitivity about her age and escapist fantasies of romance; she is filmed in soft focus throughout until the close-up in which Mitch holds the bare bulb to her face.[145] With regard to the inferred rape, Yacowar highlights that the scene is filmed via the reflection in the mirror, now broken by the bottle Blanche smashed to protect herself. It is as though the scene "were too powerful to be viewed directly and needed to be deflected."[146]

Christine Geraghty draws on the classical film theorist André Bazin's ideas concerning film adaptation in her analysis of key scenes from *Streetcar*.[147] Though Bazin accepted that differences exist between stage and screen and must be considered, unusually he did not privilege the theater's "physical presence of the actor" over the cinema's absent, recorded actor. Bazin's focus was the "organization of space"[148]: the theater's bounded space versus cinema's access to limitless space. He was against using cinema to "open up" a play, however. He believed that a film adaptation must be "faithful to the original and respect the different dramaturgical system which it was written for."[149]

For Geraghty, Bazin's approach provides "a way of looking at how a film adaptation can both exploit the resources of cinema and acknowledge its source in theater."[150] In *Streetcar*, the filming of the apartment is organized and functions as a theatrical set. In terms of editing, the lack of reverse-shots in a number of sequences encourages or constructs a "theatrical" rather than a "cinematic" viewer, avoiding identification with specific characters via point-of-view. In the scene in which Stanley pulls items from Blanche's trunk while Stella tries to tidy up around him, the prevalent shot is the two-shot. Both characters are in continual motion: what little editing there is, is associated with reframing the action as a character moves to another segment of the space. This camerawork moves viewers into the space within the proscenium arch, "but we are not implicated with the viewpoint of either character."[151]

Geraghty notes that the same scene adds to our insight of the relationship between the couple: "They are conducting an argument but
their movements and the framing indicate a complete harmony between
them. As in a dance they move together and away, weaving an elabo-
rate pattern around each other […] here we see the relationship between
them given physical form through space and movement but are not
invited to share it."[152] The emphasis on the two-shot continues into the
following sequence between Blanche and Stanley, though here reverse-
shots are also used, sometimes in close-up, as when Stanley grasps
Blanche's arm to stop her spraying perfume over him. Although we
return to a more cinematic form of editing at certain points in which the
viewer is implicated, Geraghty points out that many of these shots are
actually of characters *watching* other characters, thus further emphasizing the film's original source on stage. That Blanche—and elsewhere,
Stella—provides a "female (albeit transgressive) cover for the camera's
gaze" supports Geraghty's view that Stanley's masculinity is not un-
dermined by these looks, which some theorists argue appear to femi-
nize him.[153] Rather, "the power of his erotic force is carried as much by
movement and proximity as by 'the gaze.' […] It is the confined space
associated with the stage which draws attention to the 'real bodies [and]
actual movements' of the actors and heightens the impact of Brando's
physical presence."[154] My analysis of early scenes in the film scored by
North that feature first Blanche and Stella, then Blanche and Stanley,
adds further support to Geraghty's arguments (see chapter 5).

Kazan's direction, choreography, framing, and editing, Ballard's
costumes, and, ultimately, the ensemble's acting all emphasize the importance of Brando's physique in our engagement with, and interpretation of, the character of Stanley. Just as he is Stella's object of desire,
so he is ours; he is the film's most alluring object. North's score emphasizes the character's magnetism, but it also encourages a sympathetic reading of his nemesis, Blanche. In this too, it echoes Kazan's
camerawork, for as R. Barton Palmer points out, in contrast to Brando,
"Leigh's body is never eroticized or glamorized in the film." Instead
she is filmed in soft-focus until her age is revealed by the bare bulb that
Mitch shines onto her face. Just as it was necessary to soften Leigh's
features, making their details slightly fuzzy—romanticized, in the manner of Blanche's magical illusions—so the ambiguities of Blanche's
past are left similarly nebulous until Stanley's, and then finally her
own, revelations. Fetishizing Leigh's body would have implied a
Blanche more consciously aware of the clash that raged within her,

between her sense of cultural refinement and propriety on the one hand, and sexual hunger on the other.

I suggested above that *Streetcar* has no single point of origin, that only versions exist. In "And Transfer to Cemetery: The Streetcars Named Desire," Leonard J. Leff highlights the openness of Williams's text, and the variety of readings it accepts. Leff argues that the reviews of Tandy's and Leigh's stage performances underscore the extremes of Blanche's characterization in terms of an interpretive continuum: where Tandy's characterization was noted for its fragility, Leigh's was more full-bodied and overtly sensual. Similarly, Brando's performance changed over the two years of the play's Broadway run: as the run continued he focused more on the character's humor, and on making him likeable. Leff suggests that the 1951 and 1993 versions of the film "not only contain traces of each interpretation but also remind us of the mutability of Williams' (or any dramatist's) play."[155] In the 1951 version of the staircase scene, shot substitutions and the scene's re-editing, in combination with the replacement music cue, support the idea that Stella "responds to her husband's aching need for her," with a string line that "evokes tenderness and reconciliation."[156] But Kazan had wanted ambivalence. In the restored 1993 version it is Stella that "fosters" her husband's need for her, and North's original cue for the scene underscores the "colored lights" of the couple's sex life, which Stella is also clearly capable of turning on.

Leff is concerned that over time the restored version will be viewed as the standard, the more "authentic" version of the film, despite the fact that this is in itself a problematic concept, given the many versions of the play that exist. He emphasizes that "'unrestored' or 'unreconstructed' works constitute an extraordinary X-ray of perceived audience taste and studio fiscal and aesthetic policy in the period of their initial release."[157] Leff thus advocates the "versioning" of cinematic texts as well as canonic literary texts. Both *Streetcar* films are "mediated variations on source texts that are themselves [...] variations on the play."[158] My approach to North's score(s) for *Streetcar* is based on this notion of "versioning." Although the score of the original/restored (1993) version forms the basis of the analysis, I conclude my study with a comparison of the two scores and their role in guiding us towards different interpretations of the film.

4

STREETCAR'S SOUNDSCAPE

Streetcar is high art in motion picture entertainment, high art in writing, directing, and action, but emotionally it is lowdown Basin Street blues—sad, glad, mad New Orleans jazz in terms of human beings. And that's the kind of music that drummed in my head. It had to be American music. No other music would do. Anything else, I felt, would be pretentious and unreal, unworthy of the integrity of *Streetcar* as a motion picture. Elia Kazan gave me *carte blanche* to compose, and I loved him for it.

Alex North[1]

I begin this chapter with a brief exploration of the role of music in Tennessee Williams's play scripts for *Streetcar*, and the play's first production, from which the sound world of *Streetcar* as film emerged. Music was present in some of Williams's earliest drafts of the play. In the transition of the play into production, the musical elements were developed extensively through collaboration with Kazan, the play's director. Some of the changes were necessitated simply by putting the play into production, with music used more frequently to cover scene changes, for example. Other transformations—including omitting, moving, and adding further cues—intensified the music's dramatic purpose and resulted in a more systematic application of musical style.[2] Music offered Kazan an additional means of balancing the performances of Brando and Tandy.

Music in the Play

A "blue piano" overheard in the Kowalskis' apartment from a club around the corner was a key component of the play script Williams sent to his agent, Audrey Wood, along with an occasional "hot" or muted trumpet.[3] Blanche's memory music also featured in the form of a "polka," but it was concentrated in the play's latter scenes where it was used to show the disintegration of Blanche's mental state, and to suggest a connection between Stanley's behavior toward her and her growing sense of desperation. Musical counterpoint was also present in early versions of the script: the chanting of the Mexican woman selling flowers for the dead punctuates Blanche's dialogue, and interjections from Blanche singing "It's Only a Paper Moon" in the bathroom are heard as Stanley tells Stella of her sister's misdemeanors.[4]

Regarding Williams's choice of the "blue piano," critics argue that in his early plays and writing, Williams's attitude towards African American culture is primitivist, even racist. As Nick Moschovakis points out, however, as Williams's writing developed he used African American music "to disrupt culturally constructed racial binaries."[5] After *The Glass Menagerie*, Williams "confronts and rejects the conviction that the primitive is a quality naturally less white than black, or brown, or any other color. For Williams [...], we are all primitives by nature, taking pleasure in the satisfaction of our instincts. This fact, if not perhaps as it ought to be, only becomes all the more destructive for being denied or forgotten."[6] Indeed, such a denial of instinct is at least partially responsible for Blanche's downfall in *Streetcar*. In these terms, it is possible to read the blue piano's unbounded permeation of the warm air in Williams's production notes for the play's first scene as corresponding to the French Quarter's special character, demonstrated by the intermingling of races.[7]

Kazan thought Williams's choice of the blues was appropriate thematically, particularly in terms of Blanche's lonely, abandoned soul.[8] In production, the piano and trumpet were augmented to a four-piece jazz band comprising clarinet, trumpet, piano, and drums, playing arrangements of jazz standards, in the main. The musicians performed in an upstairs dressing room, ostensibly the band from the Four Deuces bar. They were cued by a light and a buzzer activated by the assistant stage manager and the music was broadcast into the theater by speakers located on the stage.[9] The assistant stage manager also cued a fifth musician who played the "polka" on a Hammond Novachord sited backstage. This, the first electronic polyphonic synthesizer, used vacuum tubes to generate and manipulate its sound, with a number of dials and a pedal in addition to its 72-note keyboard.[10] The Novachord could imitate a variety of acoustic instruments, as well as generating a number of wholly original sounds through the manipulation of the various dials and pedal, enabling variability in attack, sustain, decay, and release.[11] The instrument was ideal for the polka: its de-familiarized and unique sound world assisted the implication that the music was subjective, that is, heard by Blanche alone.[12]

The association between Blanche and the polka was intensified through collaboration with Kazan: the polka cues indicated in Williams's pre-production scripts were developed, and further cues were added. Where Williams had concentrated the Varsouviana in the latter portion of the play, it was now heard, in different arrangements, in scenes 1, 2, 6, 8, 9, 10, and 11, motivated primarily by mention of Blanche's late husband or her memory of him.[13] Placing these cues throughout the play suggested that Blanche's mental state was fragile prior to her arrival in New Orleans. It is entirely possible that Kazan increased both the number and length of the polka cues to elicit sympathy for Blanche given his decision to emphasize her behavior as negative early on in the play. Kazan replaced the blue piano and trumpet of Williams's ending with the Varsouviana, ensuring that the audience was left thinking of Blanche.

The Varsouviana was an appropriate choice.[14] The dance originated in France in the mid-nineteenth century, and traveled to America soon after. It is described as "a genteel variation of the mazurka, incorporating elements of the waltz"[15] and would have been danced to a variety of songs or tunes that featured appropriate rhythms. A commentator from the period stated that the dance, in triple time, "combines the *mazourka, polka* and *polka redowa*," and this may explain why Williams described the Varsouviana's tune as a polka, though a polka is generally danced to music in duple meter.[16] In both the play and the film, composers and arrangers offered triple meter music for the dance, and in both cases the American traditional song "Put Your Little Foot (Right There)" appears as a key source.[17] Indeed a sound recording of a spoof version of the play's final scene made by Williams himself with friends in 1947 or 1948 includes sung extracts of both "Put Your Little Foot" and "It's Only a Paper Moon."[18]

The music cues played by the jazz band set the atmosphere of New Orleans; they built on well-understood conventions that associated such performances with the city's French Quarter.[19] The cues were used primarily to cover scene changes, though starting the cues during action or beneath lines prior to the end of scenes enabled Kazan to emphasize subtext, or offer dramatization in addition to setting the geographical context.[20] Elsewhere, the placement of jazz elements emphasized a connection with Stanley: first, as he wails for his wife to return from the apartment upstairs (sc. 3); second, when he reminds Stella of their previous physical relationship and their happiness prior to Blanche's arrival (sc. 8); third, the rape (sc. 10). Here it articulates carnal desire. The first two cases suggest the importance of sex in the couple's relationship, the last the potential for sexual violence when desire is unrestrained by morality. Also, an additional cue, a "slow, whimsical, sexy" version of "Sugar Blues," is played on solo piano under dialogue during part of scene six, and forms an ironic counterpoint to Blanche's statement that she has "old-fashioned ideals."

Kazan's changes amplified elements already present in Williams's scripts, notably the use of music in juxtaposition or counterpoint with dialogue, emphasizing the dramatic purpose of these devices more pointedly, as with "Sugar Blues," for example. Kazan also changed the placement of the flower seller's chanting ("flores para los muertos...") to emphasize particular elements of Blanche's speech in scene nine. The addition of the Varsouviana during the same speech added another layer of texture and semantic richness, possibly also suggesting a further deterioration in Blanche's mental state. The decision to introduce the Varsouviana throughout the play also integrated it further with the source music produced by the band at the Four Deuces which, as Barbara Murphy highlights, "[embedded] the play's juxtaposition of subjectivity and objectivity in the production's musical code."[21] That the band played from a room offstage, out of sight of the theater audience, anticipated the ambiguity of source that North would develop in several of his simulated jazz cues for the film.

In the film, source cues and Varsouviana fragments together generate around 23 minutes of music.[22] In addition, North's score runs to almost half of the film's 120 minutes. In the context of this substantially enlarged role for music, North's score develops and intensifies the vision Kazan and Williams developed for the play's music, most notably in the use of jazz-inspired elements, the Varsouviana, and the technique of musical layering and/or juxtaposition. The score's dynamic gives a particular shape to the film: asserting a three-act structure, and directing the score towards a musical climax which, in turn, impacts upon the notion of the film's dramatic climax. North's score emphasizes Williams's tragic and ambivalent characterization of Blanche and Stanley in musical terms, and does so without moralizing or resorting to sentimentality. In places it also *re*-balances the film's dynamic in order to ensure the preservation of this fraught equilibrium—an equilibrium disturbed by a number of factors, including the changes and compromises that were required to appease first the PCA, and then the Catholic Legion of Decency.

The Production of the Film Score

In December 1950, *Streetcar*'s rough cut received the PCA seal and North began his contract to compose the film's score. The contract required that he compose the score by 22 January 1951, that is, within six weeks; he would not be needed for more than nine weeks. It stipulated that North supply the cues asked for by the producer—including any additional cues—at no extra cost. Although the contract required that the composer surrender all claim on "motion picture synchronization rights," North was to be paid royalties from sales of his music as per the agreement. However, if his music for the film was not published within a year of the film's release, copyright of the music would revert to the composer.[23] Any cues that were unused in the general release print would also be returned to the composer. A quitclaim clause was included, which enabled North to regain the rights to his score should his contract be terminated and/or his score thrown out, on the condition that he repay any monies received.

North had already discussed the score with Kazan in New York.[24] By the time he arrived on the West Coast he had written "several thematic ideas on the basis of the script."[25] Working in the same manner as he had on Broadway productions, North used the script rather than the edited film for inspiration, noting the importance of titles and phrases such as Belle Reve and Della Robia Blue.[26] At Kazan's behest, North also visited New Orleans. Kazan had shot his previous film on location in the city—*Panic in the Streets* (1950)—and was passionate about the music he heard there.

> New Orleans was full of the music I love. [...] After dark the city was full of pulsing sound. I'd walk down a street lined with "joints" out of which jazz flooded into the soft night air. I tried to fill the sound track of the film with this music, but I didn't do as well as I should have. [...] In New Orleans, on *Panic in the Streets*, I learned the importance of music in film, and I would never again leave my sound track to a producer and his musical director. Often it's as important as anything except the sequence of pictures that will tell the basic story.[27]

Table 4.1. Cue Sheet Information for Streetcar[28]

Cue	Title	Composer	Extent of Use	How Used	M.S.	[Reel: Part]
1	Belle Reve	Alex North	E	B I	1:25	MAIN
2	Somebody Loves Me	Gershwin–DeSylva	P	V W	0:10	
3	Limehouse Blues	Furber–Braham	P	B I	1:25	
4	Japanese Sandman	Egan–Whiting	E	B I	1:34	
5	Belle Reve Reflections	North	E	B I	2:04	R2:P2
6	Stan	North	P	B I	2:06	R2:P3
7	Varsouvienne	Arr. North	P	B I	0:20	
8	Stan Meets Blanche	North	E	B I	3:25	R3:P1
9	Varsouvienne	Arr. North	P	B I	0:46	
10	Reaction to Birth	North	P	B I	0:40	R4:P1a
11	Samiotassa		P	V V	0:10	
12	I Gotta Right to Sing the Blues	Koehler–Arlen	E	B I	3:20	
13	Girl with the Spanish Drawl	Camacho–David	P	B I	0:24	
14	Blanche and Mitch	North	P	B I	1:50	R4:P1b
15	Blanche and Mitch	North	P	B I	1:10	R5:P1
16	Vienna Dreams	Sieczynski	P	B I	0:25	R5:P2
17	Stan and Stella	North	E	B I	3:35	R5:P3
18	Blanche and Mitch	North	P	B I	0:59	R5:P4
19	Medley: a) Stan b) Ad-lib whistling (over above)	North	P E	B I V W	1:34 0:40	R6:P1
20	Soliloquy	North	E	B I	2:37	R7:P1
21	Blanche and Mitch	North	P	B I	1:05	R7:P1a
22	Medley: a) Collector b) Varsouvienne c) Varsouvienne d) Varsouvienne	North arr. North arr. North arr. North	E P P P	B I B I B I B I	2:53 0:27 0:47 1:05	R7:P2
23	Sweet Georgia Brown	Bernie–Rinckard–Casey	P	V I	0:04	

24	Medley: a) Somebody Loves Me b) Blue Room	Gershwin–DeSylva Rodgers–Hart	E E	B I B I	3:20 2:3	
25	Medley: a) Blanche and Mitch b) Varsouvienne	North Arr. North (over above)	E P	B I B I	2:54 1:2	R8:P2
26	Varsouvienne	Arr. North (over above)	P	B I	0:23	
27	Varsouvienne	arr. North	P	B I	1:24	
28	Consummation	North	E	B I	0:15	R9:P1a
29	It's Only a Paper Moon	Rose–Arlen–Harburg	P	V V	0:2	
30	It's Only a Paper Moon	Rose–Arlen–Harburg	P	V V	1:25	
31	It's Only a Paper Moon	Rose–Arlen–Harburg	P	V V	0:06	
32	Birthday Party	North	P	B I	2	R9:P2/ R10:P1
33	Birthday Party	North	P	B I	2:12	R10:P1a
34	Medley: Birthday Party Blanche's Solitude	North North	E E	B I B I	2:15 0:48	R10:P2 R10:P3
35	Varsouvienne	arr. North	P	B I	0:26	
36	Revelation	North	E	B I	4:25	R11:P1
37	Scherzo	North	E	B I	1:09	R11:P2/ R12:P1
38	Goodnight Ladies	North [sic]	P	B I	0:32	
39	Medley: a) Stan b) Soliloquy	North North	E E	B I B I	3:05 1:45	[R3:P1] R12:P6
40	Seduction	North	E	B I	3:54	R13:P1
41	Soliloquy	North	P	B I	1:55	R13:P2
42	Doctor	North	E	B I	1:05	R14:P1
43	Chord	North	E	B I	0:09	
44	Affirmation	North	E	B I	2:48	R14:P2
45	Belle Reve	North	P	B I	0:2	

North orchestrated the cues he had written for the opening reels himself, but Maurice de Packh took over in the week ending 20 January 1950.[29] De Packh orchestrated the remaining cues and the film's trailer over the next five weeks, while also orchestrating cues for *The Travelers* (1951).[30] With the exception of Reel 1: Part 1 (the Main Title) which was completed in the final week, de Packh's orchestrations were undertaken in chronological order.[31] Copyists worked on the score during the same period, though the parts for the trailer were not copied out until late March.[32] The score was recorded between 11 January and 22 February 1951, with an additional recording session on 27 March 1951, most likely for the trailer.[33]

On 13 March 1951, Kazan wrote to North to congratulate him on the "great score" for *Streetcar*: "the picture is certainly lucky that you were on it."[34] Kazan praised the composer for possessing the rare combination of "great imagination" and "real technical proficiency."[35] In his reply, North thanked Kazan for the "latitude and freedom" he was given: "It was a real joy to do the score [...] it's a beautiful accomplishment on your part."[36]

As was the norm, a cue sheet of *Streetcar*'s music was prepared indicating all uses of music, whether source, score, or ad-lib. The cue sheet lists composers/lyricists and publishers, where relevant. The length of each cue is given in minutes and seconds, along with whether the music's source is seen on screen (V, visual), or not (B, background), whether the music is vocal or instrumental (V or I), and whether the music is presented in full (E, entire) or in part (P, partial). Such information must be recorded because it affects the copyright payments. Information from the cue is given below, with each cue identified by a title and a reel and part number (see Table 4.1, above).

Although North composed most of the cues for *Streetcar*, and is also listed as arranger of the film's Varsouviana cues, he did not provide labels for the cues; this was done by Warner Bros.' Joe McLaughlin. Thus, the titles do not necessarily indicate or reflect North's intentions, nor his views about the cues. They perhaps tell us more about McLaughlin's views and interpretation of the characters, as with the troubling label he provides for the cue that precedes the rape: *Seduction*. However, North *did* label the tracks that appeared on the soundtrack album released by Capitol Records, and this complicates the issue somewhat.[37] To avoid confusion, I use McLaughlin's titles as they appear on the Warner Bros.' cue sheet, along with the reel and part number (e.g., *Belle Reve*, R1: P1), though I also refer to North's track labeling, where appropriate. I provide a comparison of the cue sheet titles and those North provided for the Capitol Records release of the music in the appendix, alongside a further comparison with Goldsmith's re-recording of North's score, which also includes a cue excised from the film (discussed below).

The Score

The score opens boldly with an episodic cue for the main titles which comprises a number of motifs, short themes, and textures heard in quick succession. Yet, rather than a juxtaposition of disparate elements, the cue generates a highly specific and consistent musical world. The same apparent contradiction describes the film's music as a whole, and North's contribution in particular. Stylistically, the soundscape combines jazz and swing, popular song, Romanticism, and Modernism with a harmonic language that ranges from simple functional harmony to complex enriched and altered chords, with moments of bitonality and atonality. Some of this variety was already built into the film's narrative, of course: the Varsouviana, the jazz standards, and "It's Only a Paper Moon," for example. Contrasting orchestration is used to emphasize the score's diversity, and a dynamic sense of rhythm is created via metrical asymmetry and syncopation. Yet North's score also favors episodic forms and song-structures, which lend themselves to development through variation and layering. Thus, while the score's stylistic variety is intensified through the use of certain compositional techniques, it is simultaneously balanced with coherence and consistency.

Much of North's music is generated from material in the main title cue, which he described as the score's "germ, the essence."[38] Here, the tritone, the flatted or diminished fifth that announces the cue's first theme so emphatically, is first presented. In fact, the cue is saturated with the interval. It is arguably the most important of the score's core materials, in both narrative and musical terms. As I explain more fully in chapter 5, the tritone epitomizes the idea of ambivalence around which the score is structured. It has a strong identity that signals both jazz and Romantic or Modernist harmony in the score, depending on the context. In North's music for Stanley, the flatted fifth takes on the identity of a persistently pounded blue note. By contrast, during the course of the film, materials from the main title cue come to signify the darkness and oppression Blanche experienced during the latter years she spent at Belle Reve. For the melody that underscores Blanche's aspirations for her relationship with Mitch, North augments the interval, forming a perfect fifth, transforming its oppression into openness, light, and possibility (though the theme's melancholy harmonic context hints at the inevitable failure of this relationship). In place of Blanche's illusions, the tyranny of the tritone—and, by extension, the reality of her life at Belle Reve—is reasserted in North's *Revelation* cue, the point at which Blanche finally ends her "performance" to secure Mitch, her last hope for protection.

Through a combination of compositional techniques, tension and relaxation are generated in individual cues, and shape is given to the score overall, not least in developing a structure that matches that of the play's debut production.[39] A key means by which North expressed the narrative's "deeply wrought conflict and frustration" musically was through re-contextualization.[40] As he stated: "you may find strident string chords over an innocent melody which is definitely going some place, to punctuate an emotional response; or brass figures interspersing a melodic line to convey the ambivalent nature of human behavior."[41] Re-contextualization also forms the basis of the score's musical development at macro-level, which is cumulative, rather than organic: the score's musical climax (*Revelation*) is generated through additive layering that includes Blanche's monologue and the flower vendor's chant. In the prelude to the rape, the interpolation of "raucous" musical fragments between and around dialogue disrupts such layering.

North's score runs beneath a great deal of dialogue in *Streetcar*, supporting its meaning, expression, and its subtext. Such moments also add to the score's cohesion since they are usually built from fragments heard elsewhere in the score. The integration of music and dialogue also extends to sound effects. In one case a low-level musical climax is reached concurrently with the sound of a train, a hysterical outburst from Blanche, and the fizzing over of a drink poured by Stella (*Soliloquy*, R7: P1). While the latter are causally related, and supported by North's score, the sound of the train passing is (seemingly) coincidental but adds to Blanche's agitation over the spilt drink. The sound of a train's whistle also punctuates the stillness as Blanche backs away from the apartment, embarrassed, after running after her sister—and Stanley—and witnessing the couple's reconciliation.

The score is also defined through the opposition of objective and subjective music. North described the main title cue as objective in that it "had nothing to do with the personalities involved, it had to do with the atmosphere of the city."[42] By contrast, subjective scoring conveys *Streetcar*'s "internal" rather than "external aspects."[43] Thus rather than create themes for specific characters, North produced "mental statements" that express the interactions *between* characters, such as "Stanley vs. Blanche, Mitch vs. Blanche and Stanley vs. Stella."[44] As a result, the score appears to run counter to the scene in places, though this is due to the attempt "to reflect the inner feeling of the personalities rather than the situation."[45] As in the play, the Varsouviana presents an extreme form of subjective music, an idée fixe from Blanche's past which only she hears, along with the audience. The Varsouviana cues are, in the first instance, distinct from the rest of North's score in terms of source, style, and orchestration. This changes with the arrival of the boy collecting for a newspaper, and the audience's firsthand experience of Blanche's unhealthy obsession with boys of a certain age.

"We danced the Varsouviana!"

Throughout the film, the repeated interjections of the Varsouviana represent Blanche's fragile mental state. To emphasize this, the dialogue that precedes the first entry of the Varsouviana is manipulated to indicate a shift to subjective hearing; we are granted access to Blanche's mind, with the implication that we hear as she hears. Echo and reverberation effects are used to repeat Stanley's questions to her about her marriage. The sound of the Varsouviana, played on accordion and strings, is also evocative in its distant and reverberant sound. The camerawork supports the shift, with a dolly-in to a close-up of Blanche's face. She covers her ears tightly in an attempt to avoid hearing the gunshot that closes the music.[46]

As discussed above, the music chosen to indicate the Varsouviana in the film is derived from the traditional song "Put Your Little Foot (Right There)." Here it comprises a sixteen-bar A section, which moves between tonic and dominant harmony every four bars, and an eight-bar B section with more frequent alternation of tonic and dominant harmony. Several of the cues are brief, halting before the move to the B section. Example 4.1 presents the song's melody and its simple harmonic framework. Although the title, "Varsouviana," refers to a dance rather than to the music, I use the term here to assist clarity.

The simplicity of the song's melody and harmonic framework emphasizes its difference from most of the film's other music, as does its instrumentation (see Table 4.2 below). Its meaning appears clear: it was the music Blanche danced to with Allan moments before his suicide.[47] It represents her grief at the loss of the boy she loved, mixed with feelings of guilt that she failed to understand him. Certainly, five of the film's nine Varsouviana fragments fit with this view: the tune intrudes when Stanley questions Blanche about her marriage and her love letters (cues 7 and 9), and when she describes Allan's death to Mitch (cues 25, 26, 27). The music's final intrusion (cue 35) is not motivated by an explicit reference to Allan, when it is heard soon after Mitch bursts in on Blanche to confront her about her "lies"; here it *triggers* her memory of Allan's suicide instead. At this point it seems to indicate her mental fragility, but perhaps it also suggests that Allan's death played a crucial role in the series of events that led her to her current situation.[48]

Example 4.1 The Varsouviana: "Put Your Little Foot (Right There)"

More complicated are the insistent interruptions of the Varsouviana during the scene in which a young man comes to collect for a local newspaper (cues 22b, c, d). Blanche is in the apartment alone, waiting for Mitch. The Quarter's cathedral bells chime. The entire scene is underscored by a North cue (*Collector*, R7: P2). At the beginning, the music is metrically unstable and harmonically complex: staggered string lines descend slowly, culminating temporarily on enriched or juxtaposed chords. A persistent crotchet figure low on the harp offers stability to the cue's continuation and acts as a reminder of the chiming bells, but also adds tension. At the moment that Blanche first sees the young man's face, a fragment of the Varsouviana begins on celeste, over a sustained chord.[49] The Varsouviana continues, though it is slowly engulfed by the return of the score's string descents. As the young man starts to leave, Blanche draws him back by asking for a light (as she did earlier with Mitch); the Varsouviana enters a second time. A third entry is heard as she calls him back once more. But each time the string descents overwhelm the tune. North's music then turns more ominous via a slow descent on muted trumpet as the pair discuss the boy's choice of soda and she tells the boy that he "makes [her] mouth water" (bb. 33–36).[50] Blanche calls the boy back a final time, emphasizing his youth: "young ... young ... young man." In an interesting reversal, the Varsouviana then colonizes North's underscore:

solo viola plays a slow version of the tune's first sixteen bars (A), here stretched into a duple meter figuration by augmenting the duration of the tune's crotchets. The celeste interjects arpeggios of unrelated major seventh chords (rising chromatically from D^Δ to F^Δ), becoming gradually more atonal, alongside similar arpeggios on harp. There is a switch to triple meter as a solo cello takes over the tune, with a lush and more harmonically fluid chordal accompaniment in *divisi* strings. During these bars, Blanche kisses the boy "softly and sweetly on the mouth," then sends him away, telling him that although she would like to "keep him" she has "to be good and keep [her] hands off children."[51]

Allan is not mentioned at any point in the scene, and the Varsouviana's closing gunshots are not heard: some late versions of Williams's play scripts indicate "blue piano" and "trumpet and drums" rather than the Varsouviana at this point, though Kazan left the sequence unscored in the stage production.[52] Initially, North's cue overwhelms the repeated interpolations of the Varsouviana. Ultimately though, this simple tune takes control of the underscore. The slowed-down tempo, rhythmic augmentation, and the dissonant interjections of harp and celeste all indicate a dreamlike, or illusory quality. So closely does the music appear to represent Blanche at this point, that it seems to emanate from her. Should we interpret these first interruptive, then overwhelming fragments of the Varsouviana as further examples of Blanche's subjective music? Does the moment represent an idealized memory of her youth and past? Does the young man remind her of Allan?

The scene is an important one. It occurs halfway through the film and offers the audience a firsthand demonstration that Blanche too has desires. It follows Stanley's warning to her that he is going to investigate her departure from Oriel, and Blanche's admission to Stella that she "has not been so awfully good" since the loss of Belle Reve. It precedes a heartfelt discussion with Mitch about the loneliness they share. But, her feelings for Mitch are sober and rational, based on the hope that he might marry her and thereby offer her protection from the world. By contrast, in this scene Blanche exhibits an obvious infatuation with the boy collector, a stranger. She appears unabashed in her desire, albeit coquettish at first. Blanche then romanticizes dreamily, but there is an undercurrent of sensuality to Leigh's performance, and the scene ends with Blanche's disturbing admission.[53] By contrast, she presents herself as "old-fashioned" to Mitch, lest he should imagine that she is not "wholesome."

The Varsouviana's naivete evokes an impression of innocence, which goes some way towards counterbalancing what we have witnessed. Indeed, throughout the film, the simplicity of the interpolated Varsouviana cues stands in marked contrast to the enriched and discordant harmonies found elsewhere in North's score. Each recurrence is more or less the same, though instrumentation differs; only when the Varsouviana is transferred to North's underscore is the theme altered. The manipulation of the Varsouviana in the latter part of this cue can be read in a number of ways. It underscores Blanche's vulnerability and neediness. It suggests a dreamy atmosphere that supports Blanche in her magical illusions, as emphasized by the slowing-up of the theme via the augmentation of the crotchets. For Blanche, the situation appears to offer a temporary moment of idealized bliss. But, the return of the dissonance of the cue's opening via the delicate arpeggios of harp and celeste adds a bittersweet taste that offsets a straightforward reading. In its polysemy, North's music for the Collector scene demonstrates the key characteristic that informs the score overall: ambivalence.

Cue	Music	Situation
7	Varsouviana: accordion and strings	At Stanley's enquiry about her marriage
9	Varsouviana: accordion and strings	At Stanley's discovery of Allan's love letters
22b 22c 22d	Varsouviana: celeste; celeste, strings, and harp	Over North's cue 22: R7: P2 "Collector" – then integrated into underscore
25b	Varsouviana: celeste then orchestra	Over North's cue 25: R8: P2 "Blanche and Mitch" – then integrated into underscore
26	Varsouviana: accordion and strings	Blanche tells Mitch of Allan's suicide
27	Varsouviana: celeste	Blanche explains her guilt over Allan's suicide
35	Varsouviana: celeste	Intrudes on her during Mitch's aggressive confrontation
38	Goodnight Ladies: orchestra	Blanche alone with her imagination, prior to Stanley's return from the hospital

Table 4.2. *Streetcar*'s Subjective Music

The same transformation—from the juxtaposition of the Varsouviana to its integration with the underscore—occurs again in the film's next scene, where the tune is superimposed over the most tonal and predictable of North's thematic material: his music for Blanche (and Mitch). Here though, its placement appears more conventional, since it underscores Blanche's account of the relationship with Allan, and thus functions in a manner appropriate to a leitmotif; it begins as she tells of her "discovery of love," aged only sixteen. However, while the Varsouviana is presented in triple time in the key of E♭ on celeste, the theme played by the orchestra beneath is in common time in the key of F minor (*Blanche and Mitch*, R8: P2).[54] The effect is disorienting, particularly as it underscores Blanche's dialogue, but it is not sustained for long. After this juxtaposition, fragments of the Varsouviana tune are developed by the orchestra, culminating in a full version of the Varsouviana's B section melody played by violas, and supported by a more fluid harmonization in the upper strings. I return to this sequence in chapter 5.

A further version of the Varsouviana appears in North's score, but was excised from the film. Creating symmetry around the Collector scene, it forms part of the cue for the scene that precedes the boy's arrival: *Soliloquy* (R7: P1). Five of the six bars cut (bb. 18–23) repeat a lush harmonization of motifs clearly derived from the Varsouviana; the motifs follow the cue's "magic-like shimmering" figure in upper strings in triple time, as Blanche explains to her sister that she can no longer "turn the trick" of looking young.[55] Had the sequence been retained in full, the placement of these motifs would have preempted the turn away from a direct association with Allan and death, toward youth, as is potentially also suggested by the Collector scene.

Source Music

The score's source cues comprise a variety of traditional jazz standards and popular tunes of the time. In the main, these are used to indicate the geographical location and period of the film's setting, a view supported by the fact that almost all the source music is heard within the film's first sixty-five minutes (with the exception of "Paper Moon"). Where, in the play, jazz numbers occasionally took on other functional roles, in the film they are replaced by North's cues, as in the staircase scene, for example. Most of the film's source jazz is performed by a small combo, the implication being that this is the same band glimpsed briefly

through the door of the Four Deuces club as Blanche searches for
Stella's apartment at the start of the film.[56] The club is located just
around the corner from the Kowalskis' apartment: its music drifts into
the apartment through the louvered shutters, alongside the flickering
light from its sign. The intrusion of music and light from the club into
the apartment emphasizes the lack of privacy.

Cue no.	Song (Composer/lyricist)	Source (apparent or implied)
2	"Somebody Loves Me" (Gershwin & DeSylva)	Sailor whistles (train station)
3	"Limehouse Blues" (Furber & Braham)	Four Deuces
4	"Japanese Sandman" (Egan & Whiting)	Four Deuces
11	"Samiotassa" (Public Domain)	Character sings (Pablo)
12	"I Gotta Right to Sing the Blues" (Koehler & Arlen)	Four Deuces
13	"Girl with the Spanish Drawl" (Camacho & David)	On radio
16	"Vienna Dreams" (Sieczynski arr. North)	On radio
23	"Sweet Georgia Brown" (Bernie, Rinckard, & Casey)	Casino band
24b	"Blue Room" (Rodgers and Hart)	Casino band
29	"Paper Moon" (Rose, Harburg, & Arlen)	Character sings (Blanche)
30	"Paper Moon"	Character sings (Blanche)
31	"Paper Moon"	Character sings (Blanche)

Table 4.3. *Streetcar*'s **Source Music**

There is more "stylized jazz" in the film's first five reels because,
as North stated, these scenes "take place mostly at night when the 'Four
Deuces' dive is in operation."[57] His intention was to "make the transi-
tions from the source music (popular tunes) to the underscoring as im-
perceptible as possible."[58] Through the use of jazz inflections, chamber
arrangements, and formal structures associated with jazz, North made
the source of these cues ambiguous: the music might issue from the
club (as source music), but could also be understood as underscore.

Some substitutions were made to keep clearance costs low, given the number of popular tunes and jazz standards to be included. The exception was the song "It's Only a Paper Moon" (Arlen, Harburg, and Rose) which Williams had written into the play and which was retained in the screenplay. The rights to use the song amounted to almost double that of the cost of the other music rights combined. It is difficult to think of a substitute that would perform quite the same role of reflexivity in relation to Blanche at this point in the narrative, however.[59] The lyrics suggest that if belief is strong enough, then what is illusory may be realized. As Blanche sings lines from the song in the bathroom, Stanley tells Stella why her sister *really* left Oriel, thus emphasising the difference between the characters in terms of the distinction between imagination/illusion and reality/truth.

"[J]azz but in that other sense"[60]: Jazz, Modernism, and America

In interview, North stated that he used jazz in the underscore whenever there was an element of sex.[61]

> I felt very strongly about the use of jazz throughout a good part of the film. I thought the play had a very sensuous ... at least the characters... a sensual feeling, and to reflect that best would be by using elements of jazz, and especially in those moments where there was a personal kind of relationship. [...] The first time that Stanley meets Blanche, there is a club ... you could see a light flashing, a little dive ... so I tried to combine the fact that there was source music, and also this sensuous, sexual undercurrent, and I just felt that jazz could best reflect those particular moments. I remember Eleanor Slatkin, the first cellist, saying to me, "Alex, such bedroom music," you know. And I'm sure jazz had been used before, but I just felt that it was the right approach. In keeping with the style of Tennessee Williams—the South. I couldn't conceive of it in any other way.[62]

In using jazz to represent and underscore sex and sensuality, North's approach appears to fit with the persistent notion of the dualism of mind and body.[63] Broadly speaking, "mind" has been privileged at the expense of "body" in Western thought for centuries, particularly in terms of the development of the Cartesian subject (after René Descartes). The Romantic aesthetic extended this valorization of mind: feelings were sublimated so that they could be expressed mentally rather than bodily. The same culturally determined ideology endured in critical writing about jazz in the first half of the twentieth century (and later, with regard to various types of popular music). Race and rhythm were mapped onto this same dualism as a result of racist fears about "other" cultures and the apparent lack of inhibition created by dancing.[64] As David Butler and Krin Gabbard highlight, the same dualism persisted in Hollywood's portrayal and use of jazz from the so-called silent era through to the 1940s.[65] But in the case of Alex North and *Streetcar*—as is true of other films in the 1950s—the choice of jazz is less clear-cut.

As Mervyn Cooke highlights, North was one of a small number of film composers for whom jazz was perceived as "an ideal vehicle for American nationalism in music, and this sentiment resurfaced at a time when [...] modernism in film music was also on the increase."[66] In the 1920s, Aaron Copland—with whom North studied in the mid-1930s—successfully combined jazz and (Modernist) concert music in works such as his Piano Concerto (1926). Although Copland soon turned to other idioms—notably, American folk—in order to forge a specifically American musical identity which would both assert its independence from European art music and communicate with a broad public, North may well have been encouraged by his teacher's synthesis of jazz with other musical languages.[67]

North had admired jazz since his teenage years, particularly the music of Duke Ellington, and critics noted the influence of jazz elements in North's music from the mid-1930s on. In 1940, they praised his ability to synthesize jazz successfully with the language of concert music in the cantata *Negro Mother*. In interview in 1943, North urged that jazz elements be "put [...] to work" in the composing of "vital, democratic, and dynamic" American music.[68] Thus it is clear that North's view of jazz was not one constrained by the stereotypical associations suggested by Hollywood:

> Jazz is by far a more authentic indigenous ingredient of American music than the folk music which is expressed in mountain ballads and cowboy songs [...]. True, jazz has become commercialized to the degree where it has lost its freshness and spontaneity, but the jazz form should not be snubbed by composers because of its occasional maudlin wanderings into Tin Pan Alley. An attempt should rather be made to extract the essence and spirit of jazz and to project it with all the resources of craftsmanship at one's command to produce an end product which will have artistic integrity as well as emotional impact.[69]

In his *Revue* for clarinet and orchestra (1946), commissioned and premiered by Benny Goodman, North again assimilated jazz—and more particularly, swing—with music for the concert hall. Features of the *Revue* can be found in the *Streetcar* score: frequent metrical changes, syncopated rhythms, an enriched harmonic language that features dissonance, chromatic alterations and short passages of bi- or polytonality, and moments of chamber-ensemble. There is also a more direct motivic link between the two works: the *Revue* opens with an accented, rising flatted fifth (tritone) figure—a quaver followed by a semibreve—played loudly and in unison across the orchestra on the first beat. The figure returns in various guises during the first movement, and again briefly in the final (third) movement, though it resolves to a more consonant fourth in the slow movement. Bluesy flatted fifths also feature during the opening and closing of the first of North's Twelve Dance Preludes (1948) for piano, though a sense of tonal center is replaced by a more chromatic sound towards the middle of the piece. Each prelude is a short character study. Here jazz characteristics in melodic line, harmonic enrichments, and rhythm are combined with modernist dissonance and atonality. The influence of Schoenberg's atonal Three Piano Pieces (Op. 11) can be heard, along with passages of Debussy-like fluid and floating harmony.[70]

On one level then, the character and placement of North's blues-based jazz cues in *Streetcar* can be read as stereotypical, suggesting not only an urban setting but also an unspoken undercurrent of sex and sensuality that may also be mapped onto notions of race. To emphasize ambiguity in terms of the source of these cues, North composed music that simulates jazz directly: in its melodies, some of its harmonic language, formal structure (albeit altered), instrumentation and arrangement. As Cooke notes, North "demonstrated the insidious suggestiveness of jazz by creating a sultry musical idiom perfectly attuned to the drama's humid claustrophobia."[71] North's quasi-jazz cues and their representation of Stanley are overtly seductive. They are vibrant, with spontaneous-sounding solos that are either "sweet" or more earthy—the latter influenced by Ellington's "jungle" sound—and notated in full, as were those performed by Ellington's players.[72] These cues emphasize the body, its power and desirability, as also suggested in North's instructional score markings: "Sexy, virile" (R3: P1), "Dirty" (e.g., R13: P2, bb. 42–43). Additional jazz players were brought in to authenticate further the score's jazzy sound.[73]

On another level, however, jazz was clearly an important feature of North's developing compositional voice through the 1940s, alongside—and frequently integrated *with*—Modernism. Jazz spoke to him of America. But *which* jazz? The jazz-inspired cues of North's *Streetcar* score synthesize elements from a variety of jazz styles. The character of the melodic lines, motifs, licks, and aspects of the performance practice invoke traditional, small-ensemble New Orleans jazz, and its development in Chicago and New York, and/or the revival of the earlier New Orleans style in the 1940s.[74] Although North's instrumentation for these cues may have been influenced by such styles, there is little of the group improvisation that characterized the early New Orleans style. The twelve-bar blues structure is evoked, but altered formally and in terms of nonstandard harmonic substitution. North adds ninths and elevenths, but frequently misses out the seventh, perhaps the strongest single indicator of a jazz sound in harmonic terms. These latter elements are more suggestive of the more complex structures and harmonies of big bands of the swing era on the one hand, and bebop combos on the other. Although Ellington made use of the flatted fifth in the 1930s, most commentators consider this "blue note" to be a relatively late addition associated most directly with bebop players in the 1940s, such as Dizzy Gillespie.[75]

Cooke suggests that North's *Streetcar* score "trod a designedly uncomfortable middle ground between populism and modernism."[76] Along with the bebop players, the music of Duke Ellington inhabited some of this same space in terms of a harmonic language of enriched chords, major/minor ambivalence, and dissonant chromaticism. As one of his favorite composers, Ellington's influence on North was formative. But the same harmonic language can be heard *throughout* North's *Streetcar* score; i.e., not just in the jazz-inspired cues. Here though the harmonic context is late Romantic and Modernist music rather than swing or bebop. In combination with elements such as orchestration, the same harmonic language takes on a nostalgic character in some of the cues associated with Blanche, for example.[77] The score's more extreme dissonance and bitonality could just as easily be interpreted as rooted in the music of bebop or Ellington and some other swing bands of the period, as that of European modernists such as Delius or Milhaud. Indeed, Ellington and other big band composers and arrangers were inspired by these and other European (and Russian) art music composers of the early twentieth century.[78] Such harmonic correspondences clearly add coherence to a score that might otherwise have sounded more fragmented. This musical connection also plays a narrative role, intimating that Blanche and Stanley are perhaps not so dissimilar after all; each is flawed and guilty of the "misunderstanding and insensitivity" from which the tragedy of Williams's play and screenplay spring.

As I explore in more detail in chapter 5, my interpretation of North's score is built on the notion that it demonstrates the ambivalence that exists at the heart of Williams's play. On a macro-level, stylistic difference in the music for Blanche and Stanley assists in setting the characters in opposition to one another. On a micro-level these differences are counterbalanced by similarities in terms of harmonic language, thematic consistency, and the unifying role played by the tritone, supporting Williams's suggestion that neither character should be blamed or considered "good" or "bad." The score also plays a key role in maintaining the Collector scene's polysemic character, standing as a counterweight to Leigh's performance of the scene. In the third and final act, however, North's score arguably tips the balance lightly in favor of Blanche, through an operatic celebration of Leigh's performance (*Revelation*, R11: P1). In making *this* the musical climax, North subtly downgrades the focus on the inferred rape as the film's dramatic climax.

Critical Reception of the Score

North's score was intriguingly described in a trade review as "unique *but* moving."[79] In the main, his music was little discussed in newspaper reviews of the film. Of course, the score's nomination for an Academy Award demonstrated that the industry held it in high regard. Sam Goldwyn, then head of MGM, wrote to North to compliment him on the "beautiful" score; he hoped they would have an opportunity to work together in the future.[80]

Just a few months after the film's initial release, Frank Lewin reviewed the score for the journal *Film Music*.[81] The essay included brief extracts from the conductor score, and a paragraph from North in which he explained his intentions. Several of the score's elements are singled out for praise by Lewin: the contrasting character of the music for Blanche and Stanley, the main title, *Revelation*, and *Scherzo*. He was critical of the scoring of three other sequences, however: the staircase sequence, where "a halo of sweet strings goes along," the short cue heard after Blanche and Mitch kiss on the pier, and the film's closing music.[82] It is clear from the review that Lewin's account is based on the 1951 release of the film; i.e., the re-edited version. He wrote to North and asked if studio policy had been brought to bear in the scoring of these cues. It seems that the composer did not reply: in the article Lewin writes, "[In] view of the sensitivity shown throughout the greater part of the score, one cannot help feeling that these are instances where the composer was acting on suggestions, or directives, other than his own judgment."[83] Clearly, Lewin was not aware of Kazan's letter to the *New York Times* published a few months earlier.

Lewin's review is not a detailed analysis, but it is perceptive, particularly given that the primary means of hearing the score again at this time involved return trips to the movie theater. In the case of *Streetcar*, excerpts from the film's score could also be heard on the soundtrack recording released by Capitol Records, though Lewin states that the blues solos, which are effective when part of the film, seem "quite long and static"[84] on the soundtrack album. By contrast, he suggests that the Capitol recording of *Flores para los muertos* (*Revelation* on the Warner Bros.' cue sheet) is "even more impressive when unhampered by the spoken word," for, on record, the listener is better able to notice the "skilful musical transformations of the various themes" in the score which may go unnoticed when watching the film.[85] On this point, I must take issue with Lewin, as my analysis of *Revelation* in chapter 5 makes clear.

An essay on the score also appeared in *Pro Musica Sana*, the magazine of the Miklós Rózsa Society, in the mid-1970s.[86] Here Ken Sutak provided a fulsome and richly evocative description of the score. Once again, the *Revelation* cue was praised, its music

> so searing, so hopeless, and so just-plain-frightening [...] that the scene winds up intoxicated with a drenching presentiment of doom. The abandoned Blanche turns facially demoniac and the music attains an internal burst of glass-smash shatter precisely at the moment when destruction is structurally settled in the drama.[87]

Sutak makes an interesting point concerning Blanche's desperation to find protection and the role of the score in this respect. He suggests that after the rape, with all sense of protection lost, North scores Blanche's loss of grip on reality in a pitying manner. As she leaves, however, Sutak argues that the score "finally assumes a protective role." Here, North composes "for the Blanche that once was, thereby inviting his audience to focus on the horror of this woman's suffering, the necessity of realizing what has been done to her, and the probability that destruction of what is personally found beautiful is a capacity which lies within all of us."[88]

Sutak criticizes the score's final flourish, which "risks a bizarre identification. It almost sounds jubilant," though he is more confident than Lewin in his suggestion that the blame for the compromised ending lies with interference from the Breen Office. Paradoxically, Sutak suggests that the compromise ultimately works in favor of *Streetcar*'s writer and director, so much so that "one can only wonder if Williams and Kazan did not consider North's musical voice their hidden ace when they agreed to revise the *Streetcar* script."[89] North's score was not composed until some time after these changes were agreed and the sequence filmed, of course, but Sutak's point is an intriguing one.

Writing in the mid-1970s, Sutak also refers to the 1951 version of the film, as Lewin had in 1952—that is, the version that includes North's replacement cue for the staircase scene, rather than the original. As is explored in more detail in chapter 5, North replaced the (censored) staircase cue with an extended version of a theme that was already part of the score, though in the original score it was first heard *after* the staircase scene. Elsewhere, it underscored moments of tenderness between Stanley and Stella (in R6: P1, R10: P1, and R10: P2). An extended version of the same theme had already been written into the score's final cue. It is heard as Blanche is driven away: Stella turns to pick up the baby, then runs away from Stanley up the stairs to Eunice's apartment, telling the baby that they will never return. For Sutak, the placement of this latter version of the theme "flatly contradicts Stella's final words," implying instead that she *will* return to him, that Stanley's tenderness towards her will win out. Sutak thus suggests that the film's closing music is not so much "jubilant" as "victorious" in that it underlines the extent of Stanley's cruel triumph, thus "structurally imbedding Williams's theme deep within the film's final frames."[90] I return to Sutak's view of this cue at the end of chapter 5, since it is key to my comparison of the two "versions" of the film, of North's score, and the impact each has on our interpretation of *Streetcar*'s ending.

5

AN ANALYSIS OF THE SCORE

In this chapter I provide an analysis and interpretation of the original version of North's *Streetcar* score, as heard in trade previews in May and June of 1951, now restored in the director's cut of the film. The larger part of the chapter explores the music that comprises the principal groups of musical materials. Since so much of the score is generated from a relatively small collection of materials, I provide a detailed analysis of this material, then discuss its re-contextualization and development through the score. This is followed by a more detailed analysis of the two musical climaxes in which I highlight the role of structure. Finally, I consider the impact of the film's re-editing in the summer of 1951 alongside the revisions to the score that North was required to make, and explore the impact of these changes.

Stylistically varied, the score's coherence is generated primarily through the recurrence and variation of principal motifs and themes, most of which are introduced within the first thirty-five minutes of the score, when most of the film's source music is also heard.[1] Ross Care identifies six major themes or motifs from which most of the score is derived, with the first three in the main title: the main title's vamp (or accompanimental ostinato); the opening melody (theme 1); the arpeggiated G♯m melody (theme 2); the Varsouviana; Blanche's theme (as heard in *Blanche and Mitch* cues); and Stanley's music ("less as specific motifs than as the through-composed jazz sequences").[2]

This thematic core is supplemented by an additional suite of elements in the film's final third: the *Birthday Party* cues. The introduction of new material at this point in the film is key to the dynamic of the score, which reasserts the three-act structure of *Streetcar* on Broadway: the first act establishes characters, the locale, the film's dramatic themes (the play's scenes 1–4); the second confirms Mitch as a last hope for Blanche, though other elements disrupt this (5–6); the third act

begins with Stanley's revelations about Blanche to Stella (7–11). Over
the course of the film the score builds slowly towards its climaxes in
the third act. Tension is generated first through the juxtaposition or
layering of different musical voices (*Collector*, R7: P2 and *Blanche and
Mitch*, R8: P2). This is followed by new musical material (*Birthday
Party*, R9: P2, R10: P1a, and R10: P2), and the mixing of materials
from different motivic groups (*Blanche's Solitude*, R10: P3). These
techniques continue into the two musical climaxes, both of which take
place in the film's final thirty minutes: *Revelation* (R11: P1)—during
which Blanche explains herself to Mitch—and *Seduction* (R13: P1)—
the prelude to the rape. Both cues represent an apotheosis in their integration of music, action, and the delivery of dialogue, albeit in different
ways. Following *Seduction*, the score enters a coda-phase and elements
from the main title return, followed, apparently paradoxically, by the
first exposition of the love theme in full. Finally, at the end of the chapter, I explore the film's ending and the role played by the score in its
sense of closure.

The main difficulty in providing a guide to this score is that it is
almost impossible to settle on a dominant reading, though this is not
entirely surprising given the play's openness to interpretation in terms
of authorial intention, performance, and criticism, as discussed in chapter 3. North's score matches Williams's ambivalence towards the key
protagonists of his play, though neither version of Kazan's film
achieves this entirely, given the changes made to accommodate first the
Breen Office (the original/restored 1993 version), and then to placate
the Legion of Decency (the 1951 release). Even in Kazan's origi-
nal/restored version, the various amendments and omissions and, particularly, the changed ending unbalance this ambivalence, though not
terminally. Indeed, in spite of these changes, the film is an immensely
successful adaptation of the play, and North's score is vital both to its
success and in defining its ambivalence. The score identifies Blanche
and Stanley as the key protagonists and antagonists. It supports and
emphasizes Kazan's and Brando's alignment of Stanley with physicality and a live-in-the-moment desire to take what is his. Leigh's alternately coquettish and sensual interpretation of Blanche on screen (by
comparison with Tandy's stage performance) brought to light a correspondence between the characters which may have been more covert
on stage. On the one hand, North's score *re*-balances this, contrasting
Stanley's virility with Blanche's melancholy romanticism and nostalgic
imagination, notably in the cues that underscore her hopes for her relationship with Mitch (the *Blanche and Mitch* cues). These hopes are
characterized by some of the score's most tonal music, often expressed

in lush string writing, though its thematic material is less dynamic and more melancholy than that of the Varsouviana. By contrast, Stanley's solid bodily presence is articulated in cues that foreground the blues scale or blue notes, supported by jazz harmony and various indicators of blues or jazz performance practice. These (musical) extremes assist in establishing Blanche's vulnerability, and her sense of being over-whelmed by Stanley's larger-than-life physical presence when she first meets him.

Williams insisted that neither Blanche nor Stanley should be de-picted sympathetically at the expense of the other, as already discussed. Kazan too emphasized the contradictions in both characters.[3] This complexity in characterization is also depicted in the score. For exam-ple, though the synthesis of jazz and concert music is itself complex, Stanley is not solely identified with jazz and with the physical and the carnal in North's score: Stanley's tenderness towards Stella is also rep-resented musically. Equally, Blanche is not solely identified as a nos-talgic or romantic dreamer, as *Revelation* makes clear. Indeed, through an association with the lost estate of Belle Reve, the score implies that the difficulties Blanche experiences are born of her situation: her sex, her class, her widowhood, her economic poverty. In this way, the score is ambivalent at a macro-level. For Blanche, as with Stanley, the other is the problem; Stella is pushed and pulled between them. But through alterations to the harmonic language associated with turn-of-the-century concert music on the one hand, and jazz and blues on the other, a correspondence between Blanche and Stanley is hinted at. As already mentioned, the score's enriched harmonies frequently lack a seventh, removing both a clear indication of the chord's pull or resolution and, in North's simulated jazz cues, the most direct reference to the chord's derivation. As a result, these chords thus slip more easily between these two possible musical contexts, as do the score's moments of bitonality, and the profusion of chords that combine both major and minor thirds (sharp ninths, in jazz parlance), which display ambivalence at a micro-level throughout the score (as in the piano vamp introduction to *Stan R2: P3*, for example). Thus, although the score develops from quite disparate, even contradictory materials, and emphasizes difference in support of the narrative, it is also highly integrated in thematic terms and harmonically unified.

Several motifs, figures, and themes are important in the thematic consistency of the score, notably the descending two-note appoggiatura figure of the main title's opening theme. The interval of the tritone is also key: indeed, it epitomizes the score's relationship to the narrative. The tritone has a strong identity in its own right: its characteristic dis-

cord and ambiguity is easily recognizable, and in this it encapsulates
the outward ambivalence of North's score towards Blanche and Stanley. Identified as a "blue note" in jazz, the interval relishes its discord, a
context emphasized in North's carnal music for Stanley: as the trumpet
rocks laconically between fourth and flatted fifth in the opening melody
of *Stan* (R2: P3); in the interval between the trumpet and piano lines in
the four-bar break in the same cue; and between the "dirty" trumpet
entries in the buildup to the rape (*Seduction*, R13: P1). The same interval forms the crux of the main title, where once—just briefly—it is
augmented upwards to form a perfect fifth (*Belle Reve*, E in bar 6).
Although this note forms the registral high point of the cue, its resolution is transitory; the pervasiveness of the tritone is reasserted almost
immediately. Over the course of the film, material from this cue comes
to signify the oppressive pull Belle Reve exerted over Blanche, so aptly
represented by the tritone's suppression of resolution; it conveys the
inescapable tragedy of Blanche's past. Elsewhere the interval indicates
the "brutal desire" that Blanche appears to repudiate. Forming a perfect
fifth in North's *Blanche and Mitch* cues, the augmentation of the interval offers respite, but—as in *Belle Reve*—it offers only temporary release.

The Score's Thematic Integrity:
Belle Reve

The first of the film's core groups of musical material is heard over the
main titles. The cue proper begins after the bars added for the Warner
Bros.' distributors card, and comprises a sequence of relatively short
themes of 2–4 bars heard in quick succession, none of which is repeated here.[4] Most of the cue underscores the film's title cards which
run over a still image master shot of the apartment building where almost all of the film's action takes place, though the final section underscores the arrival of a steam train (implicitly, Blanche's train), and the
hustle and bustle of the station. The cue's episodic character adds interest to the stillness of the first background image, while its musical coherence offers continuity as the title cards change. Harmonically, the
cue wanders: it opens with enriched chords (added ninths, added sixths)
of F♯m, moves up to G minor, then to the dominant, D, then on to G♯
minor as the image dissolves to that of the approaching train, closing
with an emphasis on G in the final bars. The tempo for the main titles

segment is relatively uniform, though less so at the start and with the move into the latter section.[5]

The use of extended chords and the abundance of flatted fifths generate a rich and discordant musical world. With the exception of the move to the dominant, there is a relative lack of harmonic functionality, which supports the ossified character of the cue's first themes. The jazzy "blues" style is over-determined by an accumulation of musical elements: pitch structures, the performance of the solo trumpet player, the warm and close inner harmonies of the enriched chords in laconic "wah-wah" rhythms, and semi-chromatic low register piano vamps, anacrustic at first, then focal with the shift to the train station. Together these elements set the atmosphere of the film with great clarity and efficiency. Indeed the results of an experiment undertaken by Philip Tagg and Bob Clarida that uses this title sequence emphasize this.[6]

Example 5.1. *Belle Reve*, **Main Title, Introduction (bars A and B)**

The cue begins, alongside the play's awards card, with an accompaniment figure that develops into a syncopated but rhythmically regular figure in low brass over open fifths in the bass (tonic and dominant). A response from trumpets interjects partway through the third beat, with glissandi between pitches; such trumpet interjections can be found throughout Ellington's oeuvre and is a characteristic of swing-band style more generally. Rocking between the tonic and supertonic, the trombone plays the scooping line (G♯–F♯) which adds the ninth to the chord of F♯m$^{\text{add9}}$. During the third beat, the bass moves from F♯ to C♯, generating the sense of a shift to the dominant (though the chord is a dissonant C♯$^{\text{6sus2}}$). This rhythmic accompaniment figure continues into the cue, albeit with some variation. The main theme enters played by upper strings alongside the film's title card (Ex. 5.2). The theme's arrival is emphasized by appearing to enter early: this is caused by a shift to 3/4 in the previous bar, which also absents the trumpet's answering phrase. After this, the meter settles down into a more regular 4/4. The theme's first note forms a tritone with the root of the chord (and a minor second with the fifth) creating strong dissonance, which dissipates as it falls to the fourth. Opening the score (and the film) with this robust motif sends out a very strong message.[7] Indeed, Tagg and Clarida state that they can find no such dramatic positioning for a ♭5–4 figure elsewhere in the repertoire for this period, though, as discussed previously, North used the same figure as the opening of his *Revue* for clarinet and orchestra (1947).

Example 5.2. *Belle Reve*, **R1: P1, bb. 1–7, Theme 1**

The melody's descent to the (perfect) fifth in bar 3 offers relief from the discord of the opening, though its stability is offset by a rising semi-chromatic anacrustic vamp, low on the piano on the fourth beat of the bar (Ex. 5.3).[8] The figure is repeated in the following bars, emphasizing each downbeat and, in bar 4, the melody's step up a tone. The vamp also retains the sense of a brief, if unemphasized, shift to the dominant.

Example 5.3. *Belle Reve*, **R1: P1, piano vamp, bb. 3–4**

The continuation of the main theme in bar 5 behaves as a consequent phrase, with the first four bars the antecedent. While it retains the shape of the theme's opening and also generates a tritone (though here between the third and the sixth—A and D♯—rather than the root and the flatted fifth), the appoggiatura-motif here descends a whole tone, rather than a semitone. In the following bar, the theme's development is again more consonant, melodically and rhythmically. The first note of this bar (E) is the highpoint of the cue in registral terms, but it does not indicate a climax. Rather, it is followed by a key change, up a semitone to G minor, closing the theme on the seventh of the tonic chord.

In the bass, the pedal of open fifths of tonic and dominant continue, with syncopated figures filling in the harmony, predominantly Gm^9. During this section, high register piano chords join with, and then take the place of, the trumpet's response figure. In the next bar, a solo trumpet takes over the melody with a triplet figure focused on the tonic minor chord, then moving to the tonic and falling to the seventh (Ex. 5.4, theme 1c).[9] This two-bar figure is then repeated, though its pitch structure is altered by augmenting the ascent of the triplet, an alteration that enables the trumpet line to continue seamlessly into the next section, in D, by voice-leading (A–G–F♯). In the same bar, a clarinet begins a two-and-a-half octave ascending glissando, landing on C natural (♭7 in D) on the first beat of the following bar; during the glissando, the title card for Alex North and Ray Heindorf appears. The supporting harmony for bars 7 and 8 is Gm^9, but in bars 9 and 10, the fifth is flatted in an inner harmonic line (D to D♭)—forming another tritone—while retaining G–D open fifths in the bass, giving Gm$^{\sharp 11(\text{no } 7)}$ (in open voicing).

Example 5.4. *Belle Reve*, R1: P1, solo trumpet (bb. 8–11), Theme 1c

Example 5.5. *Belle Reve*, R1: P1, D section (bb. 11–14), Theme 1d

While the triplets and performed glissandi on trumpet add to the languorous and rather sleazy feel (bb. 7–10), with the move to D in bar 11 the melodic line takes on a more imposing and direct quality, not least due to the strings' octave doubling and the avoidance of triplets. Initially the line favors pitches of the tonic triad, but then falls from G♯ to C. The G♯ generates a tritone against enriched tonic chords (D^{13})—it is stressed by its position in the bar and here too forms the first of a two-note descent—while C forms a minor seventh. The stability generated by a return to the third in bar 13 is soon undone via the syncopated chromatic slide from B to G♯ over the dramatic jolt of a sudden move to G♯m^9 (bar 14). The segment in D can function as an extended dominant seventh in G minor, though this is followed by a tonicization of G♯m^9, rather than Gm^9, in bar 15. A tonic pedal is repeated through the next three bars, with emphasis on an altered version of the bass vamp (which, in turn, adds emphasis to each downbeat). During the last bar of this section, Kazan's title card and the image of the apartment beneath dissolve to a black screen. Alongside the registral shift that signals the move to the next section, the previous static image changes to one of movement: an overhead shot of a steam train moving through a warehouse area next to a large river (the Mississippi) at dusk, accompanied by sound effects. The words "New Orleans" appear on the screen.

Example 5.6. *Belle Reve*, R1: P1 (bb. 15–17), Theme 2

Though the octave doubling continues, the melody (in strings and woodwind) now reaches higher with a focus on stable pitches: octave leaps, and intervals of fourths and fifths. The shift to semiquavers generates a sense of momentum, though motion is intermittent. Where notes are sustained, trumpets again interject, here resolving a suspension from supertonic to tonic, over a tonic chord. The low brass accompaniment and vamp are replaced by sustained chords and, on trombone, a semi-chromatic line in crotchets that wanders between the fifth and the major seventh over chords of G♯m^{add9} (bb. 15 and 16), finally sliding to a complex chord that might be read as D^{11}/E bass. There is a cut to a shot of taxis pulling up into the station as a train arrives. The two pianos begin a low syncopated boogie-woogie line in octaves (playing out the blues scale on G) with brushes on cymbals, though this is barely audible over the scene's sound effects. Blanche emerges from the steam.[10]

Example 5.7. *Belle Reve*, Main Title, Trombone, b. 15

Belle Reve Through the Film

At this point in the film, Joe McLaughlin's label for the main title cue—i.e., after the lost DuBois estate—seems odd, not least since Tagg and Clarida's experiment highlights the clarity with which the cue emphasizes an association with cities, clubs, tension, melancholy, and prostitution, for example.[11] The motivation is clear when the next North cue is heard, however. *Belle Reve Reflections* (R2: P2) is almost identical to the main title in terms of musical material though it is placed a semitone lower and its instrumentation is completely different.[12] It is heard as Blanche tells Stella of the loss of the estate. In some respects, Blanche is as much the object of the cue as Belle Reve is: both are symbols of a way of life that can no longer be sustained. North scores Blanche's active subjectivity, her aspirations regarding Mitch, with a different set of musical materials (the *Blanche and Mitch* cues). Ultimately, however, these are supplanted by the return of *Belle Reve*, underlining Blanche's inability to escape from her tragic situation.

North's *Belle Reve Reflections* (R2: P2) follows two short source cues: "Limehouse Blues" and "Japanese Sandman."[13] Its orchestration here presents a subdued rather than a strident sound: solo violin and solo woodwind replace string and brass tuttis. The cue's solo lines and warm, harmonically enriched accompaniment figures supply an intimate mood for Blanche's revelation, at least initially. The music is quite low in the mix at points during the scene, but in places it pushes through to the foreground, largely due to dialogic pauses, and here comments on the sisters' exchange. The cue's placement also emphasizes the theme's melancholic potential. Blanche appears astounded by Stella's admission that she "nearly goes wild" when Stanley is away, and on his return, cries "in his lap like a baby." Blanche closes the subject with an observation: "I guess that's what's meant ... by being in love." Her comment is underlined by the cut to a mid-close-up and the music's entry.

The cue's episodic quality echoes the parsing of the discussion in visual terms; the scene is segmented similarly in terms of framing, and movement within and around the apartment. The sequence begins with the mid-close-up of Blanche as she introduces the subject and moves across to Stella, seated at the table. The camera moves down to frame the sisters in a claustrophobic two-shot. Blanche begins quietly, asking her sister not to reproach her, but through a gradual increase in the tempo, amplitude, and emphasis of her speech, she develops a more accusatorial tone. She compares their behavior directly: Stella left, Blanche stayed; Stella made her own way in New Orleans, while Blanche struggled to keep the estate together. The first key change (*Belle Reve*, b. 7) is reached as Blanche states that although she does not mean to admonish her sister, and here she is more emphatic, "all the burden descended on my shoulders."[14] Her line is supported by the triplet figure previously heard on trumpet (*Belle Reve*, b. 8). Stella stands and turns. There is a cut to a mid-shot: again, both women are tight inside the frame. Stella tells her sister that looking after herself was the best she could do in the situation, but Blanche reiterates her point: "You [...] abandoned Belle Reve, not I." Finally, exasperated, Stella asks Blanche what she's talking about: "About what? Please?" Her lines are delivered at high pitch but more slowly and emphatically than Blanche's accumulated frenzy, and alongside the next key change (*Belle Reve*, b. 11). Blanche stops and withers, almost fainting into the seat beneath her. The low register semi-chromatic anacrustic piano vamp pushes through the silence into the foreground. Finally, at a much lower pitch, she explains: "Loss. The Loss." There is a reverse-shot of Stella's shocked reaction, which returns to Blanche for confirmation. The sound of a steam train creeps in. There is a second reverse-shot as Stella asks what happened, and the final key change occurs along with the entry of the melody in semiquavers in octaves, high on the piano (*Belle Reve*, b. 15; hereafter *Belle Reve*, theme 2). Blanche becomes defensive once more, and runs outside to the staircase as the sound of the train intensifies. We see the train's steam rise from the alley, and for a moment the music seems to dissolve into it.

The final part of the cue introduces new material, primarily developments of *Belle Reve*; first of the trumpet-led triplet episode, then interjections of theme 2 on piano. Blanche lists the deaths she waited for; Stella returned only for funerals. Harmonically, the sequence alternates between Dm^7 and $E\flat m^\Delta$, then between Dm^7 and Em^Δ, finally moving to C^6 before a return to F minor. The melody is played warmly on sax, but moves only between the fifths of these alternating chords. A return of the cue's opening theme follows, also on sax, as Blanche states that funerals are too expensive for a schoolmistress's tiny salary. She berates her sister, for all the while she was here with her "Polack." The cue closes on a chord of Fm^9/D♭ bass, which generates yet another tritone (between D♭ and G). Stella runs inside to the bathroom crying and shuts the door.

The cue's placement forms a connection between the musical materials and the loss of the estate, the deaths that Blanche witnessed there, and the passing of her youth. The loss of Blanche's youth is emphasized by the next cue in the collection—*Reaction to Birth* (R4: P1a)—which follows Stanley's revelation that Stella is pregnant. Blanche sits before the mirror, her head in her hands. Several elements from *Belle Reve* return in this nine-bar cue: a descent from supertonic to tonic on cup-muted solo trumpet, a minor added ninth chord (Gm^{add9}), a variant of the semi-chromatic trombone line (*Belle Reve*, bb. 15–16), here in minims, played by cellos, bass clarinet, and harp. This slow-moving, low-register figure imparts inevitability and resignation, and moves the harmony from Gm^{add9} through $Gm^{\Delta 9}$, Gm^7, and $Gm^{\sharp 13(no7)}$. As Blanche whispers, "Stella? Stella's going to have a baby?" she looks up at the mirror, interrogates her tired face and sighs. A solo flute plays the opening of theme 2 (*Belle Reve*, b. 15). The trumpet completes the theme as Stella re-enters, and the ex-trombone descent is repeated in crotchets. Blanche rushes towards Stella to congratulate her, but the music is dissonant: a chord of $Fm^{9♭5}$. A solo bass clarinet plays a searching dotted rhythm melody that emphasizes minor seconds and recalls the piano boogie at the end of *Belle Reve*. These elements add an unnerving quality to the end of the scene as another impact of the years Blanche spent at Belle Reve comes into focus: the loss of the opportunity to become a mother.[15]

Elements of *Belle Reve* also emerge when Blanche realizes that Stanley may soon discover the truth about her life in Oriel. The cue *Soliloquy* (R7: P1) begins as Blanche asks Stella whether she's heard any gossip about her past. The cue opens with a slow variant on *Belle Reve*'s minor ninth accompaniment figure. Theme 2 enters on piano though the line is fragmented, as in *Reaction to Birth* (R4: P1a). A solo violin plays a melancholy *obbligato* line above, then a new theme is introduced by violins, solo viola, solo cello, and celeste (initially), marked "magic-like shimmering" (Ex. 5.8) Musically, the sequence is unlike any other in the score, though its triple meter evokes the Varsouviana. Three lines of *divisi* violins move in parallel through a rolling descent and partial ascent, returning to the same pitches in the main. The vertical harmony of the upper string lines glides between C♯m, F♯m, G♯m, and A in a circular fashion.[16] In bar 14, a major triad on B♭

descends chromatically, following the rhythm of bar 12. The solo viola and cello lines—with their emphasis on E♭—seem only distantly related, if at all.[17] Starting each bar with two quavers creates a sense of gently persistent pulsing or circular motion.

MAGIC-LIKE, SHIMMERING

Example 5.8. *Soliloquy*, R7: P1, Strings, bb. 11–14

During this sequence Blanche reveals her doubts that she can continue to "shimmer and glow." She needs to court the support of others, those with the tough outer shell that she lacks, but she is now losing the only means that she knows by which to find protection: her looks. As she moves across the room she passes the lantern that covers the bare bulb. We glimpse her reflection in the mirror she has ornamented. She is framed in mid-close-up against flimsy voile curtains, behind which rain falls heavily, providing a glistening backdrop. These discordant string lines generate a sense of fragility or ethereality imbued with nostalgia, colored by Blanche's tragic recognition that she is "fading now." At her spoken acknowledgment, the sequence is halted and the cue returns briefly to the familiarity of the cue's opening accompaniment figure. This is followed by discordant stingers provided by seventh chords with flatted fifths ($D^{♭9♭5}$ and $A^{7♭5}$) over a D pedal, as Blanche asks Stella if she has been listening, the move to the dominant underscoring her question. Stella's reply signals the return to a more stable G minor harmony, a development of theme 2 in violins, and a passing reference to the semi-chromatic ex-trombone line. Stella busies herself by opening a coke for her sister, but when Blanche asks for a shot in it, an oboe begins a chromatic descent, commenting on Blanche's reliance on alcohol for refuge. As their discussion turns fondly to Belle Reve, the music stabilizes once more: the melody emphasizes fourths and fifths and chords alternate between Gm^7 and C^9, culminating on $C^{9\flat 5}$. Here the cue builds to its melodic climax via a sequence of increasing intervals, each of which pulls further away from the tonic until it reaches the tonic an octave above.[18] Agitated, Blanche speaks of leaving soon. Stella tries to calm her sister but pours her drink too quickly: Blanche screams hysterically as it fizzes over onto her dress as the rising leaps finally reach the octave above. The moment recalls an earlier eruption by Blanche during *Belle Reve Reflections* (R2: P2). Her anxiety here comes at a crucial point in her relationship with Mitch, her last desperate hope of shelter. With Stanley's suspicions, her aspirations are now in jeopardy.

The original placement of *Belle Reve*'s theme 2 signaled a move away from the static image of the Kowalskis' apartment to the arrival of a steam train into New Orleans. The train—and by extension, theme 2—connects Blanche from the world of Belle Reve to her sister in New Orleans, her last resort. The theme returns during Blanche's birthday party, when Stanley presents his sister-in-law with a bus ticket back to Oriel, forcing her from his home, back to where she cannot go (*Birthday Party*, R10: P2, b. 4).[19] Crucially, the stable character of the theme's opening—the tonic and the fifth of G♯m in *Belle Reve*—is here altered to an arpeggiation of $D^{\flat 13}$, over $Ab^{\sharp 11}/C$ bass and is left unresolved as Blanche runs into the bathroom sobbing. A brief quotation from *Belle Reve*'s theme 1 follows when Stella berates her husband for his cruelty toward Blanche. She tells him of her sister's innocence when she was younger, before she was changed by the treatment of others, adding an association of cruelty to the theme, alongside those of the estate, its loss, and the impact of the years Blanche spent there.

Theme 2 returns with Mitch's appearance later that night (*Blanche's Solitude*, R10: P3), heralded by a figure on cup-muted trumpet that combines the lazy supertonic-tonic trombone motif of *Belle Reve*'s accompaniment figure with the two-note appoggiatura descent of theme 1. Here though it descends a whole tone (supertonic to tonic), adding a ninth to the cue's F minor harmony alongside resignation. The semi-chromatic trombone line also returns, moving the harmony through to Fm^Δ, Fm^7, and Fm^6. These bluesy sounds are heard as Blanche looks across the empty apartment, lit by the flickering neon of signs nearby, searching for the source of the knocking that woke her from a drink-induced stupor. As she asks who is at the door, a slower version of the theme enters low in the violins (tutti), now rhythmically augmented and more measured. It is supported by a harmonium-like chordal brass accompaniment that moves fluidly from F minor to C^{b9} via G^{7b5} and other neighboring chords. When she hears that it is Mitch, Blanche looks heavenward, as if in thanks: "Gracious." This move to the dominant seventh seems to mirror Blanche's flicker of optimism—perhaps he will still marry her?—though the theme itself, with its overall motion downward from C to G works against the harmony's unresolved question.

Example 5.9. *Blanche's Solitude*, **Violins, R10: P3, bb. 6–9**

The same theme returns briefly during *Revelation* (R11: P1, bb. 22–25). It takes the same form as in the previous cue (*Blanche's Solitude*, R10: P3), but with the tonic (F) replaced by G (third quaver in each phrase), suggesting the theme is rooted in C minor, rather than F minor. The sequence is accompanied by alternating major triads at the distance of a tritone (C and Gb), suggesting bitonality and endorsing the semantics of Blanche's dialogue: the complexity of the human heart. I return to the cue in detail in my discussion of the score's musical climaxes below.

This same more measured version of theme 2 is heard twice in the film's final cue, *Affirmation* (R14: P2). After a hysterical breakdown and struggle with the Matron, the Doctor re-dignifies Blanche by addressing her directly as Miss DuBois. The cue begins with theme 2 in upper strings resolutely in D minor, over a tonic pedal. Extending the duration of the crotchet in the second phrase to a dotted minim (bar 3), means that the quavers that follow now fall on the downbeat. This latter part of the phrase now seems to balance the first, finally, where previously it had always sounded hurried; the last three notes (F–D–E) now refer more directly to the last three of the first phrase (G–F–G).

Example 5.10. *Affirmation*, **R14: P2, Horns, bb. 1–4**

Above this, two flutes, two clarinets, and two oboes together play three slowly descending lines, two of which are chromatic. The oboe line emphasizes its chromaticism via an accented appoggiatura figuration which references the opening of *Belle Reve*'s theme 1. These descents continue as theme 2 develops in a meandering manner, with various pitches flatted. During bar 5, a slowly rising chromatic scale in the bass replaces the tonic pedal, adding an un-rooted character to the bars that follow. Blanche rolls onto her back and closes her eyes in defeat, but the Doctor reopens them.[20] A plea follows, and he instructs the Matron to free her. As the Doctor helps Blanche to her feet, the oboe's appoggiatura figuration is harmonized and passed between sections of the orchestra in turn, in some cases falling, in others rising. The chromatically inflected bass line slowly wanders upward, replaced by a dominant pedal (on A), beneath a chord of A^9 (bar 12). The Doctor removes his hat and offers his arm to Blanche. Solo wind lines slowly ascend independently, mirroring the opening of the cue, while timpani and harp repeat a dominant pedal. Blanche accepts the Doctor's arm and delivers her infamous line: "Whoever you are, I have always depended on the kindness of strangers." The extended dominant sequence is now finally rewarded with a return to the tonic, emphasized by a melodramatic anacrustic octave leap on A, high in the violins, that lands on the downbeat. A quaver later, the cadence is completed with a return to the tonic as four horns repeat theme 2 majestically in D minor in unison. Another three-line descent features, now lower, played by trombones, bass clarinet, bassoons, celli, bass, and piano in octaves. Again, one of these descents emphasizes its chromaticism via an accented appoggiatura figure, here too invoking the ♭5–4 opening of the main title's first theme. With the return of these principal elements of *Belle Reve* at the close of the action, North underlines the inevitability of Blanche's situation, but offers her the dignified exit that befits her character.

North's score thus works with the other elements of the screenplay and film to suggest that Blanche's demise is the result of her situation and the position of women in society, rather than solely pointing the finger at Stanley's cruelty toward his sister-in-law which culminates in a horrific act of sexual violence, or towards Blanche's own behavior. Importantly, the development of theme 2 into a slower, more poignant form occurs after Stanley unearths Blanche's past. The theme now appears more reconciled, although its harmonic context when (a) Mitch arrives (*Blanche's Solitude*, R10: P3), and (b) Blanche queries how a heart can be "straight" (*Revelation*, R11: P1), contradicts this. Only when Blanche responds to the Doctor's formal invitation—"Miss Du-Bois?"—does the harmonic context of the theme echo its dignified acceptance, confirming it after Blanche's final line.

Stanley, the Four Deuces, and Lust

This group of cues is clearly indicated as blues-based jazz-simulation, as is reflected in their instrumentation, the number of players, the musical style, and performance practice. The similarity of these elements to those presented in the jazz standards that (apparently) issue from the Four Deuces creates ambiguity in terms of their source. This is further supported by references to formal structures such as the twelve-bar blues, though here in altered form. These cues appear to be musical works in their own right, with an expected form of continuation oblivious to the film's ongoing narrative. The use of both straight and cupmutes for the trumpets acts as another obvious jazz signifier. North's own label for the first of this suite of cues, "Four Deuces," emphasizes this ambiguity further.

The first of the cues—*Stan* (R2: P3)—underscores Stanley's first meeting with Blanche; Stella is in the bathroom throughout. The music begins with a repeated slow vamp on piano and bass; a two-bar sequence in A minor, with a familiar step-wise descent from tonic to dominant in the bass. A sharp ninth is added to three of the four repeated chords (giving both major and minor thirds), a sharp eleventh is added to the other, creating a tritone.[21] A languorous melody line enters on saxophone two bars later in a style of bluesy extemporization, though the solo is notated. Its pitches are drawn wholly from the blues scale on A (minor pentatonic plus diminished fifth): A C D [Eb] E G A. Tonic, dominant, and flatted fifth (also spelled as sharp four) are emphasized, the latter through appoggiatura-type figures that again echo the opening of *Belle Reve*'s theme 1. Motion is added by means of laid-back dotted rhythms that rock between minor seconds, and again emphasize a quasi-jazz element.

Example 5.11. *Stan*, **R2: P3, Sax, bb. 3–7**

The cue is clearly divided into sections. The introduction is followed by a thirteen-bar sax solo (the A section), which it is possible to read as an altered twelve-bar structure with the penultimate bar augmented (though there is little reference to the usual harmonic structure of the twelve-bar blues). A four-bar B section follows. This is closely related to the opening material but develops a more jagged line, with quaver rest interruptions, and is supported by the return of a variant of the opening vamp. The return of the A section is announced at bar 20, though here the sax's solo material is compressed into nine bars, followed by a second four-bar B section, which interrupts the A section's more fluid and relaxed sensibility.

Section:	Intro	A	B	A'	B'	Coda
Bars:	2	12 + 1	4	9	4	4

Table 5.1. Outline Structure of *Stan*, R2: P3

After the first eight bars, chromatic alterations creep into the solo line (notably E$\sharp$, F$\sharp$, G$\sharp$, B$\flat$, and B), and the piano's chordal accompaniment begins to slide around, away from the A minor feel of the sax line. With the recapitulation of the A section (b. 20), piano and bass start another shifting vamp: here a syncopated alternation between Am^{6add9} and F$\sharp$m$^{\flat9\flat5}$/E bass, then Am^{6add9} and E$^{\Delta\sharp911}$. The tonal function of the E chords is effectively eradicated by the inclusion of both major and minor thirds, along with both the major seventh and ninth. A dotted quaver figure that falls from A to F$\sharp$, then from G to E is related to the melodic line and offsets some of the discordance. With the second B section, the vamp is replaced by a variant of the cue's opening: Am^{add9}, G^{add9}, F$^{\Delta}$, E.[22] With the return of the opening sax motif and its variants (b. 33, the coda), the piano vamp is replaced by enriched chords that descend twice through a cycle of fifths progression from A^7 through to B$\flat^{9add13}$.

The cue is seductive in its relation to the action. The piano vamp enters over a cut to an internal shot of Blanche watching Stanley enter the apartment. Two silent reverse-shots follow as the pair look at one another. At this point Blanche has the upper hand; she knows who he is. As Stanley remembers the expected visit from his sister-in-law the balance of power shifts: with the support of the score and camerawork, Stanley dominates the scene entirely. In the main, the camera remains positioned centrally in the apartment, alongside Blanche. From this vantage point it follows Stanley's expansive movement through the apartment's space, his mobility only halted when he finally moves toward Blanche. The camera's position exaggerates the contrast between Stanley's height and solid muscular physique and Blanche's fragile, petite build: the camera is positioned higher for the reverse-shots of Blanche from Stanley's point of view; he seems to loom over her. The same contrast is emphasized in the cue's strong saxophone line and the more delicate descant on flute that floats above it.

The B section accompanies Stanley's momentary pause in the kitchen, as he pours himself a shot. With the recapitulation of the A section, A', he moves across to the bedroom. In a reverse-shot, the camera reveals Blanche's surprise and embarrassed fascination at the display of his naked torso while he changes from one close-fitting T-shirt to another. Her gaze—and that of the audience, via the camera—is underlined by her halting delivery of the line "and here ... you are" as Stanley turns to face her, revealing his flesh. A structural shift a little later, indicated by the second B section, B' (b. 29), signals the end of small talk: "How long are you here for?" Stanley asks. During the coda, Blanche is startled by the screech of a cat. Her hand instinctively reaches out to reestablish her balance and she clutches at Stanley's bare arm. Catching herself, she pulls away. Stanley spins around to shout to Stella in the bathroom. Blanche stumbles away toward a chair and crumples into it.

The music fulfills several functions here. It is a good example of North's use of jazz to suggest source ambiguity, through its stylistic elements, approximation of formal structure, and its mainly jazz-band based chamber scoring. The soloists' note bends and swooping glissandi, the piano vamps, and other elements clearly signal jazz and blues performance practice, and this includes the flute line, its *obbligato* line suggestive of the clarinet's role in traditional New Orleans jazz ensembles. Nevertheless, the cue's structural divisions accentuate those of the scene's action and dialogue; thus it also fulfills a key criterion of dramatic underscore. The character of the cue intimates a mood that is laid-back yet confident, self-satisfied perhaps, or a suggestion that "this-is-how-it-is" and "it-shall-not-be-otherwise." The same mood is generated by Stanley's repeated dismissal of Blanche's answers to his questions: "Oriel. That's not my territory"; "I never was a very good English student." The cue's stylistic markers bring the carnal, the bodily into focus. North's music is one of several elements that assert that Stanley's muscular physique is the focal point of the scene, along with the camera's eagerness to follow him, and Stanley's scratching of his chest and back, which also draws attention to his body and the sweat-drenched T-shirt that sticks to it.

The next cue in the collection, *Stan Meets Blanche* (R3: P1), begins as Blanche opens the bathroom door to see Stanley staring back at her. It is marked "sexy, virile" and begins with a triplet figure played by cup-muted trumpet that recalls the dotted quaver figure that leaned on minor seconds in the previous cue, *Stan* (R2: P3) (compare Ex. 5.12 below with Ex. 5.11). Beneath this, a D major harmony is established by a repeated tonic pedal on bass (played pizzicato), and a rising chromatic triplet figure (in tenths) on piano that recalls the anacrustic semichromatic piano vamp of *Belle Reve* (Ex. 5.3). *Stan Meets Blanche* is more obviously built on the model of a twelve-bar blues, though even here it does not form a straightforward framework, as shown in Table 5.2 below. Chord substitutions are expected in a twelve-bar blues, which, in its most basic form is built from tonic, subdominant, and dominant chords (that is, chords I, IV, and V). Here, substitutions are sometimes anticipated, as with the subdominant chord heard on the third beat of the fourth bar, and less common substitutions are used (chords on the mediant and flatted mediant are substituted for dominant and subdominant chords in places). In one case the twelve-bar structure is shortened by the contraction of its last four bars into two (A2), and in the final version the last four bars are simply omitted (A4), leaving the sequence unresolved.[23] The B section is an interruptive four-bar break on enriched chords of B^7. Instrumental forces are gradually increased throughout, with different soloists taking the lead in each section; the exception is the first section, in which saxes take over from trumpet in bar 9. A2 and A4 both feature the same "sweet" trombone solo, though in A4 it is played on sax. The clarinet solo in A3 inverts the trombone solo, in terms of shape.

Example 5.12. *Stan Meets Blanche*, R3: P1, Trumpet, bb. 1–3

Section:	A	B	A2	A3	A4
Bars:	4+4+4	4	4+4+2	4+4+4	4+4
Lead:	Tpt–Sax	Tpt	Trb	Cl	Sax
Support:	Pno, Bass	Pno, Bass, Dr, Sax, Tbs, Fl	Pno, Bass, Dr, Sax, Tpt, Fl	Pno, Bass, Dr, Tpt, Tbs, Sax	Pno, Bass, Dr, Tpt, Tbs, Sax, Fl

Table 5.2. Structure and Instrumentation, *Stan Meets Blanche*

As with the previous cue, *Stan*, the opening solo is less a melody than a collection of melodic fragments or motifs that emphasize certain pitches: here, tonic and flatted supertonic (notably via the rocking triplet figure), fifth, sixth, and major seventh. After a brief interruption by saxes, the trumpet returns with an anacrusis into the next section, signaled by the dramatic shift to a chord of B^7. Here the trumpet develops the opening motif: first, augmenting its interval to a minor third (F natural)—which forms a tritone against the root of the chord—then diminishing it to a major second, and finally a minor second. Meanwhile the piano repeats the trumpet's original triplet rocking motion between D and E♭ in octaves, generating both major and minor thirds against the root. After two bars, the piano motif is shifted down a flatted fifth, generating a further tritone with the trumpet. This startling and dissonant four-bar break begins as Blanche realizes her trunk has been disturbed. The bravado that marked her entrance into the room is knocked off balance. As she regains her composure, the music stabilizes again, and the performing ensemble continues its enlarged scope through the repetition and development of the A section.

Example 5.13. *Stan Meets Blanche*, R3: P1, Trombone, bb. 17–20

Immediately after the disruptive break, a solo trombone plays the first extended theme of the cue high in its register. This "sweet" legato solo bears the influence of Lawrence Brown, trombonist with Ellington's orchestra. It is built from straightforward four-bar phrases, though the third phrase is compressed into two bars. During the first bar, there is a prominent slide from flatted third to major third. The solo is followed by another altered twelve-bar blues structure in which clarinet takes the lead, supported by harmonies that focus on tonic, dominant seventh, and subdominant chords, frequently enriched with sixths and sharp ninths. The same major/minor third confusion is emphasized by the clarinet, which leans on each pitch in alternate bars. The melody heard in A2 signals the return of the more straightforward twelve-bar structure, though here the solo is played on tenor sax. It is cut short when Stanley shouts at Blanche: "How about cutting the re-bop!"

In this scene Blanche tackles Stanley the only way she knows how: she flirts. But Stanley's focus is directed elsewhere. She explains that clothes are her "passion," but he is interested only in the cost of the items in her trunk. She repeatedly invites him to compliment her, telling him she is "fishing for a compliment" when he manages only a basic grunt of approval: "Your looks are ok." His view is that women know whether they are attractive or not without the need for confirmation. Blanche tries another tack: she flatters him. He is a real man, a man who cannot be manipulated by women. He demonstrates that she is correct by shouting at her to stop.

Blanche appears to control movement in the scene. First she asks Stanley to move into the back of the apartment and closes the curtain while she dresses. She then moves around the room and around Stanley when she tells him he may enter and asks for his help with her buttons. The music does little to support Blanche's attempts to manipulate Stanley, however. Perhaps it is better to understand the cue as underscoring Stanley's imperviousness to her charms, his rejection of her efforts, as the music continues regardless. Its regular structure, relative lack of response to the moment-to-moment exposition of the action, and the low level it assumes in the mix emphasizes ambiguity over the cue's source, more so than was the case with *Stan* (R2: P3). Although the cue's solo lines are rooted in the blues and are relatively simple, the supporting harmonic language is complicated by enriched and altered substitution chords that obscure the framework's functionality at times (though less so than with *Stan*, R2: P3). On the Capitol Records' soundtrack album of the score, the cue is combined with *Seduction* (R13: P1), and labeled "Lust" by North. In purely musical terms, the label certainly fits, though arguably it fits *Stan* (R2: P3) or *Stan and Stella* (R5: P3) better.

The next cue in the Stanley group is that of the infamous staircase scene: *Stan and Stella*, R5: P3. It begins with an eight-bar introduction on solo clarinet, played *rubato*, which outlines a series of upward "scoops" followed by major seventh descents. The third descent describes a more meandering line, with leaned-on minor seconds combined with emphatic downward leaps of a minor seventh then a major seventh, leading to a final semi-chromatic triplet figure that descends slowly, landing on E on the first beat of bar 9 over a tonic pedal on A. From this point the cue restates the earlier *Stan* (R2: P3) cue almost directly: the vamping piano accompaniment is the same, but the alto sax line is varied slightly over the section's first nine bars, though it retains the same basic shape, as shown below. After this the line matches that of the earlier cue exactly; the same augmentation of a twelve-bar blues into thirteen bars, followed by a four-bar B section.

Example 5.14. *Stan and Stella*, **R5: P3, bb. 11–20 (with R2: P3 bb. 3–12 above)**

During the clarinet solo and the first part of the *Stan* variant we see Stanley emerge from the shower and remember what has happened. First, he searches for Stella in the apartment, then telephones Eunice, and finally shouts to his wife directly from the bottom of the stairs in the courtyard. The flute enters, taking over the lead two bars into the four-bar B section, and continues with a further recapitulation of *Stan*'s opening gesture (*Stan and Stella*, b. 28). At the same point, a solo tenor sax enters, and the piano and bass accompaniment drop out: for the next four bars we hear only tenor sax, flute, and barely audible brushes on cymbals. The restatement of *Stan* is interrupted by the interpolation of these bars (bb. 28–31) (Ex. 5.15 below).[24] With the entry of the flute in bar 26, playing a figure we already associate with Stanley, we see a mid-shot of Stanley, desperate. The camera is positioned high above him, emphasizing his vulnerability and apparent lack of power. Stanley screams once more for his wife from the bottom of the staircase. As the tenor sax enters there is a cut to a mid-shot of Stella, seated by the door in Eunice's apartment. She stands, then moves slowly but with purpose. Her expression is enigmatic but seems to blend calm resolve and revulsion as she practically sashays to the door and moves out onto the porch. Blanche reaches out for her, but Eunice steps between them, closing the door behind Stella: "I wouldn't mix in this if I were you." It is tempting to interpret the counterpoint of the two solo instrumental lines as an embodiment of Stanley and Stella and their interrelation at this point, particularly given the marked absence of most of the rhythm section in these bars. The tenor sax line is marked by descending figures with dotted rhythms followed by leaps of sevenths (major and minor), chromatic slippage, and an emphasis on the first and third beats of the bar. The meandering flute line is less regular, but the lines combine effectively: one moves while the other is sustained. Harmonically, however, the lines diverge: the flute maintains a connection to A minor, while the tenor line begins to move away from it.[25]

Example 5.15. *Stan and Stella*, R5: P3, **Flute (above) and Tenor Sax (below), bb. 26–32**

There is a cut to a reverse-shot of Stella at the top of the staircase in a long-shot from below, as though from Stanley's point of view. An alto sax enters, leaning on minor second alternations in a relaxed dotted rhythm, to which Stella's hips seem to sway briefly. Piano and bass re-enter with the second (syncopated) vamp figure, and the cue resumes its restatement of *Stan* from the point at which it was interrupted (*Stan*, R2: P3, bar 20), with the earlier cue varied only slightly; first when flute and sax swap lines briefly, then when sets of descending minims on flute in the B section are here ornamented.[26]

Stella's silent descent is halting but inexorable. She moves slowly, first leaning against the wall for support, then the ornate iron banister. At the halfway point she seems to stop and a reverse-shot of Stanley below shows him looking up enquiringly. She is partially in shadow, but her eyes remain on Stanley throughout. As she nears the bottom of the stairs, a mid-shot shows that her expression remains inscrutable. The recapitulation of the B section signals a brief return to straight crotchets in the rhythm section, partway through which Stanley falls to his knees contrite with his head bowed in tears. Now on the bottom step, Stella pushes her fingers into his hair as she pulls his head in towards her stomach. A dotted quaver figure reenters on piano, off-kilter with accents on beats two and four. Stella leans down over Stanley pushing her hands down his broad bare back as he grasps her around the thighs. As their bodies meet and they begin to kiss passionately, for the first and only time in the cue the flute and saxophone briefly play in unison, emphasizing the convergence of bodies, a variant on the opening sax motif over the same descending circle-of-fifths sequence that culminates on a sustained chord of Bb^{9add13}. This chord signals the end of the restatement of *Stan*. Stanley carries Stella into their apartment. Sax and flute riff gently on related motifs until the chord finally resolves on a sustained $A^{\sharp 9}$ chord. A pattern low on the piano recalls the chromatic triplets heard at the start of *Stan Meets Blanche* (R3: P1), and the semi-chromatic anacrustic triplet figure that rumbles in the low-register of the piano in *Belle Reve* (Ex. 5.16). The figure plays with the chord's juxtaposition of both major and flatted thirds, but also indicates a return to the dotted rhythm minor seconds, ubiquitous in this group of cues.

Example 5.16. *Stan and Stella*, R5: P3, Piano entry, b. 50

The scene's combination of music and image is pure sex, though it is difficult to articulate quite how this effect is created beyond highlighting specific musical characteristics, the editing of the image, and performative elements of the music and the acting. On the one hand such elements emphasize Stella's corporeality and her power over Stanley, yet she also appears somewhat disembodied in terms of the inevitability of her staircase descent. The whole adds up to more than the sum of its parts. Where the earlier cue, *Stan* (R2: P3), emphasized Stanley's bodily presence in contrast to Blanche's fragility, and added a sleazy backdrop to their meeting, here the cue underscores the magnetic pull between Stella and Stanley and the physical character of their bond. Their closeness has already been established in scenes that emphasize their physical proximity, but this scene makes explicit what other films of the period denied, or indicated via other means. With North's music added, along with the possibilities afforded by close-ups, this sequence likely went further than its equivalent on stage. That the cue is ostensibly a recapitulation of *Stan* (R2: P3) tells us something interesting about its censorship. Perhaps Jack Vizzard and Martin Quigley failed to notice that much of this music had already been presented as part of the score? For if it were really only the *music* that offended their sensibilities so powerfully, one would expect them to ask for its removal from the score entirely. Instead, their difficulties with this scene in particular demonstrate that it was the interaction of music, camerawork, editing, and acting that emphasized the scene's "carnal" implications, and the importance of the couple's sexual activity to their relationship.

Stanley's musical material returns in the scene that takes place the morning after: *Stan* (R6: P1). While he is away working on the car, Blanche takes the opportunity to urge Stella to leave him. The cue begins with whistling, which implies Stanley's return. The women look at one another, anxious that he may have heard them talking. The familiar cup-muted trumpet figure rocks between tonic and flatted supertonic in a dotted rhythm, followed by a variant on the motif that opens *Stan* (R2: P3). Beneath this, a slow harmonized ascent on piano and low woodwinds is repeated through eight bars: a one-bar figure that moves from a chord of $A^{add\sharp9}$ to $Cm^{\Delta9}$ via $Bm^{\Delta9}$. This is followed by a lighter, dotted rhythm walking-bass figure on piano and cello played *pizzicato*. Violas add an ominous rising and falling line, with staggered entries of a falling appoggiatura figure on trumpet and trombone, both above and below the viola line. Stanley opens a beer bottle and calls to Stella. He asks if Blanche is back, and strings play a rich, two-chord figure that veers towards atonality, marked by a hit-point in the score: its harmony seems to float, suspended, assisted by the upper strings which sustain a unison on B through the bars that follow. Beneath this, a searching dotted rhythm motif on enters on horn (Ex. 5.17). Together these elements generate anticipation, and contribute to a growing sense of tension.

Example 5.17. *Stan*, R6: P1, Horn entry, bb. 14–15

Then Stanley smiles at Stella. Lush and uplifting string chords descend over a bass pedal on G, relieving the tension. The chords are a harmonization of a two-note whole-tone descent that is repeated and extended in the following bar (see Ex. 5.18 below). A "twinkly" octave descent on piano lightens the tone further. Stella smiles warmly at Stanley, but becomes briefly self-conscious when she acknowledges Blanche. Stella runs to Stanley, jumps up at him, and throws her arms around him, almost knocking him over. Thus she makes clear where her allegiance lies. Lower strings extend the whole-tone descent, while the upper strings mirror her actions through a harmonized ascent followed by a hurried semiquaver descent, landing on a closely voiced chord of D+$^{\Delta 9}$, to which the major seventh adds warmth. A thirteenth chord on F follows (with a particularly dissonant flat ninth), over an accented appoggiatura descent from E♭ to D on horns. Stanley grins at Blanche over Stella's shoulder as he hugs his wife tightly. The scene fades to black as the camera turns to Blanche's horrified expression. This new thematic line can be considered another development of *Belle Reve*'s theme 1, though here the connection is with the whole-tone descent in bar 5, rather than ♭5–4 of bar 1.

Example 5.18. *Stan*, R6: P1, Strings, bb. 16–17

When Stanley returns from the hospital in good spirits, interrupting Blanche's "Goodnight Ladies" fantasy, another cue from this collection is repeated almost in its entirety: *Stan Meets Blanche* (R3: P1). As with its first appearance, the cue's instrumentation, its low auditory level and relative autonomy all suggest it may be source music, a view enhanced by the excision of the dissonant four-bar break (the B section). Here the cue underscores the sequence in which Blanche tells Stanley that Shep Huntleigh has invited her on a cruise to the Caribbean. Buoyant at his impending fatherhood, Stanley seems genuinely pleased for Blanche. Spraying beer into his mouth, he extends an olive branch: "You wanna bury the hatchet and make it a loving-cup?" The question is more or less concurrent with a return of the "sweet" trombone solo, and the shift away from the minor second triplet figure. Blanche refuses, however. Stanley pursues the point for a moment, but is distracted. He is happy at their combined good fortune: "You're having an oil millionaire and I'm having a baby." By contrast, Blanche's "joy" is bitterly expressed; she looks forward to the return of her privacy. The cue ends in the same unfinished manner as previously.

Musical elements from the same group are also heard in the midst of the music that builds to the implied rape (*Seduction*, R13: P1). Dotted quaver figures that rock between minor seconds are heard on trumpet and trombone, sometimes with cup mute, sometimes marked "dirty." I consider the cue in more detail below in relation to the score's musical climaxes.

Blanche's Music: *Blanche and Mitch*

As discussed above, in one sense Blanche is the focus, the object, of the score's *Belle Reve* cues. However, North also makes her the subject of the *Blanche and Mitch* group of cues; labeled "Blanche" by North for the soundtrack album. These cues underscore Blanche's aspirations regarding her relationship with Mitch. After Stanley has called a halt to this romance by revealing her recent past, Shep Huntleigh replaces Mitch as her possible savior; she conjures Huntleigh from her memories and imagination.

The poker party forms the backdrop for the first of these cues: *Blanche and Mitch* (R4: P1b). Source music features earlier in the scene: first, Koehler and Arlen's "I Gotta Right to Sing the Blues," apparently from the Four Deuces; then a frenetic Latin-American dance band version of Camacho and David's "The Girl with the Spanish Drawl," heard on the radio, to which Blanche dances dreamily in her slip. The radio is noticeably louder than the music from the Four Deuces, and Stanley is put off his game. He barges in to the curtained-off bedroom and switches off the radio. *Blanche and Mitch* (R4: P1b) is heard, quietly, immediately after Stanley switches off the radio, implying that the music was already playing. As with "I Gotta Right to Sing the Blues," the cue appears to be source music that drifts into the apartment from the Four Deuces: the cue has an autonomous structure, and "sweet" jazz instrumentation and styling on solo clarinet and piano, with an improvisation on piano at the start. Beneath the clarinet's simple, emphatically tonal melody, the piano's pseudo-improvised accompaniment articulates a progression of enriched chords in F minor. The cue is slow and melancholy, and the structure straightforward: AABA'. Each section is sixteen bars long, except the last, which is just eight bars. Table 5.3 outlines the basic chord progression of the A section.

With the B section, there is a move to the relative major: A♭. Initially chords of A♭$^\Delta$ and D♭^{9} alternate, then a meandering route is taken back to F minor through a series of more ambiguous altered seventh and flatted ninth chords. The cue ends with a melancholy plagal cadence in F minor.

Bars 1–4:	iv^7	V+^{7}	i^9	i^9—i$^{9\sharp13}$
5–8:	II$^{7♭5}$	V$^{11♭9}$	V^7/i bass —i	V/i bass—i
9–12:	i^7	i^7/iv bass	VII$^{\Delta9}$—VII$^{\Delta13}$	vii$^{\Delta9}$
13–16:	i^7	i$^{7\,(♭5-6-\sharp6-7)}$	ii^7–ii^6	II–II$^{♭5}$

Table 5.3. *Blanche and Mitch*, R4: P1b, Basic harmonic progression

Example 5.19. *Blanche and Mitch*, R4: P1b, Melody

Mitch leaves the poker game, using a return trip to the bathroom as an excuse to meet Blanche again. She prolongs their exchange by asking for a cigarette, which leads to a discussion of the Browning inscription inside his cigarette case, which reveals a mutual interest in poetry. Mitch is clearly fascinated by Blanche, and is unfazed by her bald lie that Stella is her elder sister. The cue ends when Mitch shouts to Stanley that he has left the game; he is talking to "Miss DuBois."

Mitch asks Blanche if she's married. When she tells him she's an "old maid schoolteacher," he jumps at the chance to flatter her. As Blanche looks up at him the second *Blanche and Mitch* cue begins (R5: P1). Here there is no question of source ambiguity: orchestrated for strings, flutes, harp, and celeste, the music is clearly underscore and is signaled as overtly romantic. The cue repeats the last twenty-four bars of *Blanche and Mitch*: the B section followed by the coda. The arrangement retains the previous cue's slow tempo, but the melody is played by a solo violin with a wide vibrato. Flutes sustain chords above slow glissandi on harp. The conversation turns to Blanche's profession. The B section reaches its climactic close (at the dominant of F minor) as she explains that she "attempt[s] to instill a bunch of bobby-soxers and drugstore Romeos with a reverence for Hawthorne, and Whitman, and Poe." The shift to the A' section is emphasized by a change in instrumentation: to solo violin, viola, and cello. Here the music is more muted, yet also more intense. The final bars underscore Blanche's more intimate discussion of the "other things" her charges are interested in: their "first discovery of love." Blanche is pensive, and though her words have the desired effect of deepening her appeal for Mitch, in the light of later revelations concerning her dismissal from the school, retrospectively we may understand her wistfulness as otherwise directed: her love for young boys.

Later the same evening, immediately after the staircase scene, another much shorter cue draws on the same materials: *Blanche and Mitch* (R5: P4). Blanche withdraws from the apartment, shocked by what she sees. The music begins as Mitch calls out to her to reassure her. After a closely voiced chord of Db^{Δ} on piano (with the major seventh as the root), a solo sax enters with an ornamented line based on the clarinet theme. It has the same emphasis on the fifth, but now also the flatted fifth in passing; the part is marked "freely—in blue style." At first the accompaniment follows the harmonic progression of the first *Blanche and Mitch* (R4: P1b) cue. Latterly, however, strings, trombone, and low winds switch to semi-chromatic figures in dotted rhythms, generating an unstable harmonic throbbing over a repeated bass pedal on F which finally comes to rest on a chord of $Gm^{7\flat5}$, as Blanche thanks Mitch for his kindness.

The next cue in this collection is heard shortly after Blanche's hysterical outburst at the spilt coke, just prior to her date with Mitch: *Blanche and Mitch* (R7: P1a). She is anxious about the date and explains her dilemma to Stella. She wants Mitch's respect, but fears that he will lose interest: "he hasn't gotten anything more than a goodnight kiss." She hasn't told him her real age, and he thinks she's "prim and proper." Blanche justifies the deception because she wants him to want her. Stella asks Blanche directly if she wants *him*. The cue begins as Blanche tells her that she wants him "very badly." Her dialogue makes explicit the tragedy of a widowed or unmarried woman of a certain class and age without an independent income, thus dependent on relatives for food and shelter: "just think, if it happens, I can go away from here and not be anyone's problem." Blanche longs for the uncertainty of her situation to be resolved, so that she can "rest" and "breathe again."

The cue is twenty-four bars long, comprising the A section and the first eight bars of its repetition, here too in F minor. It is richly orchestrated, with violins taking the melody in unison at first, then *divisi*. An additional *obbligato* line characterized by step-wise motion augments the texture, passing from solo clarinet to horn and back to clarinet. Chromatic alterations to the line function as suspensions, intensifying the relatively simple progression of the harmony.

The longest of these cues is heard as Blanche and Mitch talk on the pier, after dancing: *Blanche and Mitch* (R8: P2). The first part of the cue presents another lush orchestration of almost all of *Blanche and Mitch* (R4: P1b): the repeated A section, followed by the B section.[27] Violins take over the melody from solo muted brass at the repeat of the A section. A flute provides a melancholy *obbligato* above the violins in the second half of this section and continues into the first eight bars of the B section, adding texture (bars 23 to 42). A discussion of Blanche's age turns into an admission from Mitch that he likes Blanche and has discussed her with his sick mother, who wants to see him settled before she passes away. As the flute enters, Blanche puts into words the loneliness he will feel after his mother's death, and reveals that she too understands loneliness, that she lost someone. The B section begins as the scene's emotional intensity builds, and Blanche tells Mitch of Allan.

Through the last eight bars of the B section, the celeste enters playing the Varsouviana while the violins continue the *Blanche and Mitch* theme beneath.[28] The two melodies are juxtaposed, as discussed briefly in the previous chapter, the celeste in E♭ and triple time, while the *Blanche and Mitch* cue continues in F minor and 4/4.[29] The interpolation of the waltz begins when Blanche reveals that she was only sixteen when she fell in love, but she was unlucky: there was something about Allan, "a nervousness, ... a tenderness, ... an uncertainty." The theme's B section is followed by two further sixteen-bar units, both of which expand elements of the Varsouviana. The focus of the first segment is a playful variant on its opening five-note figure, followed by several beats rest, giving an impression of halting or faltering, thus providing a musical analogue to Blanche's description of her husband's "nervousness" and "uncertainty" (see Ex. 5.20 below). After a simple section that moves between tonic and dominant in E♭, there is a jump to the unexpected key of G major for the final sixteen bars. Violas play the Varsouviana's melody, with cellos and harp supporting with arpeggios of tonic and dominant chords. Above this violins play triads *divisi*, sliding between them via step-wise movement. The fluidity of these mobile triads, delicately played, evoke a childlike quality, as Blanche describes hearing Allan crying at night, "the way a lost child cries." The cue ends with her confession: "I killed him."

Example 5.20. *Blanche and Mitch*, R8: P2, Flutes, b. 55

As Mitch kisses Blanche at the end of the same scene, the *Blanche and Mitch* theme is quoted again: *Consummation* (R9: P1a). A compressed variant of the theme's opening eight bars, this four-bar version of the theme suggests G major, rather than F minor. Intriguingly, the act of sharpening the third results in a reference to Max Steiner's Tara theme, from *Gone with the Wind*, in which Leigh also played the lead Southern belle. The harmonization of the sequence is different, though it still retains an emphasis on seventh and ninth chords built on the dominant, subdominant, and tonic. The lack of a third in the penultimate dominant chord—though the pitch is heard briefly, though delayed, in the melody line above—weakens the cue's closing perfect cadence: in removing the tritone (here, between F♯ and C) that urges resolution of the chord, the cue's closure is more subdued. The intimacy and fragility of these closing moments are emphasized by the contrast created by a noisy scrap between Mitch and Stanley at the factory which follows immediately.

After this point, only fragments of the *Blanche and Mitch* theme appear. Violins play the opening melodic figure loudly and aggressively, in octaves and sixths, as Mitch bursts through the door of the apartment at the end of *Blanche's Solitude* (R10: P3) (see Ex. 5.21 below). Here it signals Mitch's hostility toward Blanche, for her "lies" led to his humiliation. Excerpts of the theme also permeate *Revelation* (R11: P1), the sequence which follows, as I discuss in detail below. The theme's opening figure is a key generative component of the *Scherzo* (R11: P2 and R12: P1), during which it is also quoted directly. The opening of *Soliloquy* (R13: P2) also makes reference to the theme, though less directly. The cue underscores Blanche's preparation for the arrival of (the imagined) Shep Huntleigh. Solo instruments play the theme's first note repeatedly, for four bars, over chords that allude to the progression heard at the opening of *Blanche and Mitch* (R4: P1b), here too, in F minor.[30] The repeated notes suggest an arrested version of the theme, which is unable to progress. The first chord returns in the fifth bar, and violins quote the figure's rising fifth (F–C) when Blanche asks Stella if Shep Huntleigh has called, the replacement for Mitch that Blanche conjures from memories of her youth. The figure proceeds no further, however. The atmosphere darkens once more ($\flat$II+$^\Delta$) when Blanche overhears Stanley mention Mitch by name; a flicker of recognition passes over her face.

Example 5.21. *Blanche's Solitude*, R10: P3, Strings, b. 13

The *Birthday Party* Cues

This group of dark, closely related cues is focused around Blanche's birthday party and signal a significant increase in tension. The first of the cues begins when Blanche realizes that something has changed: *Birthday Party* (R9: P2 and R10: P1). After a sinister and dissonant introduction[31] a new melodic idea begins in unison on viola and cello: a winding two-bar theme that stutters rhythmically and is then repeated with some pitch variation. Flutes, bassoons, and harp accompany the theme with pulsing chords that alternate between F♯+$^\Delta$, G♯, and G♯ minor harmonies.

Example 5.22. *Birthday Party*, R9: P2, Cello/violas, bb. 5–8

Blanche attempts to hide her anxiety by chattering; neither Stella nor Stanley has much to say. As the cue continues the tortuous quality of the viola/cello theme is developed further, while harmonically the sequence slides between added eleventh chords on F♯ and F. Violins answer the cello's opening theme, while the cello line continues in a developed form. The similarity between the rhythm and contour of the two themes is disguised by a two-beat displacement (compare Ex. 5.22 and Ex. 5.23). The violin theme develops, and briefly mirrors the cello line, a tenth above it.[32] The meandering string lines are halted by the ringing of a telephone. Blanche stops chattering, expectantly; a repeated crotchet pulse on timpani emphasizes the tense atmosphere. When she realizes the ringing telephone is upstairs, Blanche continues with her "parrot story." The first bar of the cello theme is heard again, though its progress is suspended. Flutes and bassoons interject with a repetition of the bassoon figure from the cue's introduction. The cello theme enters again, an octave lower, but is again halted, as trumpets and trombones play alternating chords. Finally, the cello completes its phrase, though in a modified form. Stella berates and insults her husband. As we watch Stanley's reaction, the orchestra brings a dissonant chord of E♭m[13♯11] to a dynamic climax, stopping only when Stanley slams his hand down on the table and throws his plate to the floor.[33]

Example 5.23. *Birthday Party*, R9: P2, Violins, bb. 15–16

The next *Birthday Party* cue begins as Stanley offers to "clear" Stella's place at the table (R10: P1a); the same chord is heard transposed a semitone higher (Em[13♯11]). The first bar of the winding cello theme emerges (marked *espressivo*), but here a twelfth lower. This is answered by a phrase on violins, which snakes then begins to leap upward through an *accelerando*. Tension continues to build as further layers are added: figures on violas and second violins interject (see Ex. 5.24, for example). When Blanche asks Stella why Mitch didn't come to the party, she is not given an answer. Blanche resolves to call Mitch to find out the truth. The violin's answering phrase (bar 3) is repeated an octave higher, harmonized, and again marked *accelerando* (bar 7).

Stella steps into the yard to talk to Stanley. The violins' earlier interjection (bar 5, see Ex. 5.24) is now played on cellos. It is repeated in the next bar with durations halved, becoming a murmur (see Ex. 5.25 below). Such examples emphasize the cue's thematic consistency: each element is derived from the winding cello entry in the first of the *Birth-*

day Party cues (Ex. 5.22 above). The violins return with another ascent, though here slower and with longer durations. Blanche places her call to Mitch.

Example 5.24. *Birthday Party*, **R10: P1a, Violins, b. 5**

Example 5.25. *Birthday Party*, **R10: P1a, Cellos, b. 10**

A decisive shift occurs in bar 13, when Stanley moves toward Stella. Here the sighing whole-tone figure heard earlier in *Stan* (R6: P1) returns, harmonized and repeated, then developed with an expressive violin line floating above. This sighing figure and the theme that develops from it, together form the first part of Stanley and Stella's love theme. Violins repeat the sighing motif a tenth higher, and develop it into a more expanded version of the theme as Stanley tells Stella that everything will be well once Blanche has left and the baby has arrived (see Ex. 5.26). That the melody is a variation on *Belle Reve* theme 1 is clearer at this point (see Ex. 5.2 for comparison). The theme is harmonized first over D♭ then A♭, providing a welcome relief from the tension generated earlier in the cue. As Stanley nuzzles against Stella's neck, she responds, and sweetly she pulls him back into the apartment by the hand.

Example 5.26. *Birthday Party*, **R10: P1a, Love theme, bb. 17–23**

The murmuring figure on cello reenters when Stella sees her sister. Blanche stops Stella lighting the candles on the cake, telling her to keep them for the baby's birthdays: "I hope that candles are going to glow in his life." The cello's murmurs continue to unsettle the atmosphere beneath an otherwise bright ascent of triads in upper strings that underscores Blanche's dialogue. The strings' ascent culminates on a chord of $E\flat^{add9}$, which hangs in the air as Stanley slams the bathroom door behind him: "What poetry."

The final *Birthday Party* cue begins soon afterwards (R10: P2). Stanley shouts at Blanche for calling him a "Polack" and presents her with "a birthday remembrance."[34] The music begins as Blanche realizes Stanley has given her a bus ticket back to Oriel. The first bar of the winding cello theme returns, followed by a development of the fragment in violas. Violins complete the theme in bar 3, over lush minor chords in strings and wind. Then the opening of theme 2 from *Belle Reve* recurs on piano over a discordant chord of $Cm^{\flat 9\flat 5}$ as Blanche flees into the bathroom.

An argument between Stella and Stanley follows, underscored by further murmuring cellos and fragments of the original cello theme, now played by bassoons in thirds and extended with each repetition. Beneath this, basses sustain a D pedal, repeated high above in violins. From a gradual descent, the slow version of *Belle Reve*'s theme 2 emerges briefly from the violin line. When he tries to leave, Stella attacks Stanley. In his aggression, he grabs her, holding her tightly by the elbows as he reminds her that although she thought him common when she first met him, she loved "havin' them colored lights goin.'" He repeats his earlier point that everything was ok before her sister arrived. The violins, now pitched higher, continue their descent, emphasizing two-note sighing motifs reminiscent of the opening of *Belle Reve*'s theme 1, and also now the love theme, while three clarinets bubble away far beneath. As Stanley mentions Blanche, strings start a low-register lurching figure (see Ex. 5.27):

Example 5.27. *Birthday Party*, R10: P2, Strings *divisi*, b. 19

Stella, self-absorbed, makes her way to the door, while Stanley continues his rant. Soon after she grasps the door, muted brass and horns play a discordant stinger chord,[35] while winds and piano repeat Bb in semiquavers in octaves. The harmony moves to Fm^{7b5}. As Stanley realizes something is wrong, a solo violin plays the love theme as muted strings sustain the discordant stinger chord below. The discord resolves somewhat with a move to $Gb^{\Delta9}$ in the next bar, but then continues to altered Db harmony, with "crunchy" pitch clusters incorporated into the accompaniment. The love theme continues its development above, finally ascending to Db. Although the theme itself retains its warmth, the harmonic alterations and discords of the accompaniment add an "unknowing" or fearful quality.

Building to the Climax

The *Birthday Party* cues are followed by *Blanche's Solitude* (R10: P3), heard as Blanche wakens to the sound of Mitch hammering on the door of the apartment. After the layering of musical voices (in *Collector*, R7: P2; *Blanche and Mitch*, R8: P2), the introduction of new material in the previous suite of cues, and the gradual expansion of the love theme, *Blanche's Solitude* increases the tension further by combining motifs and materials from a range of cue groups. The opening triplet semitone figures refer to the triplets at the start of *Stan Meets Blanche* (R3: P1), bars 1–2. In bar 4, trombones play the minim accompaniment figure from *Reaction to Birth* (R4: P1a), here transposed down a tone, bringing in material from the *Belle Reve* group of cues. This is followed, in bar 6, by a version of *Belle Reve*'s theme 2 in *tutti* violins, here in F minor rather than G♯ minor (Ex. 5.28 below). Also transposed down a semitone, in bar 10 cellos enter with a repetition of the first three notes of the winding cello theme (bar 5, *Birthday Party*, R9: P2 and R10: P1), though its development here owes more to the second of this group of cues: R10: P1a, bb. 12–13. This theme's stuttering character, rise in pitch, and diminution of note values builds the tension further, generating a sense of agitation. Allusions to the *Birthday Party* cues close with a further reference to theme 2 from *Belle Reve*: cf. the last four pitches of the cello line in bar 12 (C Bb Ab Bb). The cue ends in the following bar with a climactic and accented harmonization of the opening of the *Blanche and Mitch* theme, here diminished in duration (R4: P1b) (see Ex. 5.21, above).

Example 5.28. *Blanche's Solitude*, R10: P3, Violins, bb. 6–9

Example 5.29. *Blanche's Solitude*, R10: P3, Celli soli, bb. 10–12

The First Climax:
Revelation (R11: P1)

Here Blanche reveals the truth of her life to Mitch; the scene signals the end of her "performances" for him. At times the dialogue is so well integrated with the music that it approaches melodrama, in the true musical sense.[36] Leigh's performance is astounding, not least due to the range of her vocal delivery in the course of the monologue, which is rhythmic and spans a thirteenth (or, an octave and a sixth). Although Blanche's speech is not notated, at times Leigh's delivery comes close to *Sprechgesang* (literally, "speech-song"). Both music and dialogue are episodic in *Revelation*. The cue slowly builds in intensity through the accumulation of textural layers culminating when Blanche, screaming, chases Mitch from the property. Table 5.4 shows the structure of the cue, making reference to the episodes of Blanche's speech (described below), and the key musical elements in the cue's accumulation of layers.

The first part of Blanche's monologue concerns her search for protection, her loneliness as a young widow, and her relief at meeting Mitch (PROTECTION). It is followed by a brief emotional exchange between Blanche and Mitch in which he accuses her of lying (LYING). Blanche is distracted by the sound of someone outside: a Mexican woman selling "flowers for the dead" (FLORES); the vendor's chanting is added into the mix as a further layer. The next section of the monologue begins as she closes the door: she tells Mitch of her life at Belle Reve, that she was enveloped by the bitter thoughts of old women

Table 5.4 Structure of *Revelation* (R11: P1)

Section 1: PROTECTION (21 bars)   **Section 2: LYING** (5 bars)

Blanche and Mitch 2 bars B + M (3rd → 4th) and dev. of min 2nd rocking, resolving (bb. 9–10) Accomp: alternates between Gm$^{\Delta 13}$ and D$^{\Delta 9}$	B + M in full (+1 bar, 15), harmony too, bb. 13–14 then more discordant (to G♭)	*Belle Reve* Theme 2 over bitonality	Chord (3/4 bar)
12 bars	8 + 1 bars	4	+1

(Links to *Stan Meets Blanche*, R3: P1, bb. 1–2)

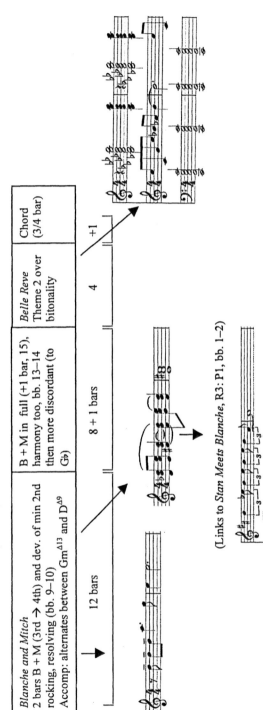

Section 3: FLORES/DIRGE (10 bars)   Section 4: DEATH (8 bars)

Dirge A (*Belle Reve*), C#m Fluid harmony	10-note chord	"Flores…" Dirge A	Transition (dev. of bb. 3–12)	Dirge A (extended) (Dm) Harmony starts D/G then rising steps
4 bars	+1	+3	+2	8 bars

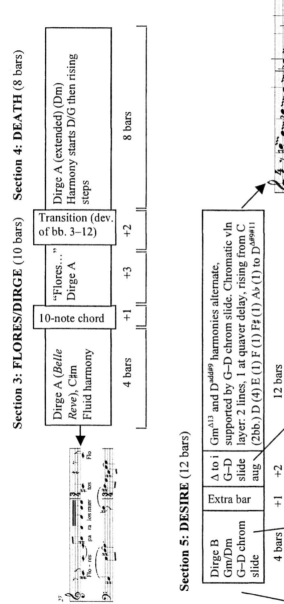

Section 5: DESIRE (12 bars)

Dirge B Gm/Dm G–D chrom slide	Extra bar	Δ to i G–D slide aug	$Gm^{\Delta13}$ and $D^{add\#9}$ harmonies alternate, supported by G–D chrom slide. Chromatic vln layer: 2 lines, 1 at quaver delay, rising from C (2bb.) D (4) E (1) F (1) F# (1) A♭ (1) to $D^{\Delta\#9\#11}$
4 bars	+1	+2	12 bars

and the nearness of death (DEATH). In the final section she talks of
desire, the opposite of death, and of the soldiers who would visit her
house drunk, calling to her on the way back to their encampment
(DESIRE). At this point, Mitch clutches her, kissing her passionately.
She begs him to marry her, but he insults her. She pushes him away and
chases him from the house.

Protection

At first Blanche dismisses Mitch's accusations, but he persists. When
he finally asks her about the Flamingo Hotel, she becomes antagonistic.
"Flamingo? No. Tarantula was the name of it. I stayed at a hotel called
the Tarantula Arms. [...] Yes. A big spider. That's where I brought my
victims." Standing only inches in front of him she tells him that she had
"many meetings with strangers." Leigh's delivery of these lines outlines the extremes of her vocal range in the monologue that follows.
North's cue, *Revelation*, begins in the shocked silence that follows,
opening with a variant of the *Blanche and Mitch* theme on flute (the
third replaced by the fourth), with octave interjections on harp on the
fourth beat of each bar (Ex. 5.30). A pulsing rhythmic figure alternates
between Gm$^{\Delta\sharp13}$ and D$^{\Delta9}$ below. After the two-bar melodic figure of the
opening, upper winds generate further figures from familiar motifs: the
first combines an alternating semitone figure with a semi-chromatic
descent, which moves to more harmonically stable pitches; the second
is characterized by a step-wise rocking motion in thirds (with some
chromatic alterations) which resolves over the tonic harmony, D$^{\Delta9}$. Al-
lusion to the *Blanche and Mitch* theme emphasizes that what might
have been is now lost. The chromatic elements in the following bars
underscore further mention of strangers and the panic that drove her to
them. With a move to rocking-thirds, she tells of the seventeen-year-old
in whose arms she also sought protection, though here the figure remains unresolved. The same figures return twice (now resolving), as
she explains that she lost her position when the relationship was re-
ported.

Example 5.30. *Revelation*, R11: P1, Flute, b. 1

At the mention of meeting Mitch, *Blanche and Mitch* returns in full (also on D, and with the fourth lowered back to the third), with an extra bar that freezes time as Blanche tells him that she "thanked God for you. You seemed gentle. A cleft ... in the rock of the world I could hide in."[37] In outline, the harmony is the same as for the theme in its original arrangement (R4: P1b), though here fourths and sixths add ambiguity. The addition of descending figures (both semi-chromatic and step-wise) drags the sequence down, as Blanche admits that she expected too much. The segment finishes on C over an Fm^{13} chord, to which a Gb triad is added, overthrowing any sense of resolution.

In terms of vocal delivery, *Protection* begins quietly, very low in Leigh's register (between Eb and Bb below middle C initially). As she describes her search for protection, the pitch of her voice rises gradually, first to pitches centered around middle C, edging higher as she expresses her outrage that someone revealed her tryst with the boy. She asks, rhetorically, whether she was unfit for her position as schoolmistress, and answers—emphatically—at the same pitch an octave lower. As she explains that she had no choice but to join her sister, her agitation and pitch rise again, peaking—at Bb above middle C—on the word "youth": "My youth was gone up the water spout." Her delivery turns gentle as she recalls meeting Mitch, staying in her upper register until she contemplates the "rock of the world" that she wanted him to protect her from, at which point she sinks down low, rising briefly only to explain that she now understands she was "asking, hoping too much."

Lying

The harmonic disjunction of the previous bar is intensified as it moves to the tritone, resulting in a bright clash: a C major triad pulses on beats 1 and 3, with Gb triads on beats 2 and 4 creating a bitonal effect (see Ex. 5.31 below).[38] Against this discordant backdrop, theme 2 of *Belle Reve* returns low in upper strings. Here Blanche responds to Mitch's complaint that he "thought [she] was straight." She queries whether the heart can ever be "straight," and flatly denies his accusations of lying, exclaiming, "I never lied in my heart," high in her register, on Gb, matching one of the episode's tonal poles.

Example 5.31. *Revelation*, R11: P1, bb. 22–26

Flores

Neither Blanche nor Mitch speaks as the music continues into the next section, marked "Dirge." The rhythmic pulsing of alternating chords continues over a pedal a semitone higher (C♯), though here chords on the second and fourth beats tend to repeat those on the first and third. The voice of the flower seller is also added: "Flores, Flores para los muertos […] Coronas, coronas para los muertos […]." Her chanting begins at the pitch of the pedal beneath, though it soon becomes more declamatory. A new theme enters on low strings: Dirge theme A (Ex. 5.32 below).[39] Melodically, the dirge theme emphasizes the tonic, minor third, fourth, and flatted fifth—again, showing a debt to the blues scale—before finally ascending to the perfect fifth. Its emphasis on the flatted fifth, its evident "blues" sound, and slow tempo connect it to *Belle Reve*, and theme 1c, in particular (see Ex. 5.4 above).

Example 5.32. *Revelation*, R11: P1, bb. 27–31

Blanche opens the door. As the woman turns towards her we hear arpeggios on the triads of F and E ascend together. She walks forward towards the open door of the apartment, Blanche's fear emphasized by a ten-note chord on piano and *divisi* upper strings, suspended over a chord of E⁶ in low strings. As the woman reaches the door, the E/F arpeggios are repeated, bringing the chord to a close. She now speaks in English: "Flowers, flowers for the dead." At this, the dirge theme returns in low strings, harmonized on brass, chorale-like, without the flatted fifth: C♯m E F♯ G♯ F♯ C♯m Dm Em D. The ascending arpeggios return once more as Blanche sends the woman away: "No, no! Not now! Not now!" She closes the door.

Death

The pitch moves up another semitone: the next section opens with a pulsing bass pedal on D on the first and fourth beats, to which the celeste adds a fifth in quavers that alternates between octaves; these figures continue. Low strings play a two-bar transition figure in thirds that is a close variant of the upper wind figure from the opening of the cue. Blanche continues her monologue: "I lived in a house where dying old women remembered their dead men." The last two words hit the downbeat of the following bar, which also signals the return of the dirge theme on violin, now in D minor. The flower seller's cry can still be heard in the background, and Leigh's delivery is again focused low in her register. Woodwind and celeste alternate between triads on D minor and G in minims. Extra weight is added to the third quaver of the bar via a repeated rhythmic figure on cello, along with added dissonance at times (see Ex. 5.33 below).

Here the pitch of Leigh's delivery changes to match the monologue's content. For the first and fifth lines, those in which she mentions the "dying old women," the focus is at the very bottom of her range (D–F below middle C). The second, third, and fourth lines, in which she speaks bitterly of "Recriminations" and "Legacies," are pitched a little higher (around Gb–C). The pitch rises further at the explicit mention of "death," falling again as she tells him that its "opposite is desire." It peaks once more, as she asks how he could wonder about her past, given that her young life was so besieged by death.

Example 5.33. *Revelation*, R11: P1, bb. 39–40[40]

Desire

A second, related theme enters: Dirge B (Ex. 5.34). Unlike Dirge A, it
is characterized by wide leaps rather than step-wise motion, building
the tension further. It emphasizes the tonic, the fifth, and major and
minor sevenths. Here too a connection with *Belle Reve* can be detected,
particularly with theme 1d (see Ex. 5.5 above). As Blanche tells Mitch
of the soldiers who would visit her, calling her name from the lawn, the
pitch of Leigh's delivery is compressed into the more narrow frame of
a fifth (E–A below middle C), exhibiting chromatic slides between
words/pitches in places. Leigh's regular rhythmic delivery of the lines
here lays emphasis on the repetition of the words "Belle Reve" in adja-
cent lines, repeating their pitch ascent too.

Example 5.34. *Revelation*, R11: P1, Dirge B, bb. 48–54

Quiet chords are added by horns, alternating between Gm$^{\Delta13}$ and
D$^{add\sharp9}$ in minims. At the same point, a low string pedal enters, repeatedly sliding between G and D chromatically (from bar 48). As Blanche
finishes her monologue and moves towards the half-open shutters, the
duration of this alternating pedal is augmented, adding gravity; each
pedal is now held for a bar, with the chromatic slide taking place on the
final quaver (from bar 53). Blanche acts out her pseudo-coy response to
the soldiers, peeking through the curtains and giggling coquettishly. A
further layer is then added: two lines of muted violins slide down a
(mostly) chromatic scale, a crotchet at a time (from bar 55). The second
line begins its descent a quaver after the first, but both entries are syncopated at the delay of a quaver. The first descent lasts two bars (from
C). The next begins a tone higher and continues the descent for four
bars. The third descent begins, again, a tone higher than the last (E),
marked *tutti*, but lasts only one bar. It is followed by three more one-
bar descents, each starting a tone higher, culminating on F. Above this,
upper strings play a high register *obbligato*: primarily a two-note appoggiatura figure, once again suggesting a return to the opening of
Belle Reve's theme 1. Here though the two-note figures both ascend
and descend, sometimes a tone, sometimes a semitone, though the last
four all ascend, also culminating on F, the same pitch as the other violin
parts. The alternating and sliding chromatic bass pedal continues until

the final chord: a highly dissonant $D^{\Delta\sharp9\sharp11}$, which is better understood as a juxtaposition of triads on C$\sharp$ and D.

As the violin descents begin, Mitch pulls Blanche towards him roughly, kissing her. She begs him once more to marry her. The one-bar descents coincide with her query of his refusal. He replies that she is "not clean enough" to live in a house with his mother. She pushes him away and chases him from the apartment, screaming over the final chord.

After the intensity of *Revelation*, North's *Scherzo* (R11: P2)—which the composer labeled "Mania" in the track listing for the album—provides a degree of respite.[41] By contrast to the heaviness of *Revelation* (in orchestration, in character), *Scherzo* is jittery and nimble: *pizzicato* strings, staccato articulation, irregular phrase lengths. The cue underscores Blanche's skittish movements as she barricades herself into the apartment having aroused the attention of the local residents by running screaming into the courtyard. There is no dialogue to speak of to compete with the cue as it whips itself into a frenzy. As mentioned above, it is organized around fragments of the opening of *Blanche and Mitch*, though the appoggiatura figure from theme 1 of *Belle Reve* can also be heard. It closes with groups of instruments creating a complex chord—a juxtaposition of $D+^\Delta$, A$\flat$, and F+.

The Second Climax:
Seduction (R13: P1), *Tempo da Rapo*

This cue underscores the moments that precede the inferred rape. Realizing that the imminent arrival of her beau—Shep Huntleigh—is a fantasy, Stanley pushes Blanche violently onto the bed, hovering over her threateningly as he tells her that he was not taken in by her illusions. He goes into the bathroom, slamming the door behind him. The cue begins as Blanche, shocked and terrified, runs about the apartment, frantically collecting handfuls of her belongings. It is clear that she plans to leave in a hurry, but as she opens the door she sees the Mexican flower seller across the street. The woman seems to float towards the open door across the mist-covered ground, as her now familiar chant is heard: "Flores para los muertos."

TEMPO DA RAPO

Example 5.35. *Seduction* **(R13: P1), Clarinet, bb. 1–7**

The cue begins with a short solo clarinet ascent that slowly winds upwards, punctuated by a chord that superimposes the triads of C and D♭ on piano and low strings. This fragment repeats and develops material from the *Birthday Party* cues. The clarinet entry is repeated three times more: with each repetition, its rhythms are diminished and more notes are added prior to the final upward ascent.[42] A chord punctuates the clarinet's second entry: D♭m$^{\Delta 11}$ (or A♭^{7} over D♭m) is played twice *pizzicato* on muted strings. At the fourth entry of the clarinet figure a bass clarinet enters and parallels the now-extended clarinet line in thirds below, both major and minor (see Ex. 5.35 above). This (approximate) parallel motion of solo clarinets suggests the influence of the opening to the second tableau of Igor Stravinsky's *Petrushka* (1910–11).[43] It is followed by a more sustained repetition of the D♭/C juxtaposition in upper strings, now bowed. Beneath, there is a brief harmonized return of the Dirge A theme (*Revelation*, R11: P1), heard when Blanche first opened the door to the flower vendor. Below that a timpani pedal on C (with field drum) articulates the rhythm of the flower vendor's chant (see Ex. 5.36). Here the theme's harmonization slides between chords of Cm, D♭, and D, with parts of each clashing with the complex chord above. The cathedral's chimes are added into this mix on C. There is a dramatic shift to another chord in which the triads of G, F, and F♯ are superimposed, high on strings, vibraphone, and piano.[44] Over this, the piano repeats the ascending arpeggio figure from bar 30 of *Revelation* (R11: P1). The music stops. Blanche shakes her head and turns the woman away.

As Blanche closes the door and moves back into the apartment, a bass clarinet completes the Dirge theme, a third higher. It is followed by another sustained chord: here a juxtaposition of an A minor triad over the tritone, B–F, and a repeated pedal on E. This chord is part of a sequence of parallel chords played quietly on strings and brass that slide upward, culminating on a dissonant chord of B♭m$^{\Delta 9}$. The sequence is punctuated by semiquaver figures played *pizzicato* high on violins. These fluttering figures underline Blanche's growing panic as she tries to place a call to Western Union.

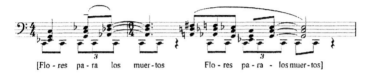

[Flo - res pa - ra   los   muer - tos   Flo - res   pa - ra -   los muer - tos]

Example 5.36. *Seduction*, R13: P1, b. 8

The next episode of the cue, and the drama, begins as Blanche hears the bathroom door shut behind her. A muted trumpet quotes the opening dotted quaver figure from *Stan Meets Blanche* (R3: P1), here rocking between C and D♭, over a chord of C/D♭ open. The harmony moves to E♭m$^{13\sharp 11}$ (or F over E♭m^7) as a solo horn enters with one of the cue's opening clarinet figures. Low strings repeat the previous chord while two cup-muted trumpets enter with a dotted quaver figure one after another, the second a tritone below the first; these entries are marked "dirty" in the sketches.[45] Two clarinets enter, repeating the same clarinet/horn motif in thirds, while bassoons grumble away below with a figure that harks back to an accompaniment figure from the *Birthday Party* cues.[46] The clarinets then repeat their extended fourth entry from the cue's opening, with bassoons now supporting the ascent, also in thirds. These elements continue in various combinations as Blanche tries to maintain physical distance from Stanley. As she asks to pass him to reach the door, a simple syncopated quaver figure is heard three times on bassoon, with decreasing rests between the figures: the figure involves extreme leaps up a tenth and down a twelfth. The clarinets continue to develop the opening motif, augmenting the intervals in places. The repetition of these fragments in thirds across clarinets and bassoons adds to the mounting sense of claustrophobia.

As occurs in the *Scherzo* (R11: P2 and R12: P1), the layering of varied rhythmic figurations that switch between quavers and triplets, repeated with rests of different lengths between, creates an uncertain and tense atmosphere. Minor second chords are sustained alternately by winds and horns, adding further dissonance to juxtapositions of F/E♭m^7

or F♯/Em⁷. Blanche attempts to rush past Stanley in a bid to escape. He clutches at her, surprised at her palpable fear that he might "interfere" with her. But his surprise is underscored by staggered entries of cup-muted trumpets playing the "dirty" dotted semiquaver figure that leans persistently on minor seconds. Again, the second trumpet enters a tri-tone below the first. Blanche's retreat is scored by a superimposition of F/E♭⁷. As she sees the open door, a further clarinet figure in thirds un-derscores her desperate move toward it. Stanley stands in front of the door and pushes it shut, as the same chord is repeated a semitone higher: F♯/Em⁷. Over this, he conjectures, "Maybe you wouldn't be bad to interfere with."

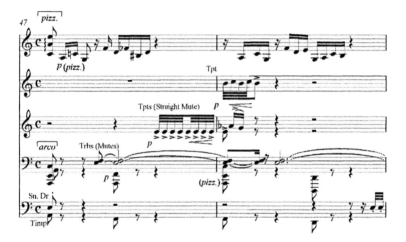

Example 5.37. *Seduction*, R13: P1, bb. 47–48

This line signals a move to the cue's final episode. Here tension is built through an accumulation of figures and a two-bar sequence that rises a semitone with each repetition. A syncopated *pizzicato* figure returns in upper strings, now extended. Trombones sustain pitches a minor second apart. Quaver pedals on timpani are sounded on the first and third beats with *pizzicato* chords above on low strings. Between these, three abrupt trumpet figures interject and overlap (see Ex. 5.37 above). While all other elements of the two-bar phrase simply rise a semitone with each repetition, the trumpet figures are slightly varied: their pitches rise, but the number of notes in the first trumpet entry changes, and the figures are repeated more frequently than every two bars, with a different rest period on each occasion. Over the course of the sequence, the two-bar phrase and irregular trumpet interpolations rise from a chord on Am through five transpositions to Dm, with the latter phrase repeated. Over the course of these bars, some elements are cut and others substituted, building tension and adding variation. For example, the trumpet figure is cut from the two-bar phrase on C♯ and the first of the Dm phrases. In its place, an appoggiatura-like figure and supporting chord are substituted on woodwinds. The return of the trumpet figure in the last of the phrases adds finality, here also extended via an additional figure. The cue ends with a highly dissonant superimposition of triads, resulting in an eleven-note chord.[47]

The relative sparseness and unpredictability of this final episode allows dialogue to be heard.[48] By contrast with *Revelation*, here dialogue is interspersed between intricate figures rather than placed atop an accumulation of layers. Blanche backs away from Stanley pleading with him not to come any closer, but Stanley continues to advance towards her. He appears playful and genuinely intrigued by her behavior. Blanche is terrified. Backed into a corner she smashes a bottle to defend herself. But Stanley interprets her actions as evidence that she wants "a little rough-house." At that moment, the sequence halts its upward ascent, static as Stanley stands before her: "Alright, let's have a little rough-house." Pianos hammer the pitches B and A♯ simultaneously (marked *martellato* and, in the sketches, "ominous"). To this is added a chord combining triads of F and D with $D+^\Delta$ and $E\flat m^7$ layered on top of one another.[49] The chords shift as Stanley seizes Blanche, *forte-pianissimo* with a crescendo as he tries to force the bottle from her hand. The camera stays focused on the view of the battle in the mirror, with the scene's—and cue's—climax as the bottle smashes against it. Through the shattered mirror we see Blanche appear to lose consciousness, with her head thrown back. Compound chords alternate as they build, culminating with trumpet chords descending from F to E, followed by a glissando down from each pitch. Additionally, recorded on a separate track and superimposed over the top, horns approximate an "animal howl" via a slow glissando ascent of an octave on F; such novelty features were common among some of the early New Orleans jazz combos. This grotesque "howl" is heard twice here. The image dissolves to black and then to a shot of a hose washing down the street, beneath which the chord slowly dissipates.

The Final Scenes

As mentioned above, the next cue, *Soliloquy* (R13: P2), begins with a reference to *Blanche and Mitch*. At Blanche's enquiry about Shep Huntleigh the melody's tonic stutters make reference to the theme's rising fifth (F–C). The stuttering continues with further pitches added in the same rhythm (C♯ and D). The chord progression beneath is similarly arrested, alternating first between juxtaposed chords on G♭ and F (♭II and i in F minor), then moving to alternations between other chordal combinations that change more quickly, but which are also separated by minor seconds. Above these shifting chords, solo winds play a gentle melancholy theme that grows from the rising fifth, emphasizing fourths and fifths, subtly underscoring the conversation between Blanche, Stella, and Eunice. When Blanche hears Stanley shout out Mitch's name, she becomes noticeably unsettled, but when reminded of her "trip," the line is brighter, and suggests major key sonority. Chromaticism creeps into the melody as she dresses, asking whether the grapes have been washed. The cue closes with the chimes of the cathedral bell, "the only clean thing in the Quarter."

The penultimate cue begins as Blanche prepares to leave with (as she believes) Shep Huntleigh. The opening of *Doctor* (R14: P1) comprises two elements: two differently spaced chords of A^{11}/D bass on beats 2 and 3, and a horn figure that rises a seventh from A and then descends an octave step-wise via a D major scale. Harmonically and melodically the sequence stalls when Blanche reaches the curtain and asks, "Must we go through that room?" Movement returns with a brief shift to Em^{11}/D bass when Stella offers to go with her. The opening scalic descent is repeated and extended in a slightly varied form. It is ornamented by an additional line on a cor anglais and then bassoon that is briefly reminiscent of elements of the love theme (see Ex. 5.38 below).

Example 5.38. *Doctor*, R14: P1, Cor Anglais, bb. 8–10

Blanche's shock at seeing that the man at the door is *not* Shep Huntleigh is expressed musically in ominous accented semiquavers on horns (on B) over a staggered slide from a D triad to a stinger chord on

Fm+$^\Delta$/A bass, repeated then replaced by a further complex chord as she whispers to Stella that the man is not Huntleigh.[50] The cue closes with a repeat of the latter chord, as Blanche tries to flee.

As with *Blanche's Solitude* (R10: P3), the film's final cue, *Affirmation* (R14: P2), also combines elements from different groups of themes, though here in the summarizing capacity of a coda, rather than the frenzied tension-building of the earlier cue. Notable among these references are those to *Belle Reve*: via the descending appoggiatura figure of the opening of theme 1, and theme 2, here presented twice, in full. As mentioned above, these references mark a return to the score's (and the film's) site of origin and the events associated with it: the main title, the arrival of Blanche, the loss of the estate and of Blanche's youth and aspirations (see section on *Belle Reve* and Ex. 5.10). In its allusions to the iconic appoggiatura at the start of *Belle Reve*, *Affirmation* functions as the score's culmination, much of it generated from this same figure. Importantly, in terms of interpreting the film's ending, the love theme also returns, here in its most complete expression.

After the second, climactic presentation of *Belle Reve*'s theme 2, a short bridge passage accompanies the close-up on Mitch (bb. 21–22). This is followed by an emphatic two-note minor-second descent in horns: Bb–A (bar 23). Blanche exits the frame and Stella is pulled forward, calling to her sister. The love theme first heard in *Stan* (R6: P1) here returns on cello, transposed down a third and in a form more developed than its second appearance in the *Birthday Party* cues: *Birthday Party* (R10: P1a), bars 19–23. Stanley blocks Stella's path. The theme begins as Stella pulls away from him: "Don't you touch me. Don't you *ever* touch me again."[51] It opens with a rising fourth (from D to G) followed by the familiar whole-tone descent, echoed immediately afterwards on strings in a lush harmonization of the figure. Stella looks toward Blanche in the car, and walks to the road to watch her departure. Here we hear only the meandering solo cello line. We see Stella in close-up with a tear in her eye underscored by a chord of C$^\Delta$ on muted brass. She is called back by the baby's cry. Upper strings play a rising figure, harmonized with lush chords, then repeated higher: Am^7 D^6 Am^7 Cm$^\Delta$. Stanley calls to her from inside the apartment. With the third repetition, the sequence pauses on the last chord; Stella hugs the baby in close to her and turns towards the camera. The love theme now reaches its second section, this time in horns and cellos (anacrusis to bar 33). She tells the baby (and herself): "We're not going back in there again. Not this time. We're never going back. Never," and runs up the stairs to Eunice's apartment as we hear Stanley continue to call after her. Suddenly, the cue builds to an "ending" climax, with upper strings and winds repeating the opening of the love theme high in the register (see Ex. 5.39 below). The cue finishes on a rich chord of $G^{\triangle 13}$, with a bass movement from D to G adding finality, the sense of a perfect cadence. But this is all wrong … isn't it?

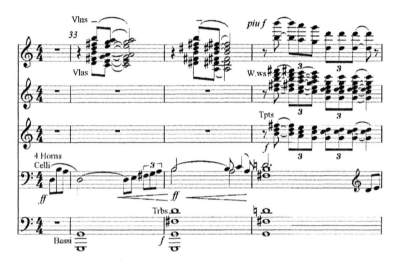

Example 5.39. *Affirmation*, R14: P2, bb. 33–38

The ending of the play continued Williams's ambivalence towards Blanche and Stanley. Stella sits sobbing on the steps, her baby in her arms. Stanley approaches and comforts her. The stage directions have him kneel beside her and caress her as she sobs. Steve ends the play with a line that indicates the card game is to continue, thus suggesting an emphatic return to the status quo, or rather, the situation as it was prior to Blanche's arrival. As explored in chapter 3, however, the play's adaptation into a film required that it abide by the constraints of the Production Code: Stanley had to be seen to be punished for the rape. Stella's conversation with Eunice makes explicit that Blanche told her sister of the rape, although on screen the act is referred to obliquely rather than depicted directly. Stella refuses to accept her sister's accusation. With a newborn baby and no other source of income, she has little choice but to remain with Stanley. Yet, despite advice from Eunice to the contrary, at the end of the film Stella appears to leave Stanley.

North's final cue performs two key functions: first, it re-dignifies Blanche via a stately version of theme 2 from *Belle Reve*; second, via the return of the love theme in an expanded version as Stella runs away from Stanley by ascending the stairs to Eunice's apartment, it potentially weakens the notion that Stella really will leave Stanley, by reminding us of the strength of their bond. An alternative reading is equally possible, however: the baby has usurped Stanley as the object of Stella's love; indeed, in one sense the placement of the theme encourages this interpretation. North's closing musical statement is equivocal. In recapitulating the couple's love theme at this point, North's score marks a return to the ambivalence of Williams's original ending, notwithstanding the enforced and inflated perfect cadence at the cue's close (albeit to an enriched chord of $G^{\Delta 13}$). These final bars (see Ex. 5.39 above) underline the retribution that Stanley must undergo. In doing so they remind me of the ideological difficulties thrown up by the final chords of Bizet's opera *Carmen*. There too a major key ending seems to champion the wrong character.

As discussed in chapter 4, Ken Sutak argues that following the musical intimation that Stella will return to Stanley, these final bars are perhaps not so much "jubilant" as "victorious" on Stanley's behalf, emphasizing the temporary nature of Stella's departure, and thus reasserting the ambivalence of the play's ending. The sudden emphatic certainty of the score's final bars comes as a shock. Indeed it is not too much of a stretch to suggest that the bombast of the score's closure indicates a knowing degree of artifice: these bars appear only nominally anchored to the rest of the score; they seem to rush in from elsewhere, closing the action in a superficially abrupt, "neat and tidy" manner that is disingenuous in the broader context of the score and the film. Here, then, North did what was required of him. But his solution allows us to have it both ways. On the surface, the cue confirms the simplified ending, with Stanley punished, but the cue also hints that its certainty is a ruse. Sutak's point is an interesting one. Crucially, however, he was not writing about the version of the film that I have focused on thus far: the version restored in 1993. Sutak's critique concerns the 1951 release, and in this final section I explain the importance of the distinction for the interpretation of the film.

The Two Scores:
Fewer Revelations and a "Purified" Love

As explained in chapter 3, through mediation and the work of Dave Weisbart, a re-edited version of *Streetcar* was produced and given a "B" rather than a "C" rating by the Legion of Decency. The excisions led to a less lust-fueled relationship between Stanley and Stella, and the representation of a more chaste Blanche.[52] Key among the cuts that changed the characterization of Blanche were lines and actions that emphasized her flirtatious behavior towards Stanley early on; lines at the end of the Collector scene, in which she makes clear that this is not the first time she has made approaches to young men, or boys; her confession to Mitch that she had "many meetings with strangers," and all of her dialogue in the *Desire* segment of the *Revelation* monologue.[53]

In the Collector scene, Blanche's lines were cut with no impact on North's cue. However, the scene's first shot was started later—to remove Blanche's "writhing"—and this cut was matched in the music: the cue begins partway through bar 4. Cuts to the scene that lead to the rape also necessitated musical excisions; cuts were made to the sequence of two-bar phrases just prior to *Seduction*'s conclusion, though in such a way that the sequence's musical logic was retained, thus reducing considerably the damage the scene could have suffered.[54] The more dramatic cuts made to *Revelation* were effected in a similar manner, retaining the logic of the cue's structure, to a degree, and thereby also concealing evidence of the scene's re-editing. Had the *Desire* segment of Blanche's monologue simply been removed from the composite print, the scene's mutilation would have been self-evident, and the cue's impact, generated by gradually increasing tension and accumulative layering, would have been severely curtailed.[55] However, the music North composed for the *Desire* sequence of *Revelation* was left intact. Instead, cuts were made to the music for the *Death* sequence that preceded it.[56] The solution is not ideal—the impact of the original/restored version of the cue/scene is unquestionably more effective in musical and dramatic terms—but in finding a *musical* response to the problem, the linearity and the impact of the cue's buildup is retained. As Leonard Leff suggests, in preserving and analyzing the 1951 version of the film, we are given insight not only into the social mores espoused by the influential institutions of the period, but also into the aesthetic policy of the creative team who worked on the film. By focusing on the re-edited score it becomes clear that despite the need to make cuts, an effort was made to safeguard the musical logic and impact of North's score.

As already mentioned, North was also required to rescore the staircase scene for the re-edited (1951) version. As North explained, this replacement cue was for "French horn and strings, and [had] a mournful quality. In a sense it worked, but the other [...] the other was more consistent with the character of Stanley."[57] The sense in which it worked perfectly was in North's decision to score the scene with an extended version of the love theme. In this way, the score's overall musical coherence was retained, along with consistent semantic associations of the theme's use elsewhere, or at least that was the case up to a point. In the original version of the score, the theme first enters in the cue *Stan* (R6: P1) in fragmentary form. Its appearance here and later in the score supports its interpretation as a love theme for the couple, expressing tenderness rather than the sexual side of their relationship, which North underscored in the simulated jazz cue, *Stan and Stella* (R5: P3).

The first part of the re-edited staircase scene retains the opening of North's original *Stan and Stella* cue, featuring both the opening eight-bar clarinet solo and the twelve bars that follow. At this point the original cue is cut, and North's replacement cue enters focused solely around the love theme (itself a variation of *Belle Reve* theme 1, as mentioned above). With the exception of a handful of supplementary bars at the beginning and the end, twelve of the cue's twenty bars (bb. 6–17) repeat directly a sequence of bars from *Affirmation* R14: P2: bb. 26–37 (see Ex. 5.40 below). Or rather, in terms of the progress of this altered score alongside the re-edited film, the theme now *originates* in these bars.[58]

The love theme begins with a whole-tone descent on solo horn at the same pitch as the fragment in *Stan* (R6: P1), here supported by a chord of $G^{\Delta13}$. Rising arpeggios on flute and harp lead to the string chord and set a calm and ethereal tone. In the next phrase the horn's descent is extended (from B–A to B–A–G–D), followed by a chord of A⁷/D bass. The melody then leaps upward from D to repeat the opening two-note descent a tone lower: A–G. These notes are repeated then meander downwards on bass clarinet for almost two octaves (to C♯) before ascending and culminating on a different, slower paced two-note descent (E–D). Above this, strings begin a sequence of sixth or seventh chords based on ii, iv/IV, and V (Am, Cm/C, D), in ascending figurations.

Example 5.40. *Stan and Stella* (R5: P3 replacement), Melody, bb. 1–10

Finally, release is achieved with the return of a cello theme that combines the D–A–G figure (from bar 5 into bar 6) with the opening B–A motif: D–B–A–D over a chord of G^Δ as the couple embrace (see Ex. 5.41 below). The melody then ascends upwards to B (they kiss) *en route* to D (Stanley's plea that Stella should never leave him). Finally, after a further ascent, the melody reaches B, the octave above, as Stanley carries Stella into the apartment. Beneath this, muted horns and strings provide a G^Δ harmony, which moves to Am⁷ and Am⁹ as he lifts her. Above this, a harmonized version of the opening of the theme is played in rhythmic diminution *divisi* in upper strings. This is similar to (and now preempts) part of the fragment heard in the scene set the morning after (*Stan*, R6: P1, bb. 16–17, see Ex. 5.18). The cue closes with the return to the opening bars: the two-note motif on horn (B–A), followed by a chord of G^Δ13.

Example 5.41. *Stan and Stella* (R5: P3 replacement), bb. 13–14

The replacement cue is shorter than the original staircase cue, as one would expect given that the scene was subject to a number of cuts. As with the edited images, this music conveys little of the ambiguity of North's original cue for the scene. Stella's ambivalence is replaced by a much less complex act of redemption on her part, and the music echoes this, connoting a more pure and uncomplicated love, rather than the original cue's carnality. Indeed, it is fair to say that Stella is the character who is most changed by the scene's re-editing and rescoring. Given that the staircase scene follows Stanley's violent abuse of his wife, this new version adds a further subtext: Stella's acquiescent acceptance of her husband's domestic abuse.[59]

In the context of the film's ending, however, the replacement cue for the staircase scene offers a symmetry which—paradoxically, given the scene's censorship—weakens the film's compromised ending further. Stella's staircase descent to Stanley to the music of the love theme in Reel 5 is now mirrored at the end of the film by Stella's flight *up* the same stairs, away from Stanley, accompanied by the same music. As suggested by Ken Sutak, this symmetry encourages the view that Stella's leaving is temporary; just as she returned to Stanley earlier, so she will return again. Thus, despite sanitizing the staircase scene, in the context of the film's ending, North's replacement cue for the scene—for the 1951 release—suggests a more emphatic return to the ambivalent ending Williams wrote for the play.

AFTERWORD

North's score for *Streetcar* was recently rated nineteenth in the American Film Institute's Top 25 Film Scores by a "jury of over 500 film artists, composers, musicians, critics and historians."[1] The score's success extends to more than half a century of recordings and performances in a variety of arrangements.[2] Notably, the music for a *Streetcar* ballet choreographed by Valerie Bettis is still performed internationally. It was arranged and orchestrated from North's score by Rayburn Wright, and includes additional music from North's *Revue* for clarinet and orchestra for the "Poker Game" sequence.[3] The orchestral suite North arranged for the 1951 soundtrack recording also formed the basis of a suite for piano, published by Witmark (c. 1953): *A Streetcar Named Desire* (Nine Piano Sequences).[4] Alan Bergman and Marilyn Keith (later, Bergman) also penned lyrics to North's *Blanche and Mitch* theme, creating the song "There'll Be Some Blues Tomorrow."[5] Keith also wrote lyrics for a second song, though "I Would Be Lost Without You" does not appear to have been released.[6]

Despite these various "spin-offs," North's score is not well known in its own right. The reason for this is that the score functions best as a key component (perhaps *the* key component) in *Streetcar*'s holistic audiovisual context. North's music is thoroughly integrated with the film's drama, as generated through the performance of dialogue, acting, the choreography of the actors, the camerawork, the editing, sound, the *mise-en-scène*, and so on. As with the staircase scene, *Streetcar*'s whole adds up to more than the sum of its parts. Most mainstream film production is highly compartmentalized. Those with a desire to create more holistic cinematic visions are faced with the industry's built-in institutional barriers. The protracted nature of the genesis of *Streetcar* as a film, the extended collaboration of a group of creative protagonists, many of whom had worked together before (and usually outside of the film industry), all contributed to the character of the film, just as the collaborative character of the relationship between Kazan and North contributed to the score. Why then was *Viva Zapata!* the last film they worked on together? As the sole American member of the Union of Soviet Composers, and for family reasons, North feared being called before the House Un-American Activities Committee (HUAC). By the time *Streetcar* was on general release in 1952, Kazan had already spoken to HUAC once, confirming his membership in the Communist Party during a period in the 1930s. When he was called back in April of the same year, he gave the names of several other Party members.[7] North and Kazan never spoke again.

Early in the 1990s, *Streetcar* made its debut in animated form, in an episode of *The Simpsons*: *A Streetcar Named Marge*, though the episode does not draw on North's score.[8] Marge auditions for a part in an amateur performance of a musical version of the play: *Oh, Streetcar!* When the director sees her relationship with Homer, which he interprets as a match for the relationship between Blanche and Stanley, Marge lands the role of Blanche.[9] The episode reaches a musical climax with the show's reinterpretation of Blanche's final line: a cheery little number entitled "A Stranger's Just a Friend You Haven't Met."

More recently, André Previn created an opera based on *Streetcar*, with a libretto by Philip Littell.[10] Here too the play demonstrated the range of interpretations it allows. Previn has said that he finds Kazan's 1951 film adaptation "dangerous" in what he reads as its seductive emphasis on Brando's performance of Stanley over Leigh's characterization of Blanche. Previn makes no attempt to counterbalance the two characters: Blanche is unquestionably the primary focus for the composer. Musically the opera is stylistically varied, also incorporating influences from the operatic writing of Benjamin Britten and Richard Strauss. A bluesy orchestrated train whistle forms a key unifying motif in the score, which also includes a number of intensely powerful lyrical arias, notably Blanche's "I Want Magic!" and "I Can Smell the Sea Air." The rape is depicted by a shocking and intoxicating musical interlude before a darkened stage.

Previn has said of Williams's play that he has always thought of it as "an opera that was just missing the music."[11] Yet, as I hope to have demonstrated, certain sequences in Kazan's film adaptation are *already* operatic: notably those in which North's music is thoroughly integrated with, and shaping of, the drama, the dialogue, the actors' performances, and so on—as in *Revelation*, for example.[12] Elsewhere Previn states that he "never understood" why North's score "goes into really triumphant music" at the end of the film.[13] One of my primary goals in writing this book was to offer a contextualized exploration of North's score for *Streetcar*, and thus to go some way towards offering an explanation for this otherwise anomalous celebratory ending. I hope readers agree that the discussion of North's music for the staircase scene provides further evidence to support Leonard Leff's view of the importance of retaining access to multiple versions of films, and what they tell us about the history of cinema.[14] More than anything, though, I hope readers will want to watch and listen to *Streetcar* again.

NOTES

Introduction

1. Vivien Leigh won Best Actress, and Karl Malden and Kim Hunter won Best Supporting Actor and Actress. Richard Day and George James Hopkins won for (Black and White) Art Direction (and Set Decoration). Bogart's Oscar for *The African Queen* was the only one of his career. George Stevens won Best Director for *A Place in the Sun*, with Michael Wilson and Harry Brown winning for best screenplay for the same film. Best Score went to Franz Waxman for *A Place in the Sun*, and *An American in Paris* won Best Picture.

Chapter 1

1. North received nominations for his scores for *A Streetcar Named Desire* (1951) and *Death of a Salesman* (1951) in the 1951 (24th) Academy Awards, and his score for *Viva Zapata!* (1952) in the 1952 (25th) Awards.

2. In an interview with Rudy Behlmer he states that he was offered "a C film to do at Eagle Lion or something" in 1947. North in Rudy Behlmer, "Alex North on *A Streetcar Named Desire*," *The Cue Sheet* 3, no. 3 (September 1986): 36.

3. See, for example, a letter North sent to Copland (10 November 1957): "Someday I will tell you why I have worked like mad out here these past five years, writing scores in three weeks, sacrificing my yen to write 'absolute'—I never knew when the axe would fall." North in Aaron Copland and Vivian Perlis, *Copland: Since 1943* (New York: St. Martin's Press, 1989), 7. More specifically, North later said that he found it particularly difficult to gain second performances of his con-

cert works. North in Sanya Shoilevska Henderson, *Alex North, Film Composer* (Jefferson, NC & London: McFarland and Co., 2003), 49.

4. As Henderson highlights, some sources give North's birth as 1909; 1910 is the officially recognized year, however. Henderson, *Alex North*, 7.

5. North in David Raksin, "The Subject Is Film Music." An interview with Alex North as a part of the Yale University oral history program (American Music Series). Transcription by Fred Karlin, 2. A transcript of the interview is held in the Alex North Files in Special Collections at the Margaret Herrick Library, Academy of Motion Picture Arts and Sciences (hereafter, AMPAS). As for possible influences that led to his becoming a musician, North highlights the musical culture in the house: his mother played early Caruso records, and sang a large repertoire of Russian songs to her children.

6. North in Raksin, "The Subject Is Film Music," 5. These bands were all popular white "swing" bands of the period.

7. North in Raksin, "The Subject Is Film Music," 4. See also Henderson, *Alex North*, 14.

8. North's eldest brother Joseph was a journalist and later a founder and editor of the left-of-center weekly *New Masses*. Henderson notes that it was through Joseph that North "made social contacts with some of the most progressive thinkers of that period. ... [and] influenced [his] radical attitude and active curiosity about the social events of the time." Henderson, *Alex North*, 12. She also notes that it was from Joseph that North was to take his stage name on his return from the Soviet Union; the elder brother had begun using the name Joe North "to protect his family from criticism of his activities." Henderson, *Alex North*, 13.

9. North cited in Larry Warren, *Anna Sokolow: The Rebellious Spirit* (Amsterdam: Harwood Academic Publishers, 1998), 29.

10. North cited in Henderson, *Alex North*, 16.

11. For a contemporaneous discussion of these composers see, for example, William Kozlenko's "Soviet Music and Musicians," in *Musical Quarterly* 23, no. 3 (July 1937): 295–305.

12. North in Raksin, "The Subject Is Film Music," 6.

13. North cited in Henderson, *Alex North*, 17; Warren, *Anna Sokolow*, 39.

14. North's time in Moscow (early 1934 to late 1935) coincided with a period of relative stability both in terms of the organization of curricula at the Conservatory and in terms of Soviet ideology concerning music, with support for more avant-garde musical tendencies and encouragement for music for the "masses." However, Stalin's atten-

dance at Dmitri Shostakovich's *Lady Macbeth of the Mtsensk District* at the Bolshoi Theatre in December 1935 was followed by an unsigned editorial in Pravda, "Chaos instead of Music," in which the work was denounced. Henceforth it was required that all Soviet art should conform to the ideals of "socialist realism." More and more works were censored and the role of the composer became much more precarious, with some sent to labor camps soon after.

15. Henderson, *Alex North*, 19.
16. North in Raksin, "The Subject Is Film Music," 5.
17. North in Raksin, "The Subject Is Film Music," 5.
18. North in Raksin, "The Subject Is Film Music," 5, and North in Christopher Palmer, "Film Music Profile: Alex North," in *Crescendo International* (April 1975): 28–29 and 32, 28.
19. Henderson, *Alex North*, 20.
20. North in Raksin, "The Subject Is Film Music," 6.
21. Finch College, New York; Sarah Lawrence College, New York; Briarcliff College, New York; Bennington College, Vermont.
22. Warren, *Anna Sokolow*, 52. Warren states that the work developed from Sokolow's "strong affinity for jazz, which grew out of her love for and endless fascination with New York, a city that pulsated with its rhythms" (ibid.).
23. Elie Siegmeister in Siegmeister (ed.), *The Music Lover's Handbook* (New York: William and Morrow and Company, 1943), 770.
24. John Martin, "The Dance: New Blood," *New York Times*, 29 August 1937.
25. John Martin, "Dance Debut Here by Anna Sokolow," *New York Times*, 15 November 1937.
26. North in Raksin, "The Subject Is Film Music," 8.
27. See, for example, the program from a Sokolow/North recital held on 18 February 1940, in Henderson, *Alex North*, 25.
28. Warren, *Anna Sokolow*, 59.
29. North in Joel Reisner and Bruce Kane interview, cited in Henderson, *Alex North*, 21.
30. See William Alexander, "Frontier Films, 1936–1941: The Aesthetics of Impact," in *Cinema Journal* 15, no. 1 (Autumn 1975): 16–28. See also the useful resource provided by Nicole Huffman, "New Frontiers in American Documentary Film," from her unpublished Master's thesis in American Studies at the University of Virginia (2001) available online: http://xroads.virginia.edu/~MA01/Huffman/Frontier/frontier.html (17 November 2006).
31. Some sources date this film as 1938.

32. In a letter to Kazan sent in May 1951, North states that Leyda was an old friend. It is possible that they met in Moscow; both were there at around the same time. Leyda studied with Sergei Eisenstein at the Moscow State Film School from September 1933, and went on to work for him "as photographer and archivist during the making of *Bezhin Meadow*" from 1934 to 1935. Their partners were also both modern dancers. See Jay and Si-Lan Chen Papers, Tamiment Archive, New York University. Leyda is perhaps best known as the translator of Eisenstein's writings.

33. Siegmeister, *The Music Lover's Handbook*, 770.

34. The film itself is framed by opening and closing sequences. These were scored for wordless chorus by Earl Robinson. The film may be viewed at the Library of Congress, in Washington, DC.

35. North in Behlmer, "Alex North on *A Streetcar Named Desire*," 37.

36. Henderson, *Alex North*, 21.

37. North, cited in Henderson, *Alex North*, 21.

38. The musical premiered in Hartford on 4 June 1943, was performed in 1949 in New York, in Los Angeles in 1953, and broadcast as the CBS Radio Workshop on 7 September 1956.

39. North's son Steven was born in 1942, when North was in the army.

40. In the first published edition of the poem, in *The Negro Mother and Other Dramatic Recitations*, it is accompanied by a colored illustration of a woman with a hand raised, against which the image of a black child can be seen. It was created by Prentiss Taylor and includes the following information regarding performance: "A poem to be done by a woman in the bandana and apron of the Old South—but with great dignity and strength and beauty in her face as she speaks. The music of the spirituals may be played by a piano or an orchestra as the aged mother talks to her modern sons and daughters." A copy of this edition is held in the Prentiss Taylor papers by The Smithsonian Archives of American Art, viewable at http://www.aaa.si.edu/exhibits/pastexhibits/treasures/0062.htm (20 November 2006).

41. Siegmeister, *The Music Lover's Handbook*, 770.

42. Martin McCall, "American Ballad Singers and Young Composer Heard in Excellent Programs," *Daily Worker* [New York], 22 February 1940, 7.

43. McCall, "American Ballad Singers," 7.

44. Henderson, *Alex North*, 33. North was drafted in early 1942 and discharged in August 1946. This relatively late discharge was due

to the need to hand over the rehabilitation project to the Veteran's Administration. North in Raksin, "The Subject Is Film Music," 9.

45. The work was premiered on 28 October 1946 and performed again in May 1947. The paper's own review of the latter performance was damning in its faint praise, though it is also possible to read it as critical of the type of commission: "North's own grasp of the idiom is respectable and workmanlike enough [...] *Morning Star* suffers from episodic conception [...] it is like so many works that are adequate to a given occasion and to communicate a given message, but have not the inner spark to survive beyond this occasion." *New York Herald Tribune*, 26 May 1947.

46. This description comes from the "Composer's Note on *Revue*," which can be found on the inside cover of North's own arrangement of the work, *Revue: for clarinet and piano* (New York: Mills Music, c. 1948).

47. *New York Times*, 19 November 1946, 40.

48. North, "Composer sends message from Camp," *Hartford Times*, 12 April 1943, cited in Henderson, *Alex North*, 31.

49. Aaron Copland, "Composer from Brooklyn," 1939, cited in Elizabeth B. Crist, *Music for the Common Man: Aaron Copland During the Depression and War* (New York: Oxford University Press, 2005), 5.

50. Copland, cited in Crist, *Music for the Common Man*, 5.

51. Copland, cited in Crist, *Music for the Common Man*, 6.

52. Crist, *Music for the Common Man*, 6.

53. Review, *New York Sun*, 22 September 1947, cited in Henderson, *Alex North*, 35.

54. Review, *New York Times*, 22 September 1947.

55. Review, *New York Herald Tribune*, 19 October 1947.

56. North stated that "it was much easier to identify with the characters in *Death of a Salesman* than in *Streetcar*." North in Raksin, "The Subject Is Film Music," 46. Although North is referring to Arthur Miller's *play*, in terms of *Streetcar* this is a reference to his work on Kazan's 1951 film adaptation. North did not score the stage production of Williams's play, which debuted on Broadway on 3 December 1947.

57. Miller, from interview with Henderson, cited in Henderson, *Alex North*, 39.

58. As Henderson points out, these constraints were most likely due to financial constraints regarding the American Federation of Musicians at the time. Adding musicians or including more music would have made the music considerably more expensive since it was played live each night. Henderson, *Alex North*, 39–41.

59. For *Salesman*, North conducted the musicians in the pre–New York tryouts and the first few nights on Broadway. Subsequently, they were cued by the voice of the assistant stage manager and a pair of red lights, with the flutist taking the position of leader. See Murray Schumach, "Play's Tunes Piped from Padded Cell," *New York Times*, 16 March 1949, XI, and Howard Taubman, "Plays with Music Between the Lines," *New York Times*, 27 March 1949.

60. For example, "The result is a finely integrated piece of work," Howard Taubman, "Plays with Music Between the Lines," *New York Times*, 27 March 1949. In his review for the *New York Times*, 20 February 1949, Brooks Atkinson writes: "Alex North has composed a stirring interpretive score which, like the direction and scenery, has the grace to melt unobtrusively into the work as a whole." Barbara Strong argued that the collaboration of Miller, Kazan, and North "resulting in so perfect an achievement, is perhaps the actual beginning of a new era in the theatre." North's music was "an integral part of the drama itself." Barbara Strong, "Theatre: Not So Incidental," *Concerto* (February 1950), 5, cited in Henderson, *Alex North*, 40.

61. Brooks Atkinson, Review, *New York Times*, 2 February 1950.

62. Henderson, *Alex North*, 40.

63. Strong cited in Henderson, *Alex North*, 40.

64. North cited in Irwin Bazelon, *Knowing the Score: Notes on Film Music* (New York: Van Nostrand Reinhold Co., 1975), 223.

65. Henderson, *Alex North*, 24.

66. See North in Behlmer, "Alex North on *A Streetcar Named Desire*," 38, and Raksin, "The Subject Is Film Music," 10.

67. North in interview with Fred Steiner, 27 April 1976, cited in Henderson, *Alex North*, 42.

68. The order in which films are released does not always correlate exactly with the chronology of North's work on a given film. For example, North adapted his *Salesman* score *after* his work on *Zapata*, though the former was released first. Also, although *Streetcar* is generally regarded as North's first score in Hollywood, it is likely that it was predated by his score for *The 13th Letter* at Fox; the latter film was released in January 1951, when North was scoring *Streetcar*.

69. Warren Sherk, "Welcome to Hollywood: Alex North's Unused Score for *Distant Drums* (1951)," *The Cue Sheet* 16, no. 2 (April 2000): 21–30. As with *Streetcar*, Warner Bros. was the releasing studio and, as with both *Streetcar* and *The 13th Letter*, Maurice de Packh was the orchestrator.

70. Cited in Henderson, *Alex North*, 44. I suspect North here refers to the only occasion he can remember of having to change his music at

the behest of Newman or someone else associated with a studio music department. As explored in chapters 3 and 5, two cues in *Streetcar* were also rewritten, though this was required by the producers rather than by Heindorf.

71. North in interview with Fred Steiner, 27 April 1976, cited in Henderson, *Alex North*, 44.

72. Hellman's play was originally staged on Broadway in the mid-1930s, but when it was adapted as a film as *These Three* (1936), the play's lesbian theme was transformed into a heterosexual love triangle due to difficulties with the Production Code. William Wyler directed both the 1936 and 1961 adaptations.

73. Other Mexican-influenced scores by North include: *The Wonderful Country* (1959) and *Under the Volcano* (1984).

74. In addition to *Streetcar*, other scores for films set in Southern states of the United States include *Hot Spell* (1958) and *The Long Hot Summer* (1958).

75. Although it is not uncommon for film composers to create works from their film scores that may be played in concert settings, such as Suites, it is rare indeed for composers to be commissioned to write an autonomous art work from which a score may be produced.

76. Relations between North and his first wife had apparently become strained during the 1960s. North's third child, Daniel, was born to Annemarie Hoellger North in 1970. Henderson, *Alex North*, 69–70.

77. North's concept for the dragon's music was not used in its entirety in the final version of the film, with some cues replaced by music from elsewhere in the score. In addition to *2001*, other rejected scores from this period include *Sounder* (1972), directed by Martin Ritt, and *Cattle Annie and Little Britches* (1981), directed by Lamont Johnson. Henderson, *Alex North*, 83–85.

78. North in David Kraft, "A Conversation with Alex North," in *Soundtrack! The Collector's Quarterly* 4, no. 13 (March 1985): 4.

79. The John Huston films North scored were *The Misfits* (1961), *Wise Blood* (1979), *Under the Volcano*, *Prizzi's Honor* (1985), and *The Dead*. North's scores for Daniel Mann include: *The Rose Tattoo*, an adaptation of Lillian Roth's autobiography, *I'll Cry Tomorrow* (1955), *Hot Spell* (1958), *Dream of Kings* (1969), a horror film, *Willard* (1971), and *A Journey into Fear* (1974).

80. At the 2006 (79th) Academy Awards Ennio Morricone was presented with an Honorary Award, only the second film composer to receive such an award. Like North, although a number of Morricone's scores have been nominated, as yet he has not won.

Chapter 2

1. North cited in Tony Thomas, *Music for the Movies* (London: Tantivy Press, 1973), 184.

2. Norman Lloyd, in *Film Music* 15, no. 2 (Winter 1955): 3.

3. North cited in Christopher Palmer, "Film Music Profile: Alex North," 28.

4. North, in Kraft, "A Conversation with Alex North," 5.

5. North cited in Palmer, "Film Music Profile: Alex North," 28.

6. North cited in Palmer, "Film Music Profile: Alex North," 28.

7. North cited in Thomas, *Music for the Movies*, 184.

8. North cited in Raksin, "The Subject Is Film Music," 13.

9. North cited in Palmer, "Film Music Profile: Alex North," 29.

10. North cited in Thomas, *Music for the Movies*, 183.

11. Both North and Kazan were living in New York at the time, but their discussions continued in California during trips to the beach. North notes that Kazan also sent him to New Orleans to "sop up the atmosphere." North in Behlmer, "Alex North on *A Streetcar Named Desire*," 36. Kazan had recently shot *Panic in the Streets* (1950) on location in New Orleans.

12. North cited in Palmer, "Film Music Profile: Alex North," 32.

13. Letter from Ingo Preminger, General Artists Corporation, to North dated 11 June 1965. Alex North Correspondence Files, Special Collections, Margaret Herrick Library, AMPAS (hereafter North Correspondence Files, AMPAS).

14. "*Cleopatra* was interesting because I was working with Joe Mankiewicz, who is a musically sensitive man. This was another exceptional experience because I was able to go to Rome and watch them shoot. Usually the composer is brought in at the end of the picture so that they don't have to pay him from the start. Mankiewicz felt differently; he wanted me to be there and amalgamate my ideas. I was able to do some research on music of the period and I tried to simulate the musical sounds of what I thought might have prevailed at the time." North cited in Thomas, *Music for the Movies*, 183–184. Of *Spartacus*, he said he found it "an unusual experience. I had lots of time to do [a] much more intricate kind of composition instead of just tossing off something and saying 'This is it.'" North in Raksin, "The Subject Is Film Music," 24.

15. A Twentieth Century-Fox press release, dated 13 October 1961, states that North is currently in Rome "to set the tempo for Cleopatra's triumphal entrance into the Eternal City. With the completion of

the sequence, he will return to New York to write music appropriate to this tempo." Attached to memo from Michael Michel, Twentieth Century-Fox Corp., North Correspondence Files, AMPAS. Letters from North to Joe Mankiewicz and Walter Wanger, also dated October 1961, indicate that a demonstration recording of North's "romantic theme" for Cleopatra was sent to them in Rome, "to acquaint you with the theme and to use for whatever purposes you see fit while shooting the picture." A letter from North dating from January 1962 states that he is still "anxiously awaiting some word concerning the love theme which was forwarded." By June of that year, a letter from North to Mankiewicz, written in Rome, states that North was in receipt of a continuity chart. He asks that duplicates of sequences be sent to Los Angeles "where I can work out more accurate timing, synchronization and recording. Naturally, I shall use a small combination of musicians for this purpose until the final cut is ready and can expand the orchestra to fit the dramatic needs of the scenes." In the same letter, North explores the essential distinction he intends to reflect in the music for Caesar and Cleopatra versus that for Anthony and Cleopatra. *Cleopatra*, North Correspondence Files, AMPAS.

16. Letter from the film's music supervisor, Joseph Gershenson, to North dated 17 June 1959. *Spartacus* (19-260), North Correspondence Files, AMPAS.

17. As already mentioned, North's score for Kubrick's *2001* (1968) was infamously rejected by the director in favor of his "temp track."

18. Warren Sherk, "Welcome to Hollywood."

19. As Sherk demonstrates, parts of North's *Distant Drums* score can be found in his score for *Viva Zapata!* and in the 1958 Cinerama film *South Seas Adventure*. Sherk, "Welcome to Hollywood," 29.

20. See Rider attached to clause 17 of North's contract with Chas K. Feldman Productions, dated 11 December 1950. *A Streetcar Named Desire* (hereafter, *Streetcar*), Folder 1507, Warner Bros. Archives, School of Cinematic Arts, University of Southern California (hereafter WBA USC).

21. *The Shoes of the Fisherman* is a case in point. The producer insisted that a Russian theme be used for the Pope, who was a Russian. Although resistant, North eventually acquiesced. He stated that "I thought it was wrong and I still do. ... However, your own ideas don't always prevail, you must compromise," for "the composer is an employee." North cited in Thomas, *Music for the Movies*, 184.

22. For example, Jack Warner allegedly barred Mike Nichols—the director of *Who's Afraid of Virginia Woolf?*—from the studio lot to

allow North to follow his own thoughts for the score through to its recording. North in Behlmer, "Alex North on *A Streetcar Named Desire*," 37.

23. Occasionally, as with "R11, P2; R12, P1" in *Streetcar*, a cue that covers a reel change is given a label that reflects its segue function.

24. Many of these are held in the "Alex North Collection of Motion Picture Music, 1951–1969," Music Library Special Collections, University of California at Los Angeles.

25. One cue in the *Streetcar* score offers an interesting exception. The surviving holograph score for R5, P3, the infamous staircase scene, is the only cue written in pen rather than pencil. This is the replacement cue written several months after North had composed the original score, and after it had been recorded. The cue is discussed in more detail in chapters 3 and 5.

26. Occasionally, as with the "Main Title" for *Spartacus*, an additional single line staff is hand-drawn beneath a score of four staves for percussion (printed).

27. Lionel Newman is credited as associate conductor on *Cleopatra*.

28. North in Behlmer, "Alex North on *A Streetcar Named Desire*," 37.

29. These are generally cataloged as "conductor scores" by archives. With reference to the use of the same system for Max Steiner's scores, Kate Daubney notes that the "lack of instrumental attribution in the template" enables the composer "to show the many changes in instrumental detail by appropriate annotation, without the complexity of a full score." Kate Daubney, *Max Steiner's Now, Voyager: A Film Score Guide* (Westport, CT: Greenwood Press, 2000), 15.

30. North in Behlmer, "Alex North on *A Streetcar Named Desire*," 37.

31. Bazelon, *Knowing the Score*, 221.

32. Bazelon, *Knowing the Score*, 221. Orchestrators, or arrangers as they are titled in some studio documents, do not always receive screen credit for their work. Studio Music Department timesheets and budget reports sometimes offer more reliable information with regard to the attribution of orchestration.

33. Henderson states that, although not given screen credit, Maurice de Packh produced the "final orchestration" of the score for *Spartacus*. Henderson, *Alex North*, 132.

34. Powell did not receive screen credit for his work on *The Children's Hour*.

35. Brant is noted particularly for developing a form of music "for spatially separated groups," with stylistic influences that include the counterpoint of Ives and the "angular melodic style of Carl Ruggles." For Brant, "space" is viewed as the fourth dimension of pitch, rhythm, and timbre—with spatial separation enabling him to create works with a large number of individual horizontal lines, while including a possible mode of perceptual differentiation for the listener through separating groups of performers. In this way, his works of the 1950s also prefigure the later works of Berio. Particularly notable was the work *Antiphony I* (1953) in which, as in Stockhausen's *Gruppen* (1955–57), the work is performed by a number of "widely separated orchestral groups"—here five, as opposed to Stockhausen's three. He was also interested by controlled improvisation, and this has continued to feature in his later works in which he combines the musics of various cultures. Kyle Gann (with Kurt Stone), "Henry Brant," *Grove Music Online*, ed. L. Macy, www.grovemusic.com (12 December 2006).

36. Brant possibly also orchestrated Virgil Thomson's on *The River* (1938), though he is not given screen credit.

37. John Martin, "Dance Debut Here by Anna Sokolow."

38. North's papers for *Under the Volcano* at the Margaret Herrick Library (AMPAS) include folders of research on Mexican folk music to be used as source music in the film, notably from the book *El Folklore y La Musicana Mexicana*, with music collected by Ruben M. Campos, and from music collected by Francisco Dominguez.

39. North in Palmer, "Film Music Profile: Alex North," 29.

40. Friedhofer cited in Thomas, *Music for the Movies,* 157.

41. North in Palmer, "Film Music Profile: Alex North," 29.

42. That North played a role in the selection of the film's source music is suggested by a letter sent from North to Kazan (dated 13 May 1951), with suggestions for Mexican folk songs ("corridos") for particular scenes. Letter tucked inside Kazan's *Zapata* script. Kazan Papers: Script, *Zapata* Box 25, Wesleyan Cinema Archives, Wesleyan University, Middletown (hereafter WCA WU).

43. The Yaqui are a Native American people who originally lived in the valley of the Rio Yaqui in what is now the northern part of Mexico.

44. Writing about the *son,* the "generic term for peasant or rural music" in Mexico, Thomas Stanford and A. Chamorro state that the most prominent trait of this musical form "is an unequal triple rhythm based on patterns of six beats." Thomas Stanford and A. Chamorro, "Mexico," *Grove Music Online,* ed. L. Macy, www.grovemusic.com (16 February 2007).

45. As mentioned above, this metric play between 6/8 and 3/4 is characteristic of the Mexican *son*.

46. North in Raksin, "The Subject Is Film Music," 19. See also Kazan's letter to North dated 30 October 1951, North Correspondence Files: *Viva Zapata!* (22-294), AMPAS.

47. It is heard as the first cue of the film (after the Main Title) in an easy piano arrangement. Rhoda is heard to play it again when her mother is informed that her daughter was the last to see a drowned boy alive and that his penmanship medal—which Rhoda felt was rightfully hers—was missing from the boy's clothing. Finally, she performs it in an increasingly loud and feverish performance as Leroy the handyman is burnt to death shortly after we have seen her sneak some matches and leave the house to buy ice cream. She also hums the tune as friends and family wait to hear whether her mother will survive her suicide attempt.

48. At the end of the story, the "End Cast" cue is heard as the cast are introduced. This cue repeats the lullaby.

49. In addition to "Au clair de la lune," both the strings' *moto perpetuo* figure and the descending chords of the cue's opening recur elsewhere in the score. The string figure is heard as Rhoda throws her shoes into the incinerator chute, thereby destroying the evidence that she caused the boy's death.

50. The first of these cues, played by soli strings and wind, begins with the B section of Varinia's theme which is subsequently developed in two further four-bar phrases—B2 and B3—after which there is a straightforward recapitulation of the first part of the original theme, A. This is followed by a brief pause during which Spartacus asks Varinia if she was hurt. The cue is completed by the repetition of A3', A4, and A5, in slightly modified arrangements. The second kitchen cue is shorter, and is heard as Spartacus gently touches then grasps Varinia's hand as she pours water into his cup: A4, A4' plus two bars of coda.

51. Henderson, *Alex North*, 153.

52. Inclusion of the scene makes clear the reason for Antoninus's escape and his willingness to join the slave army. In the years since the film's release the recording of Laurence Olivier's dialogue for the scene had been lost. Anthony Hopkins re-recorded Olivier's dialogue for the scene.

53. That is, with a scale organized according to the following intervals: Semitone-Tone-T-T-S-T-T.

54. Henderson lists the melody as played by vibraphone, marimba, crotales, tuned bongos, Novachord, with the repeated accompaniment figure performed on harp tremelo, lute, guitar (counter-beats) and Chinese bell tree glissandi. Henderson, *Alex North*, 148–149. North's

sketch for this scene is scored only for Novachord, fixed piano, two harps, guitar, tuned sleigh bells, Chinese bell tree, crotales, and boobams.

55. North in Palmer, "Film Music Profile: Alex North," 29.

56. North in Palmer, "Film Music Profile: Alex North," 29.

57. Within a jazz context such chords would likely be understood as sharp ninth chords, though a flatted seventh would usually also be expected, while the fifth may be dropped. Despite Anthony's intoxication, there is little reason to hear these chords as jazz inflected.

58. North said of the cue, "I think it has some kind of purpose that is essential to this particular scene in terms of building slowly the suspense. And also, it gave me an opportunity to do certain complex things that, if I hadn't had the amount of time (again, in this situation I was fortunate enough to have close to a year to work on this)." North in Raksin, "The Subject Is Film Music," 28. NB: The film's soundtrack album conflates "Premonition" (Reel 19: Part 1) and "Assassination" (Reel 19: Part 1A) under the single title "Caesar's Assassination." Here I refer to the conductor score for "Assassination."

59. North in Raksin, "The Subject Is Film Music," 34.

60. North in Raksin, "The Subject Is Film Music," 34.

61. George Burt, *The Art of Film Music: Special Emphasis on Hugo Friedhofer, Alex North, David Raksin, Leonard Rosenman* (Boston: Northeastern University Press, 1994), 12.

62. Burt, *The Art of Film Music*, 101.

63. Burt, *The Art of Film Music*, 101.

64. North in Bazelon, *Knowing the Score*, 220.

65. North in Raksin, "The Subject Is Film Music," 20.

66. Burt provides a lengthy and insightful discussion of the sequence which includes a detailed timing sheet and score of the scene with dialogue included. Burt, *The Art of Film Music*, 100–111.

67. Several bars were cut from the cue during production. This is reflected in the version of the cue presented here. I have retained the original numbering for clarity.

Chapter 3

1. Irene Selznick was the daughter of film mogul L. B. Mayer (of Metro Goldwyn Mayer), and the recently estranged wife of film producer David O. Selznick. *Streetcar* was only her second production; her first—a play by Arthur Laurents called *Heartsong*—closed during tryouts, though its failure was not considered to be a reflection of her new-

found skills as a theatrical producer. See letter from Audrey Wood to Williams, dated 18 April 1947. Harry Ransom Humanities Research Center, University of Texas at Austin (hereafter HRHRC UT).

2. Elia Kazan cited in Gene D. Phillips, "*A Streetcar Named Desire*: Play and Film," in *Confronting Tennessee Williams's* A Streetcar Named Desire*: Essays in Critical Pluralism*, ed. Philip C. Kolin (Westport, CT, and London: Greenwood Press, 1993), 225. Kazan filmed four scenes away from the apartment: the arrival of Blanche at the train station; meeting Stella at the bowling alley (rather than waiting for her return in the apartment); the scene in which Blanche tells Mitch about her late husband takes place at an amusement park at Lake Pontchartrain, rather than after their return home from the date; finally, we see Mitch respond violently to Stanley's accusations about Blanche while the men are at work at the factory.

3. As Brenda Murphy explains, the balance of this collaboration changed over time: Williams began to resent the controlling role Kazan required as director, which later included making suggestions much earlier in the gestation of Williams's plays. See Brenda Murphy, *Tennessee Williams and Elia Kazan: A Collaboration in Theatre* (Cambridge: Cambridge University Press, 1992).

4. Elia Kazan, *A Life* (London: André Deutsch, 1988), 339.

5. Tennessee Williams, *A Streetcar Named Desire* (New York: New Directions), 1947/2004, 6 (sc. 1).

6. Williams, *A Streetcar Named Desire*, 81 (sc. 4).

7. Williams, *A Streetcar Named Desire*, 45 (sc. 2).

8. Williams, *A Streetcar Named Desire*, 149 (sc. 9).

9. Williams, *A Streetcar Named Desire*, 162 (sc. 10).

10. Williams, *A Streetcar Named Desire*, 178 (sc. 11).

11. Elia Kazan, "Notebook for *A Streetcar Named Desire*" (abridged), in Toby Cole and Helen Krich Chinoy (eds.), *Directors on Directing: A Source Book of the Modern Theatre* (London: Peter Owen, 1973), 370.

12. The stimulus for the letter had been the stalling of negotiations between the play's producer, Irene Selznick, and Kazan's lawyer. The delays were caused by Kazan's request for twenty percent of the profits and a co-production credit. Selznick eventually agreed, and the "cult of the director" was advanced further.

13. Letter from Williams to Kazan, reprinted in Kazan, *A Life*, 329–330. Emphasis in original.

14. Arthur Miller, "Introduction" to Tennessee Williams, *A Streetcar Named Desire*, x.

15. Tennessee Williams, *The Glass Menagerie* (Acting Version), (New York: Dramatists Play Service, 1948), 7. Cited in Murphy, *Tennessee Williams and Elia Kazan*, 8.

16. See Penny Farfan, "Music," in *The Tennessee Williams Encyclopedia*, ed. Philip C. Kolin (Westport, CT, and London: Greenwood Press, 2004), 156–157.

17. Murphy, *Tennessee Williams and Elia Kazan*, 9.

18. Murphy, *Tennessee Williams and Elia Kazan*, 10.

19. Meyerhold later developed his own Method or System in opposition to Stanislavski's, focused on a rigorous training for the actor's body: biomechanics. See Foster Hirsch, *A Method to Their Madness: The History of the Actors Studio* (New York and London: W. W. Norton and Co., 1984), and Alma H. Law and Mel Gordon, *Meyerhold, Eisenstein and Biomechanics: Actor Training in Revolutionary Russia* (Jefferson, NC, and London: McFarland & Co, 1996).

20. Murphy, *Tennessee Williams and Elia Kazan*, 13.

21. Murphy, *Tennessee Williams and Elia Kazan*, 25.

22. Kazan in *Kazan on Kazan*, ed. Michael Ciment (New York: Viking Press, 1974), 32. Also cited in Murphy, *Tennessee Williams and Elia Kazan*, 14.

23. Kazan, "Notebook," 364–365.

24. Kazan, "Notebook," 365, 371.

25. Kazan, "Notebook," 365.

26. Kazan, "Notebook," 375.

27. Kazan, "Notebook," 366.

28. Kazan, "Notebook," 367.

29. Kazan, "Notebook," 370.

30. Kazan, "Notebook," 369.

31. Kazan, "Notebook," 369.

32. Kazan, "Notebook," 371.

33. Kazan, "Notebook," 374.

34. Kazan, "Notebook," 375.

35. Kazan, "Notebook," 375.

36. Kazan, "Notebook," 375.

37. Kazan, "Notebook," 374.

38. Kazan, "Notebook," 372.

39. Kazan, "Notebook," 372.

40. Kazan, "Notebook," 372.

41. On the fourth day of rehearsals Williams sent a note to Kazan highlighting the difference between the sisters' behavior: "Blanche is the quick, light one. Stella is relatively slow and almost indolent. . . . I

think her natural passivity is one of the things that makes her acceptance of Stanley acceptable." Williams in Kazan, "Notebook," 374.

42. Kazan, "Notebook," 378.

43. Williams in Kazan, *A Life*, 346.

44. Kazan, *A Life*, 344.

45. Murphy, *Tennessee Williams and Elia Kazan*, 27.

46. See, for example, the letters sent from Warner Bros.' Steve Trilling to director Vincent Sherman on 19 November 1948 and 5 February 1949. Reprinted in Rudy Behlmer (ed.), *Inside Warner Brothers (1935–1951)* (London: Weidenfield and Nicolson, 1986).

47. See, for example, the chapters on Warner Bros. in Thomas Schatz, *The Genius of the System: Hollywood Filmmaking in the Studio Era* (New York: Pantheon Books, 1988).

48. See Ben Winters, *Erich Wolfgang Korngold's* The Adventures of Robin Hood (Lanham, MD: Scarecrow Press, 2007), 6.

49. Schatz, *The Genius of the System*, 300.

50. Warner Bros. Inter-Office Communication dated 29 November 1949. *Streetcar*, Legal 2857, WBA USC. Williams was paid a further $30,000 to write the screenplay.

51. Letter from Audrey Wood to Williams, dated 1 March 1949. The sale of film rights to *Streetcar* were discussed by Wood and Kazan over dinner. HRHRC UT.

52. Kazan, *A Life*, 383.

53. Warner Bros. Weekly Production Cost Summary (*Streetcar*), week ending 29 September 1951. *Streetcar*, Legal 2857, WBA USC.

54. Inter-office memos dated 29 November 1949 and 14 December 1949. *Streetcar*, Legal 2857, WBA USC.

55. R. Barton Palmer suggests that gossip concerning Leigh's private life, particularly an extramarital affair, also made her an apt choice for Blanche. R. Barton Palmer, "Hollywood in Crisis: Tennessee Williams and the Evolution of the Adult Film," in *The Cambridge Companion to Tennessee Williams*, ed. Matthew C. Roudané (Cambridge: Cambridge University Press, 1997), 219.

56. Linda Costanzo Cahir, "The Artful Rerouting of *A Streetcar Named Desire*," *Literature Film Quarterly* 22, no. 2 (1994): 72–77, 73.

57. Kazan, *A Life*, 387.

58. As Cahir explains, "[The] acting does show in those opening scenes. Kazan is right; but it is Blanche's acting, not Leigh's, that seems artificial, disharmonious, contrived; Blanche whose tone is unsteady, whose gesturing is overblown. Blanche hasn't had time to gauge her audience." Cahir, "The Artful Rerouting of *A Streetcar Named Desire*," 73. See also notes made by Kazan in preparation for

directing the play, in which he states that Blanche should play different characters in different scenes (9.18). Kazan Papers: *Streetcar* notebook, B19 F1. WCA WU.

59. Kazan, *A Life*, 384.

60. Kazan, *A Life*, 384.

61. Kazan, *A Life*, 384.

62. Warner Bros.' overhead costs were additional to this figure, and included salaries for Ray Heindorf (head of Music Dept.), Joe McLaughlin (copyright), a secretary, and a librarian. These salaries amounted to $1,015.28 a week.

63. Behlmer, "Alex North on *A Streetcar Named Desire*, 37.

64. Shurlock in Murray Schumach, *The Face on the Cutting Room Floor: The Story of Movie and Television Censorship* (New York: William Morrow, 1964), 72.

65. MPPDA: Motion Picture Producers and Distributors of America; MPAA: Motion Picture Association of America.

66. Richard Maltby and others highlight Hollywood's own hand in the mythologizing of the history of the Production Code, however. In the early 1930s censorship offered the industry a means of diverting attention away from what it feared most: "the passage of legislation outlawing block booking and imposing federal regulation of the industry's business practices." Maltby argues that changes made to the Code in 1934 were more apparent than substantial and thus an exercise in public relations in which it seemed that the industry was forced to apologize for its previous failed attempt to control moral depravity in the movies. Richard Maltby, "More Sinned Against Than Sinning: The Fabrications of 'Pre-Code Cinema,'" *Senses of Cinema* Issue 29, Nov.–Dec. 2003, www.sensesofcinema.com/contents/03/29/pre_code_cinema .html (6 February 2007).

67. Leonard J. Leff and Jerrold Simmons, *The Dame in the Kimono: Hollywood Censorship, and the Production Code*, revised edition (Lexington: University Press of Kentucky, 2001), 54, and particularly, "Appendix: The Motion Picture Production Code," 285–300.

68. Memo from Russell Holman, dated 13 December 1947, *Streetcar* Files, MPAA PCA Records. Special Collections, Margaret Herrick Library, AMPAS (hereafter MPAA PCA Records, AMPAS).

69. Memo from Russell Holman, 1.

70. Memo from Russell Holman, 1–2.

71. Memo from Russell Holman, 2.

72. Memo from Russell Holman, 4.

73. Memo from Russell Holman, 5.

74. Memo from Russell Holman, 6.

75. Memo from Russell Holman, 7.

76. See, for example, Gregory Black, *The Catholic Crusade Against the Movies, 1940–1975* (Cambridge: Cambridge University Press, 1998), 109–115; Linda Constanzo Cahir, "The Artful Rerouting of *A Streetcar Named Desire*"; Leff and Simmons, *The Dame in the Kimono*, 167–189; R. Barton Palmer, "Hollywood in Crisis"; Frank Walsh, *Sin and Censorship: The Catholic Church and the Motion Picture Industry* (New Haven: Yale University Press, 1996), 244–246; Ellen Dowling, "The Derailment of *A Streetcar Named Desire*," *Literature/Film Quarterly* 9, no. 4 (1981), 233–240. The original documents are held in the *Streetcar* Production Files, WBA USC and in the *Streetcar* Files, MPAA PCA Records, AMPAS.

77. Letter from Joe Breen to Irene Selznick, dated 19 July 1949. *Streetcar* Files, MPAA PCA Records, AMPAS.

78. However, it seems that Kazan and Williams were slow to find a way to make it clear that Allan Grey's problems are something *other* than homosexuality. Letter from Breen to Jack Warner dated 13 September 1950. *Streetcar* Files MPAA PCA Records, AMPAS. Kazan wrote to Joe Breen the next day to explain the "misunderstanding." He states that he "wouldn't put the homosexuality back in the picture, if the Code had been revised last night and it was now permissible. I dont [sic] want it. I prefer the delicately suggested impotence theme; I prefer debility and weakness over any kind of suggestion of perversion." Letter from Kazan to Breen dated 14 September 1950. *Streetcar* Files, MPAA PCA Records, AMPAS. While it is possible that Kazan was honest in his statement, it seems equally plausible that he was dealing with PCA politically; by operating in a genial manner over most of the required changes, Kazan—and Williams—were in a relatively strong position when disagreements came to a head over the rape scene.

79. Letter from Williams to Breen dated 29 October 1950. *Streetcar* Files, MPAA PCA Records, AMPAS.

80. Letter from Kazan to Jack Warner dated 19 October 1950. *Streetcar*, Folder 2257, WBA USC.

81. See the letters from Charles Feldman to Kazan and Jack Warner dated 27 February 1951; cutting notes dated 15 and 26 February 1951; letter from Kazan to Jack Warner dated 1 March 1951. *Streetcar*, Folder 2257, WBA USC.

82. Letter from North to Kazan, dated 13 May 1951. Kazan Papers: Script, *Zapata* Box 25, WCA WU.

83. Letter from North to Kazan, dated 13 May 1951. Kazan Papers: Script, *Zapata* Box 25, WCA WU.

84. Letter from North to Kazan, dated 13 May 1951. Kazan Papers: Script, *Zapata* Box 25. WCA WU. NB: Due to the handwriting, it is difficult to tell whether the final word in this sentence is "respect" or "aspect," hence my use of square brackets.

85. Letter from Kazan to Breen, dated 18 May 1951. *Streetcar* Files, MPAA PCA Records, AMPAS. Letter from Kazan to Warner dated 7 December 1950, cited in Leonard J. Leff, "And Transfer to Cemetery: The Streetcars Named Desire," *Film Quarterly* 55, no. 3 (Spring 2002), 30.

86. As with a recent case in the U.K., changes to the film's soundtrack were made to appease a group(s) who had the means to judge the film harshly and thereby rate it to the dissatisfaction of the film's distributors. Sony had hoped for a 12A certificate from the BBFC (British Board of Film Classification) for Ron Howard's film *The Da Vinci Code*. The BBFC's director initially viewed a print of the film which included very little of the film's final soundtrack. When the film was screened again for the Board with the full soundtrack it was felt that the score "was making things too tense for a very young audience" and that the film's sound effects had a high "crunch factor" which "[accentuated] the violence to a degree which was unacceptable for a young audience" as a result of the mix. A 12A certificate was granted only after an agreement was made over changes to the soundtrack. Chris Hastings, "Da Vinci Code music—not the killing—is too scary for children, say censors," Telegraph Online, www.telegraph.co.uk/news/main .jhtml?xml=/news/2006/05/07/ncode07.xml (2 January 2007).

87. It is possible that the Polish and French origins of Stanley and Blanche, respectively, also had an impact on these reviewers, suggesting that both characters were likely Catholic.

88. As Gregory Black points out: "Catholics comprised only one-fifth of the population, but they were heavily concentrated in cities east of the Mississippi River. Chicago was one-half Catholic, as was Boston. New York, Buffalo, Philadelphia, Pittsburgh, Cleveland, and Detroit had sizeable Catholic populations. These cities were also important to the movie industry because they were home to huge studio-owned, first-run theatres, which exhibited their films before they were released in general run. An effective Catholic boycott in a few selected cities could thus seriously hurt the industry, which was already reeling from the financial losses suffered during America's deepening economic depression." Gregory Black, *The Catholic Crusade Against the Movies*, 22.

89. Letter from Jack Vizzard to Breen dated 5 July 1951. *Streetcar* Files. MPAA PCA Records, AMPAS.

90. Looram told Vizzard that she was risking a great deal in passing this information to him. He told Breen that "it would be curtains for [her] if any inkling of this information she has given us were to get out." Letter from Vizzard to Breen, dated 9 July 1951. *Streetcar* Files. MPAA PCA Records, AMPAS.

91. At this point Vizzard's view was that "if we can do just enough to get this picture squeaked over into a 'B,' I think that's all we can expect this time." In a handwritten PS to which he added the exclamation "Ouch!," Vizzard noted that some of Looram's reviewers had classified the film as a "D," that is, off the scale. Letter from Vizzard to Breen, dated 9 July 1951. *Streetcar* Files. MPAA PCA Records, AMPAS.

92. Albert S. Howson (Warner Bros., New York) to Vizard [sic] dated 11 July 1951. *Streetcar* Files. MPAA PCA Records, AMPAS.

93. Fathers Masterson and Little told Vizzard that they would have to "condemn this picture because of its overall gross emphasis on sex and carnality." Letter from Vizzard to Breen, dated 12 July 1951. *Streetcar* Files. MPAA PCA Records, AMPAS.

94. Letter from Vizzard to Breen, dated 12 July 1951.

95. Letter from Vizzard to Breen, dated 12 July 1951.

96. Letter from Vizzard to Breen, dated 12 July 1951.

97. Letter from Vizzard to Breen, dated 12 July 1951.

98. Letter from Vizzard to Breen, dated 12 July 1951. Emphasis as per the original. He continues: "This impression was further heightened by some trimming of the scenes we saw (by cutting down here and there on Stanley and Blanche, the character of Stella begins to come out more forcefully) as well as by the addition of a scene which I do not remember having seen when we reviewed the picture. It has to do with some lines of dialogue which reprise, in the body of the picture, the idea of the title—that desire (lust) is a Streetcar, on which you climb for a ride (to the Elysian Fields). It puts the whole thesis of the picture in sharp focus, and makes it a story about desire—sex desire, specifically—and this is the quintessence of the objection by the Legion. The illustration of the thesis is done by way of showing the savage, carnal relationship between Stella and Stanley, which is much more clear and forceful in the finished picture than it was when we saw it."

99. Warner Bros. Inter-Office Communication from McCord to Allen Bassett, dated 17 July 1951.

100. Letter from Vizzard to Breen, dated 17 July 1951. *Streetcar* Files. MPAA PCA Records, AMPAS.

101. Letter from Vizzard to Breen, dated 17 July 1951.

102. Letter from Vizzard to Breen, "Sunday" [21 July 1951]. *Streetcar* Files. MPAA PCA Records, AMPAS.

103. Letter from Vizzard to Breen, "Sunday" [21 July 1951].

104. Letter from Kazan to Steve Trilling, dated 27 July 1951. *Streetcar*, Folder: Story 2257, WBA USC.

105. Letter from Kazan to Trilling, dated 27 July 1951. *Streetcar*, Folder: Story 2257, WBA USC.

106. Letter from Kazan to Martin Quigley, dated 16 August 1951. Kazan Papers: Folder B23–F5, WCA WU.

107. Letter from Kazan to Quigley, dated 16 August 1951. Kazan Papers: Folder B23–F5, WCA WU.

108. Letter from Kazan to Quigley, dated 16 August 1951. Kazan Papers: Folder B23–F5, WCA WU.

109. Letter from Feldman to Kazan (duplication of message phoned from Bridgeport—mail confirmation), 20 August 1951. Kazan Papers: Folder B23–F5, WCA WU.

110. Letters from Quigley to Kazan, dated 20 August and 11 September 1951. Kazan Papers: Folder B23–F5, WCA WU.

111. Kazan's statement was published the following month. Elia Kazan, "Pressure Problem: Director Discusses Cuts Compelled in *A Streetcar Named Desire*," *New York Times*, 21 October 1951.

112. Kazan, "Pressure Problem."

113. Kazan, "Pressure Problem."

114. Kazan, "Pressure Problem."

115. North in Behlmer, "Alex North on *A Streetcar Named Desire*," 36. NB: Feldman's statement concerning the need to "substitute old score" for the music in the staircase sequence has the potential to confuse matters: did he mean to imply that an earlier cue existed for this scene, or did he simply expect that the simplest solution would involve playing music from another cue over this scene? North's confirmation that he rescored the scene, along with the existence of a holograph sketch for the replacement cue, suggests the latter.

116. Additional charges to certain music budget heads during this period supports this view. Budget breakdowns highlight that additional payments were made to the following budget heads after April 1951: musicians payroll and music supervisor/synchronizer. A music synchronizer (Hal Findlay) and a music supervisor (Phil Score) both had fees charged to the *Streetcar* budget in the week ending 25 August 1951, and the supervisor returned the following week with his fee charged to the trailer budget. *Streetcar* does not reappear in the Music Department's recording schedules during this period, however, though it is possible that not all of the documentation has survived.

117. North in Behlmer, "Alex North on *A Streetcar Named Desire*," 37.

118. See, for example, John S. Bak, "Criticism on *A Streetcar Named Desire*: A Bibliographic Survey, 1947–2003," *Cercles* 10 (2004): 3–32; Alan S. Chesler, "*A Streetcar Named Desire*: Twenty-Five Years of Criticism," *Notes on Mississippi Writers* 7 (1973): 44–53; Philip C. Kolin (ed.), *Confronting Tennessee Williams's* A Streetcar Named Desire: *Essays in Critical Pluralism* (Westport, CT, and London: Greenwood Press, 1993); Jac Tharpe (ed.), *Tennessee Williams: A Tribute* (Jackson: University Press of Mississippi, 1977); Philip C. Kolin, "*A Streetcar Named Desire*"; Felicia Hardison Londré, "A *Streetcar* Running Fifty Years," in Roudané (ed.), *The Cambridge Companion to Tennessee Williams*, 45–66.

119. For a selection of the reviews of the tryouts, and initial reviews of the Broadway opening, respectively, see Philip C. Kolin, "The First Critical Assessments of *A Streetcar Named Desire*: The *Streetcar* Tryouts and the Reviewers," in *Journal of Dramatic Theory and Criticism* 6, no. 1 (Fall 1991): 45–68, and Jordan Yale Miller (ed.), *Twentieth Century Interpretations of* A Streetcar Named Desire: *A Collection of Critical Essays* (Englewood Cliffs, NJ: Prentice-Hall, 1971).

120. John Chapman, "Streetcar Named Desire Sets Season's High in Acting, Writing," *The New York Daily News*, 4 December 1947. Reprinted in Miller, *Twentieth Century Interpretations*, 29–30 (29).

121. Richard Watts, Jr., "Streetcar Named Desire Is Striking Drama," *New York Post*, 4 December 1947. Reprinted in Miller, *Twentieth Century Interpretations*, 30–31 (30).

122. Irwin Shaw, "Masterpiece," *The New Republic*, Issue 117, 22 December 1947, 34–35. Reprinted in Miller, *Twentieth Century Interpretations*, 45–47 (45).

123. Vivienne Dickson, "A Streetcar Named Desire: Its Development Through the Manuscripts," in Tharpe (ed.), *Tennessee Williams: A Tribute*, 154–171. See also Sarah Boyd Johns, "Williams' Journey to 'Streetcar'": An Analysis of Pre-Production Manuscripts of 'A Streetcar Named Desire,' PhD thesis, University of South Carolina, 1980, for a fascinating account of the evolution of the play prior to production. During the play's development Williams changed the characters of both Blanche and Stanley dramatically, deciding on the tragic ending only relatively late in the process.

124. Murphy, *Tennessee Williams and Elia Kazan*, 16–63.

125. Kolin, *Confronting Tennessee Williams's* A Streetcar Named Desire, 6. In a survey written twenty years earlier, Alan S. Chesler states: "Scholars do not agree about a precise meaning, a single idea

that informs the thematic framework of *Streetcar*. They do, neverthe-less, see the play as dramatizing basic human conflicts—struggles not peculiar to twentieth-century man [or woman], but common to all hu-manity." Chesler, *A Streetcar Named Desire*, 49. In a more recent sur-vey, John S. Bak argues that "for all its attention, *Streetcar* remains a riddle no closer to being solved today than it was nearly a half-century ago." Bak, "Criticism on *A Streetcar Named Desire*," 21.

126. See Kolin, *Tennessee Williams: A Guide to Research and Performance,* 51–52, for a summary of some of these accounts. Kazan too noted the similarities. Blanche (6.13). Kazan Papers: *Streetcar* notebook, B19 F1. WCA WU.

127. Ruby Cohn, *Dialogue in American Drama* (Bloomington: Indiana University Press, 1971). Cited in Kolin, *Tennessee Williams: A Guide to Research and Performance*, 52.

128. For example, John Clum, *Acting Gay: Male Homosexuality in American Drama* (New York: Columbia University Press, 1992), 151.

129. See, for example, Thomas P. Adler, *A Streetcar Named Desire: The Moth and the Lantern* (Boston: Twayne, 1990), and C.W.E. Bigsby, *A Critical Introduction to Twentieth-Century American Drama, Vol. 2. Tennessee Williams, Arthur Miller, Edward Albee* (Cambridge: Cambridge University Press, 1984).

130. See, for example, Nancy Tischler, *Tennessee Williams: Rebel-lious Puritan* (New York: Citadel Press, 1961).

131. See, for example, Anca Vlasopolos, "Authorizing History: Victimization in *A Streetcar Named Desire*," *Theatre Journal* 38 (Oc-tober 1986): 322–338, and Pamela Ann Hanks, "Must We Acknowl-edge What We Mean? The Viewer's Role in Filmed Versions of *A Streetcar Named Desire*," *Journal of Popular Film and Television* 14, no. 3 (Fall 1986): 114–122.

132. Kolin, *Confronting Tennessee Williams's* A Streetcar Named Desire, 4.

133. Dowling, "The Derailment of *A Streetcar Named Desire*," 237.

134. Chesler, *A Steetcar Named Desire*, 45, cited in Dowling, "The Derailment of *A Streetcar Named Desire*," 238.

135. Cahir, "The Artful Rerouting of *A Streetcar Named Desire*," 72.

136. Cahir, "The Artful Rerouting of *A Streetcar Named Desire*," 76.

137. Williams in a letter to Breen. Cited in Cahir, "The Artful Re-routing of *A Streetcar Named Desire*," 75.

138. Cahir, "The Artful Rerouting of *A Streetcar Named Desire*," 76.

139. Maurice Yacowar, *Tennessee Williams and Film* (New York: Ungar, 1977), 24.

140. Gene D. Phillips, *The Films of Tennessee Williams* (Philadelphia: Art Alliance Press, and London and Toronto: Associated University Presses, 1980), 78.

141. Kazan, *A Life*, 381.

142. Letter from Kazan to Warner, dated 19 October 1950. *Streetcar*, Folder 2257, WBA USC. Emphasis as per the original.

143. Yacowar, *Tennessee Williams and Film*, 17.

144. Yacowar, *Tennessee Williams and Film*, 17.

145. As does Cahir, Yacowar sees this act as "an anticipation of Kowalski's rape." Yacowar, *Tennessee Williams and Film*, 18.

146. Yacowar, *Tennessee Williams and Film*, 20. Yacowar and others also note the coarseness of the visual pun in the shot that follows immediately after: the "forceful" and "phallic" hose cleaning the decaying rubbish from the street.

147. Christine Geraghty, "Tennessee Williams on Film: Space, Melodrama and Stardom," in Geraghty, *Now a Major Motion Picture: Film Adaptations of Literature and Drama* (Lanham, MD: Rowman & Littlefield Publishers, 2008), 73–102.

148. Geraghty, *Now a Major Motion Picture*, 75.

149. Geraghty, *Now a Major Motion Picture*, 76.

150. Geraghty, *Now a Major Motion Picture*, 77.

151. Geraghty, *Now a Major Motion Picture*, 79.

152. Geraghty, *Now a Major Motion Picture*, 79.

153. See, for example, Kristen Hatch, "Movies and the New Faces of Masculinity," in *American Cinema of the 1950s: Themes and Variations*, ed. Murray Pomerance (Oxford: Berg, 2005): 43–64.

154. Geraghty, *Now a Major Motion Picture*, 82.

155. Leff, "And Transfer to Cemetery," 32. For example, the restored version returned some of Blanche's carnality, as expressed in the difference between the Collector Scenes in the two films.

156. Leff, "And Transfer to Cemetery," 33.

157. Leff, "And Transfer to Cemetery," 31.

158. Leff, "And Transfer to Cemetery," 31.

Chapter 4

1. North, cited in Henderson, *Alex North, Film Composer*, 98.

2. No complete recordings of the Broadway production exist. The brief exploration of the play's music in this chapter draws primarily on archival research, including the drafts and fragments that demonstrate the development of *Streetcar* prior to production, then rehearsal scripts, cue lists for the production's music and sound effects, and scores of the play's music not previously considered. Brenda Murphy provides a detailed account of the musical changes. Hers is an excellent account, though she mistakenly attributes authorship of the play's music to North, likely following Kazan's account of the play's production as published in his autobiography, *A Life*, 339. A detailed discussion of the play's music can be found in Davison, "The Sound of *Streetcar* on Broadway: The Debut Stage Production of *A Streetcar Named Desire*" (forthcoming).

3. Williams's name for the club—The Four Deuces—may well have been influenced by The Three Deuces club on 52nd Street in New York. The club was central to the dissemination of bebop: Dizzy Gillespie and Charlie Parker played there for several months in 1945 in a quintet formed by Gillespie. Alyn Shipton, *A New History of Jazz* (London and New York: Continuum, 2001), 469–479.

4. The "reading version" of the play (New Directions, 1947) is the closest in published form to these early versions by Williams, though, as Murphy notes, among the key differences are a number of changes to the use of music.

5. Nick Moschovakis, "Tennessee Williams's American Blues: From the Early Manuscripts through *Menagerie*," *Tennessee Williams Annual Review* 7 (2005), para. 2, www.tennesseewilliamsstudies .org/archives/2005/02moschovakis.htm (27 April 2007). See also Rachel van Duyvenbode, "Darkness Made Visible: Miscegenation, Masquerade and the Signified Racial Other in Tennessee Williams' *Baby Doll* and *A Streetcar Named Desire*," in *Journal of American Studies* 35, no. 2 (2001), 203–215. Van Duyvenbode interprets Stanley as a disguised racial other via his ethnic marginalization as immigrant: Williams's "veiled fantas[y] of the dark Africanist other," a view supported by Williams's instructions for the play's music. Although Blanche's "whiteness" is exaggerated, in the tradition of Gothic horror—through her name, her virginal pose, and with "death, sterility and debased/ perverse sexuality"—Stanley's disguise both affirms "racial typecasting and seek[s] to break down the permanence of racial boundaries."

Stanley relinquishes his ethnic identity in favor of Americanness, and
thus attempts to present himself as white, but Blanche reminds him of
his inferiority, and thus must be destroyed. This displacement of
Stanley's whiteness and Stella's "overt sexual desire" invert "racial
[...] roles," and those of gender in Stella's case. Van Duyvenbode,
"Darkness Made Visible," 207, 212.

    6. Moschovakis, "Tennessee Williams's American Blues," para.
50.

    7. Eunice converses with a black woman as Blanche approaches.
Williams, *Streetcar*, Scene 1, 3.

    8. "[The] blue piano catches . . . the miserable unusual human side
of the girl which is beneath her frenetic duplicity, her trickery, lies, etc.
It tells, it emotionally reminds you what all the fireworks are caused
by." Elia Kazan, "Notebook for *A Streetcar Named Desire*," 371.

    9. Robert Downing, "Streetcar Conductor: Some Notes from Back-
stage," *Theatre Annual* 8 (1950): 28–29.

    10. The Novachord was only in production for a short time be-
tween 1939 and 1942: just over a thousand were made. Although initially very popular, they were soon considered unreliable, too complicated for the time. Few Novachords remain in working order. For
further information see Phil Cirocco, The Novachord Restoration Project, www.discretesynthesizers.com/nova/intro.htm (17 June 2008).

    11. The Novachord demanded a specialist performer. For the New
York run of *Streetcar*, this was Max Marlin. For more on Marlin's role
in the score for the play's debut production, see Davison, "The Sound
of *Streetcar* on Broadway."

    12. After it was revealed at the World's Fair in New York in 1939,
the Novachord was heard both in theatrical productions on Broadway—
Paul Bowles's score for Rostand's *Cyrano de Bergerac* (1946), North's
score for *The Innocents* (1950)—and in film scores in Hollywood—
Franz Waxman's score for *Rebecca* (1940), Erich Wolfgang Korngold's score for *The Sea Wolf* (1941). Although the Novachord *can*
sound similar to the theremin in some of its settings, it is quite different: where the Novachord is a keyboard instrument, the theremin's
sound is produced via the placing of the player's hands between two
metal antennae, with one hand generating pitch, and the other, amplitude. Through the history of film scoring, the unusual electronic sounds
of both instruments have been used to indicate "otherworldliness,"
though in the case of the Novachord, this has perhaps tended more towards the ghostly and the supernatural—the body not present—than
towards science fiction.

13. The composer/arranger of these cues for the production labeled them "Varsuviana." However, I use the spelling "Varsouviana" throughout, as used by Williams in the reading version of the play. The Warner Bros. cue sheets use "Varsouvienne," which I use only when quoting directly from these documents. According to Maurice J. E. Brown, it may be spelled thus: Varsovienne and Varsoviana. See Maurice J. E. Brown, "Varsovienne (Fr.; It. varsoviana)," *Grove Music Online*, ed. L. Macy, www.grovemusic.com (5 July 2006).

14. A period commentator suggests that the Varsouviana is a "rather boisterous sort of performance, more suitable for the casino than the private ball-room," which fits Williams's plot neatly, since the characters "danced the Varsouviana" at the Moon Lake Casino. See [n.a.] *Ball-room Dancing Without a Master, and Complete Guide to the Etiquette, Toilet, Dress and Management of the Ball-room; With All the Principal Dances in Popular Use* (New York: Hurst and Co., c. 1872), 47–48. *An American Ballroom Companion: Dance Instruction Manuals* project developed by the Music Division of the Library of Congress provides short video clips of reconstructions of a number of dances from the Renaissance period through to Ragtime, including the Varsouviana (clip number 59). The clips may be viewed at the following website: http://memory.loc.gov/ammem/dihtml/divideos.html (6 July 2006). Instructions for two versions of the dance's steps can be found in Betty Casey, *Dancing Across Texas* (Austin: University of Texas Press, 1985), pp. 97–103.

15. Maurice J. E. Brown, "Varsovienne (Fr.; It. varsoviana)." Brown adds that "its name—from the French form of 'Warsaw'—was intended to remove the exotic connotations of 'mazurka.'"

16. Edward Ferrero, *The Art of Dancing, Historically Illustrated* (New York: Edward Ferrero, 1859), 147.

17. In an early draft of the play, Williams referred to the Varsouviana as Var Sou Vienna: the waltz of Vienna. See Johns, "Williams' Journey to 'Streetcar,'" 82, and Dickson, "A Streetcar Named Desire," 166. The song, "Put Your Little Foot," is one of several suggested as suitable for dance by resources for traditional and folk musicians, such as Andrew Kuntz, *The Fiddler's Companion: A Descriptive Index of North American and British Isles Music for the Folk Violin and Other Instruments*, http://ibiblio.org/fiddlers/index.html (accessed via "V" in the Alphabetical Files) (5 July 2006).

18. A copy of the recording is held by the Rodgers and Hammerstein Archives of Recorded Sound, New York Public Library for the Performing Arts. The recording was made at the New Orleans Penny Arcade. Williams's co-performers on the disc are introduced as Joanna

Albus and John Mehegan: the stage manager from the Broadway production of *Streetcar* and the pianist. Mehegan is best known today as an
important jazz theorist and pedagogue. See, for example, his series on
jazz improvisation, the first of which is *Tonal and Rhythmic Principles*
(New York: Watson-Guptill Publications, 1959). He taught improvisation at the Juilliard School in New York.

19. The jazz that was selected and arranged, and in at least two
cases composed or improvised, was representative of music associated
with New Orleans. See Davison, "The Sound of *Streetcar* on Broadway."

20. See Davison, "The Sound of *Streetcar* on Broadway."

21. Murphy, *Tennessee Williams and Elia Kazan*, 31.

22. Several of the Varsouviana fragments overlay sequences of
North's score.

23. Thus North almost retained copyright of his music for the film
by accident, due to an oversight by the publisher, Warner Bros.' Music
Publishers Holding Company (MPHC). See letter to Herman Starr,
MPHC dated 27 June 1952. *Streetcar*, Folder 1507, WBA USC.

24. According to North, they would go to the beach and "walk and
discuss music and the approach." North in Behlmer, "Alex North on *A
Streetcar Named Desire*," 36.

25. North in Behlmer, "Alex North on *A Streetcar Named Desire*,"
36.

26. North in Behlmer, "Alex North on *A Streetcar Named Desire*,"
36.

27. Kazan, *A Life*, 381–382. After expressing his dissatisfaction
with the musical approach for *Panic in the Streets* (it was scored by
Alfred Newman), Kazan states: "Next time! I said. And on *Zapata* I did
better." Of course, *Zapata* was also scored by North, but several
months after he scored *Streetcar* (ibid., 382).

28. Cue sheet, dated 10 May 1951. *Streetcar*, Folder 1507, WBA
USC.

29. This explains why only the sketches for cues to Reels 6
through to 14 survive, alongside those for the Main Title and the replacement cue for Reel 5: Part 3 (Music Special Collections, UCLA).
This adds further weight to the idea that the replacement cue was composed after the score was already complete (very probably during August 1951). It was not unusual to compose a film's title cue after com-
pleting the remainder of a score.

30. Timesheets for Maurice de Packh, Music Department, Arrangers 1951, Box 074A, WBA USC. *The Travelers* was also a Warner

Bros. picture. It was directed by Raoul Walsh, scored by David But-
tolph, and was also known as *Along the Great Divide* (1951).

31. De Packh's orchestrations begin with Reel 5: Part 4 then R5:
P3 and continue through to the end of the film.

32. Requisitions for the copyists who worked on *Streetcar* are
dated: 13, 20, and 27 January 1951; 3, 10, 17, and 24 February 1951;
and 31 March 1951 for the trailer. Music Department, Copyists 1951.
Warner Bros. Archive. Copyists who worked on the score included:
Charles Eggett, Jaro Churain, Simon Bucharoff, Leo Damiani, Rex
Dunn, Arthur Grier, Einar Nilson, Joseph Weisenfreund.

33. Timesheets for Musicians, Music Department, Recording 1951,
Box 074A, WBA USC. It is possible that the score was also recorded
on other dates, but that the timesheets have since been lost.

34. Letter from Kazan to North, dated 13 March 1951. North Correspondence files, *Streetcar*, AMPAS.

35. Letter from Kazan to North, dated 13 March 1951. North Correspondence files, *Streetcar*, AMPAS.

36. Letter from North to Kazan, dated 28 March 1951. Kazan Papers: *Zapata* correspondence files (B25–F3). WCA WU.

37. These recordings were made in July 1951, conducted by Ray
Heindorf.

38. North in Raksin, "The Subject Is Film Music," 13.

39. In the Broadway production, a ten-minute intermission followed scene 4, and a five-minute intermission followed scene 6. Play-
bill, *A Streetcar Named Desire*.

40. North cited in Frank Lewin, "*A Street Car Named Desire*,"
Film Music 11, no. 3 (Jan.–Feb. 1952), 13.

41. North cited in Frank Lewin, "*A Street Car Named Desire*," 13.

42. North in Raksin, "The Subject Is Film Music," 13.

43. North cited in Lewin, "*A Street Car Named Desire*," 13.

44. North cited in Lewin, "*A Street Car Named Desire*," 13. Years
later, North took the same approach in his score for *Cleopatra*.

45. North cited in Lewin, "*A Street Car Named Desire*," 13. Similar situations can be heard in the theatrical score for *Death of a Salesman*.

46. The same echo and reverberation are applied to dialogue spoken by Stanley and the Matron towards the end of the film, when
Blanche sees that the man who has come to take her away is not Shep
Huntleigh. Here it indicates the extent of her mental fragility in the
moments before her breakdown. After the revelation scene with Mitch,
Blanche retreats into her powerful imagination, and we hear the voices
of her friends distantly murmuring at an imaginary ball that she con-

jures, along with the music "Goodnight Ladies" to indicate the end of the evening's dancing.

47. In the play, this is the same night that Blanche discovers Allan in bed with another man. As discussed in chapter 3, direct reference to homosexuality was removed from the film script, but Allan's suicide and the Varsouviana remain, along with the sound of the gunshot that closes several of the fragments.

48. Indeed, if her marriage to Allan had been happy and had endured, she may well not have returned to Belle Reve to nurse dying relatives, and would not have needed to seek comfort and protection in the arms of strangers.

49. Rather than celeste, Ross Care hears the Varsouviana played on a Novachord throughout, as in the play production. This may well be the case. Although the conductor score and parts cue in these interpolations on celeste, the instrumentation has clearly been changed in a number of cases through the score, likely at the recording. These interpolations would have been recorded ahead of the score, however. The indication of celeste perhaps refers to the kind of sound the Novachord was to produce. Ross Care, "Hot Spell: Alex North's Film Score for *A Streetcar Named Desire*," in *Performing Arts Annual* (1989): 4–23.

50. The choice of muted trumpet here is perhaps significant, given its indelible association with jazz. It is possible that North is here making a subtle comment that emphasizes a darker, more predatory reading of Blanche's "mouth-watering" line.

51. The sequence for this B section of the Varsouviana is: I^Δ IV^Δ IV^6 V^7 IV^6 V^7 IV, iii, ii, I. This slide down through the scale diminishes the sense of affirmative closure.

52. Rehearsal Script, Kazan Papers: *Streetcar* (The Play), B19–F4. WCA WU. Music and Sound Cue Sheets. Sent with memo from Joanna Albus to Irving Schneider, dated 26 December 1947. Box 45, Folder 38. Irene M. Selznick Collection (#443), Howard Gotlieb Archival Research Center at Boston University.

53. Malden, who played Mitch to both Leigh's screen Blanche and Jessica Tandy's stage performance, noted that Tandy played the scene quite differently to Leigh: where Leigh played it in a sensual manner, Tandy played it as a schoolmistress. Malden on DVD Commentary to Special Edition DVD of *A Streetcar Named Desire* (Warner Bros., 2006).

54. It should be noted that the section of *Blanche and Mitch* with which the Varsouviana is juxtaposed is the most harmonically divergent of the theme's structure: the last eight bars of the B section. See chapter 5 for a more detailed analysis of this cue.

55. These bars can be heard on the re-recording of the score conducted by Jerry Goldsmith for Varese Sarabande (see appendix). This
recording includes bars, and in one case an entire cue, written by North
but excised from the film's release print. In places the instrumentation
used on the recording of the score for the film has been changed, however (R5: P3, for example).

56. Another small jazz band provides the music for dancing at the
Casino.

57. North in Lewin, "*A Street Car Named Desire*," 13.

58. North in Lewin, "*A Street Car Named Desire*," 13. He adds
modestly that "I don't say this was entirely successful, but it was worth
trying."

59. Billy Rose initially asked for $10,000 for use of the song, but
the rate McLaughlin finally negotiated was half that. The amount was
split three ways between Rose, Harold Arlen, and Yip Harburg. By
contrast, $3,100 was paid to Harms and Remick for all of the other
source music rights. Due to the costs involved, during August 1950
there was discussion of substituting "Paper Moon" with another song:
Fred Coots's "You Go to My Head." See Music Department Files,
Folder 2069A, USC WBA.

60. Jack Vizzard to Joe Breen dated 17 July 1951. *Streetcar* Files,
MPAA PCA Records, AMPAS.

61. North in Palmer, "Film Music Profile: Alex North," 28–29.

62. North in Behlmer, "Alex North on *A Streetcar Named Desire*,"
36.

63. See, for example, David Butler, *Jazz Noir: Listening to Music
from* Phantom Lady *to* The Last Seduction (Westport, CT: Praeger,
2002); Simon Frith, *Performing Rites: On the Value of Popular Music*
(Oxford: Oxford University Press, 1996); Richard Dyer, *White: Essays
on Race and Culture* (London: Routledge, 1997).

64. Simon Frith summarizes such views thus: "Because 'the African' is more primitive, more 'natural' than the European, then African
music must be more directly in touch with the body, with unsymbolized
and unmediated sensual states and expectations. And given that African
musics are most obviously different from European musics in their uses
of rhythm, then rhythm must be how the primitive, the sexual, is expressed." Frith, *Performing Rites*, 127.

65. See Butler, *Jazz Noir*.

66. Mervyn Cooke, *A History of Film Music* (Cambridge: Cam-
bridge University Press, 2008), 215. See also Cooke's "Anatomy of a
Movie: Duke Ellington and 1950s Film Scoring," in *Thriving on a Riff:
Jazz and Blues Influences in African American Literature and Film*,

edited by Graham Lock and David Murray (New York: Oxford University Press, 2009).

67. Speaking of jazz, Copland felt "[he] had done all [he] could with the idiom," by the 1930s. Aaron Copland, "Composer from Brooklyn," 1939, cited in Crist, *Music for the Common Man*, 4.

68. North, "Composer Sends Message from Camp," *Hartford Times*, 12 April 1943, cited in Henderson, *Alex North*, 31.

69. North in Thomas, *Music for the Movies*, 182.

70. North's *Pastime Suite* for clarinet with piano accompaniment (in five movements) was also published in 1948. Intended for student clarinettists, the work is also influenced by swing. The publisher states that "*Pastime Suite* was written to provide for the clarinet a set of simple, melodic and rhythmic pieces in quasi-jazz style" [inside flyleaf]. Mills Music, 1948.

71. Cooke, *A History of Film Music*, 215.

72. Indeed, North noted that orchestrator Herbert Spencer described his music for the staircase scene as written in "early Duke Ellington style." North in Behlmer, "Alex North on *A Streetcar Named Desire*," 36. Spencer is best known for his lengthy collaboration with film composer John Williams.

73. These players were Ziggy Elman (trumpet), Babe Russin (tenor sax), Buddy Cole (piano), and Nick Fatool (drums). Both Elman and Russin played with the Benny Goodman orchestra and Tommy Dorsey's band before heading their own orchestras and bands in the 1940s. Cole worked with Bing Crosby and Nat King Cole. Fatool also played with Benny Goodman and a number of other bands between periods as a studio musician.

74. Williams would likely have heard this revivalist style when he began to write *Streetcar* in New Orleans and New York in the mid-1940s.

75. None of these distinctions are clear-cut, however. For example, particularly in its earliest manifestations, several members of Ellington's orchestra emphasized their New Orleans heritage and/or that of Chicago in the character of their sound; such players included Sidney Bechet and Barney Bigard on clarinet, and bassist Wellman Braud. Also, in works such as "Mood Indigo," for example, Ellington created new sound worlds from a pared-down wind and brass line-up that echoed that of the New Orleans sound, albeit inverting the traditional lines of the players. Shipman, *A New History of Jazz*, 272–274.

76. Cooke, *A History of Film Music*, 216.

77. See Caryl Flinn's *Strains of Utopia: Gender, Nostalgia, and Hollywood Film Music* (Princeton, NJ: Princeton University Press, 1992), for a more wide-ranging study that addresses the issues of nostalgia in relation to film music.

78. Examples include Bill Challis's arrangements for the enlarged Paul Whiteman band of the late 1920s, one of the bands North cites as being among his favorites of the period. See Gunther Schuller, "Arrangement," *Grove Music Online*, ed. L. Macy, www.grovemusic.com (19 June 2008).

79. Review, *Variety*, 14 June 1951. My emphasis.

80. Letter from Sam Goldwyn to North, dated 18 May 1951. North Correspondence Files, *Streetcar*, AMPAS.

81. Lewin, "*A Street Car Named Desire.*" See also letter from Frank Lewin to North, dated 26 January 1952. North Correspondence Files, AMPAS.

82. Lewin, "*A Street Car Named Desire*," 19.

83. Lewin, "*A Street Car Named Desire*," 19.

84. Lewin, "*A Street Car Named Desire*," 20.

85. Lewin, "*A Street Car Named Desire*," 19.

86. Ken Sutak, "The Return of A Streetcar Named Desire," (1/3) *Pro Musica Sana* 3, no. 1 (Spring, 1974): 4–10; (2/3) *Pro Musica Sana* 3, no. 4 (Winter 1974–75): 9–15; (3/3) *Pro Musica Sana* 4, no. 2 (1976): 18–24.

87. Sutak, "The Return of A Streetcar Named Desire" (3/3), 22.

88. Sutak, "The Return of A Streetcar Named Desire" (3/3), 23.

89. Sutak, "The Return of A Streetcar Named Desire" (3/3), 24.

90. Sutak, "The Return of A Streetcar Named Desire" (3/3), 24.

Chapter 5

1. The exception here is the source music heard when Mitch takes Blanche to Lake Pontchartrain to dance, an hour into the film.

2. Though Care, too, points to the importance of the rocking semitone triplet figure in North's music for Stanley. Ross Care, "Hot Spell," 9.

3. See, for example, Kazan's characterization of Stanley and Blanche in the notebook in which he outlined his preparation for the play, particularly 9.19 and 6.16. Kazan Papers: *Streetcar* notebook, B19 F1. WCA WU.

4. In a video version of the (re-edited) 1951 version of the film distributed by Twentieth Century-Fox, the additional bars are replaced by

Alfred Newman's Fox fanfare. In the original/restored version, the "Warner Bros. Pictures presents" card is underscored by additional bars that feature the cue's first melody, here scored more brashly for brass, heralding the coming film. The function is similar to that of the Fox fanfare, albeit with a musical fragment specific to the film rather than the studio. It seems likely this brief introduction was added at a late stage. As it appears in the conductor score, the cue begins two bars later with the accompaniment figure heard alongside presentation of the title card listing the play's prizes and awards. Here though, the cue opens with the cue's first melodic entry played slowly and stridently by upper brass. The accompaniment, an accented and sustained low brass chord ($F\sharp m^{add9}$ in an open voicing) is delayed until partway through the second beat. Here it is only at this point that the pitches of the descending appoggiatura figure are understood as a flatted fifth falling to the fourth (C–B). The pitches are then reiterated as the melody is developed briefly: a descent over the sustained chord, landing on the seventh (E). In the next bar, tucked between the sustained low chord and the theme above, mid-range and upper wind interject a repeated harmonized quaver figure preceded by grace notes.

5. There is some metrical instability in the introductory bars, and the agile string line heard over the steam train sequence suggests a quicker meter. The final boogie-woogie piano entry ushers in a change of tempo.

6. Philip Tagg and Bob Clarida, *Ten Little Title Tunes: Towards a Musicology of the Mass Media* (New York and Montreal: Mass Media Music Scholars' Press, 2003): 540–606. A group of subjects who had no prior knowledge of the cue were asked to record the "visual-verbal associations" (VVAs) elicited by the music; this cue was one of ten title tunes the subjects were asked to respond to. The goal of the project was to identify concrete links between the musical elements, or "musemes," and the responses gathered, via musical analysis and semiotics. The *Streetcar* cue generated more VVAs than any of the other nine title tunes, and more unanimity among respondents' VVAs. Among the highest-scoring of the VVAs were: big city, dramatic, dark, clubs, threatening, slums, USA urban, smoke, sweat, tense, suspicion, fighting, heavy, loneliness, melancholy, street girl (547–548). Although the cue is short, it consists of excessive audible variety, and thus produces a relative plenitude of possible VVA triggers. That this diversity results in comparatively coherent (rather than incoherent) responses from the subjects highlights the compatibility of the VVA triggers. Given too that the VVA most frequently offered by respondents was "film," Tagg and Clarida's study goes some way towards demonstrating the "ability

of 'classic' scoring to elicit numerous tightly focused associations."
Tagg and Clarida, *Ten Little Title Tunes*, 554.

7. In the additional bars that underscore the distributors' card prior
to the start of the cue proper, an even stronger emphasis on the two-
note appoggiatura-figure is created through delaying the entry of the
accompaniment (though this also makes recognition of the tritone retro-
spective). See note 4 above.

8. Towards the end of bar 2, the melody emphasizes the neighbor
notes of the seventh and ninth before passing through the root of the
chord to the fifth at the start of the next bar.

9. In his sketch for the main title, North marks this solo trumpet
line for "Sullivan," suggesting an awareness of the Warner Bros. studio
orchestra's lead trumpet player, Larry Sullivan.

10. Kazan stated that he "stole" the opening from *Anna Karenina*.
Kazan, *A Life*, 384.

11. See note 6 above.

12. The main title cue may well have been composed last by
North; certainly it was the last to be orchestrated. Such a practice was
not unusual, since main title music often functioned as an "overture,"
introducing several of a score's key themes.

13. The cue begins with the last two bars of the introduction, then
matches the material of *Belle Reve* for the next fourteen bars, with the
addition of a filler bar at this point. A close variant of the semiquaver
theme is then heard, after which North produced additional material for
the remainder of the cue.

14. The first two key changes of *Belle Reve* are not marked as
changes of key signature in the conductor score of *Belle Reve Reflections*: accidentals are used instead.

15. That the cue is preceded by an exchange between Blanche and
Stanley concerning the loss of the estate adds weight to this interpretation.

16. The triads are all in second inversion, as are those in the celeste
part, where the absence of passing chords emphasizes functionality
more directly.

17. Neither the sketch for the cue nor the conductor score indicates
a key signature; accidentals are used throughout. In terms of vertical
harmony, minor triads on C♯, F♯, and G♯ are the most prominent, but the
focus of the lines is horizontal.

18. The exception is B natural, which is incorporated into the leap
to C natural, after B♭.

19. The fact that it is a bus ticket, rather than a train ticket, adds in-
sult to injury for Blanche.

20. Note the disorientating camera angle here: Blanche appears upside-down, via an overhead shot.

21. The repeated progression is: i — $^\flat$vii — IIc — V, with a sharp ninth added to the first, third, and fourth chords; the second chord is a sharp eleventh.

22. Here enriched chords of i $^\flat$vii VI V replace the opening i $^\flat$vii ii V.

23. Although eight- and ten-bar blues forms exist, in this case melodic and harmonic elements suggest that the twelve-bar format is still the point-of-reference here, despite elisions and contortions to the framework. Indeed, the disruption of formal symmetries through the insertion or elision of odd bars is typical of Ellington.

24. The tenor sax sounds an octave lower than the score suggests.

25. That the flute here plays the motif from the opening of *Stan* (R2: P3)—which would be the expected continuation of the restated cue at this point (*Stan*, R2: P3, bar 20)—initially conceals that the repeat of *Stan* has been interrupted.

26. *Stan* (R2: P3), bb. 29–32 and *Stan and Stella* (R5: P3), bb. 41–44.

27. Indeed, North's sketch for the cue states explicitly that bars from R4: P1b should be used. The first bars written out in full on the sketch are the last eight bars of the B section; i.e., from the entry of the celeste.

28. In the sketch for the cue, North writes "celeste in sus. Seeps thru love music."

29. The last eight bars of the B section are harmonized differently in this cue. The eight-bar alternation between Ab^Δ and Db^9 continues, but here with an alternation between cluster chords which then move through altered seventh and ninth chords on G, ending on sustained augmented chords on C extended over several bars as the Varsouviana is completed.

30. Here the chords are Bbm^7 F^{7sus4} Gb^Δ F^Δ. Both cues open with chord iv in F minor and return to the tonic, though in this cue a major chord on $\flat$II replaces reference to the dominant.

31. Muted horns sustain major thirds on F, then G♯, then G. Beneath this bassoons play a syncopated rising quaver figure, also in thirds, suggesting harmonies a minor or major second away from the horns: F♯, A, then F.

32. See *Birthday Party* (R9: P2 and R10: P1), bb. 16–17.

33. The score indicates a hitpoint here.

34. The third cue (R10: P2) is combined with *Blanche's Solitude* (R10: P3) for the fifth track on the Capitol album, which North entitled

"Della Robia Blue," the shade of the jacket Blanche is to leave the apartment wearing at the end of the film.

35. *Birthday Party* (R10: P2), b. 21. This chord might best be described as $Ebm^{\Delta 13}$.

36. Where melodrama is understood as "the technique of using short passages of music in alternation with or accompanying the spoken word to heighten its dramatic effect, often found within opera, or as an independent genre, or as a sporadic effect in spoken drama." Anne Dhu Shapiro, "Melodrama," *Grove Music Online*, ed. L. Macy, www.grove music.com (18 June 2008). Music accompanies the spoken word in the case of Blanche's *Revelation* monologue. As Shapiro highlights, the term *melodrama* has "lost its musical meaning, through its association with the popular Victorian dramatic entertainment, with its sentimental and sensational plots and life-and-death rescues characteristic of that genre."

37. The theme continues, an octave lower, as she reaches "rock of the world."

38. The pitches of these clashing triads can also be understood as generated from a single octatonic scale (on C), but such an interpretation does not fit with the pitch-content of the theme. The registration of the triads seems also to assert distance and difference rather than unity.

39. Metric instability is generated by a 3/4 bar here (bar 28), though from the roughness of the "edit," it seems likely that a beat was excised as a consequence of image editing, rather than removed as the result of a musical decision.

40. Here I retain the bar numbering as it appears in the conductor score for the sake of clarity. As heard in the film, however, the following bars have been excised: bb. 37–38, 46, 57–58.

41. This scene was edited after the first previews: bars 33–56 are cut from the film version. The cue is sixty-two bars long in both North's sketches and the conductor score.

42. At first this line appears to establish an octatonic scale—that is, a scale generated by alternating whole tones and semitones—though this is disrupted during the sextuplet semiquavers of the fourth bar.

43. Rehearsal figure 95, Stravinsky's *Petrushka*. There is also a clear distinction, however: in *Petrushka* the clarinets outline major triads a tritone apart. Considered for some years as an exemplar of bitonality or polytonality, Arthur Berger then highlighted that the pitches of both triads were part of the octatonic scale on C. Drawing on the work of Berger, and also Richard Taruskin and Pieter van den Toorn, Kenneth Gloag suggests that C and F♯ operate as poles of attraction, and that "what is most relevant is that these triads [...] are at one and

the same time octatonic subsets and residual emblematic reflections of common-practice tonality. They are now conceptually distinct from the functions and purpose that gave a precise meaning to such elements within an earlier tonal context." Kenneth Gloag, "Russian Rites: *Petrushka, The Rite of Spring,* and *Les Noces,*" in *The Cambridge Companion to Stravinsky* (Cambridge: Cambridge University Press, 2003), 83. Stravinsky's *Petrushka* was reissued in a revised orchestration in the United States in 1947. North may thus have reacquainted himself with the work at that time.

44. This sudden jump is at least partially explained by excision of several bars from the film at this point: the music track is cut from the second half of bar 9 through to bar 16.

45. The first trumpet line is also marked for Sullivan, indicating that North had at least one specific player in mind.

46. The bassoon figure refers to the bassoon entry heard in bars 1–2 in the first of the *Birthday Party* cues (R9: P2 and R10: P1), later developed as per the strings in bar 19 of the next of this suite of cues (R10: P2).

47. The complex chord comprises Dm^7, C^Δ, and triads on F♯ and E. *Seduction* (R13: P1), b. 64.

48. Of this cue, North stated in interview that "there were pauses of about four or five seconds in between dialogue, where I brought on these raucous trumpets [...] and they were dissonant. And the music built and built and built, these trumpets, in just the phrase that was consistent with what I felt about the sex drive of Stanley, justified these little statements interspersed between dialogue. And, [...] thanks to Ray Heindorf, who had years and years of experience of timing the phrase, so that particular jazz statement was made at the right time." Here, he refers to the fact that Heindorf conducted the recording of the score. North in Behlmer, "Alex North on *A Streetcar Named Desire,*" 37.

49. However, since each of these chords shares two pitches with another, although the resultant complex chord is discordant, it is perhaps not as discordant as one might assume. *Seduction* (R13: P1), b. 61.

50. This chord appears to combine Fm/A bass with F♯^{7} and Bm. *Doctor* (R14: P1), bar 16.

51. In the film, several bars are cut from North's original cue for this sequence (*Affirmation,* R14: P2): from the last beat of bar 23 through to the first three of 25.

52. See, for example, Leff, "And Transfer to Cemetery," and Cahir, "The Artful Rerouting of *A Streetcar Named Desire.*"

53. Letter from Vizzard to Breen, "Sunday" [21 July 1951]. *Streetcar* Files. MPAA PCA Records, AMPAS.

54. The two-bar phrase on B—bars 51 and 52—was removed from *Seduction* (R13: P1); the rising sequence here moves from A to B♭, then on to C, C♯, and D, rather than rising from A to D chromatically. In addition, the third and fourth beats of bar 49 were also removed; this gives the impression that a 4/4 bar has been replaced by one in 2/4. The cuts to the score were made to accommodate those made to the image to shorten sequences of Stanley's "leering" and the removal of his line, "Maybe you wouldn't be bad to interfere with."

55. Specifically, the Dirge B segment would have been lost, removing the melodic, timbral and registral bridge between the previous section and the next, along with the start of the alternating tonic/dominant bass and its chromatic slides (bb. 48–54).

56. The two-bar transition (bb. 35–36), heard as Blanche closes the door to the flower seller in the original/restored version, was cut, along with the first two bars of the eight-bar recapitulation and extension of Dirge A that follow, and which start the previous section, *Flores.*

57. North in Behlmer, "Alex North on *A Streetcar Named Desire*," 36. NB: Feldman's statement concerning the need to "substitute old score" for the music in the staircase sequence has the potential to confuse matters: did he mean to imply that an earlier cue existed for this scene, or did he simply expect that the simplest solution would involve playing music from another cue over this scene? North's confirmation that he rescored the scene, along with the existence of a holograph sketch for the replacement cue, suggests the latter.

58. The numbering of the bars for the replacement cue refers to the conductor score for the cue. This excludes the re-used material from the original R5: P3 cue, which was already recorded.

59. Additionally, rather than fearing for Stella's safety, as Blanche's rush to her side implies in the original version of the staircase scene, here, given the comparative chasteness of the couple's display of their love, her hasty descent to the apartment below seems motivated by loneliness, and the fear that Stella's primary loyalty is to Stanley rather than to her sister.

Afterword

1. See "AFI's 100 Years of Film Scores," www.afi.com/tv events/100years/scores.aspx (31 January 2008).

2. The tracks from the original soundtrack recording conducted by Heindorf in July 1951 have been reissued on CD, most often also featuring extracts from some of Max Steiner's scores: Capitol Records

CDP0777 7 95597 2 5 (1992), DRG Records 19090 (2006). A more recent recording conducted by Jerry Goldsmith, produced by Robert Townson, is available on Varese Sarabande LC6083.

3. See letter from Wright to North, dated 22 October 1952 in *Streetcar* Ballet Correspondence (28–413), North Correspondence Files, AMPAS. Wright's piano sketch for the ballet is held in the Valerie Bettis Estate Music Scores, at The New York Public Library for the Performing Arts, New York City. The ballet was first performed by the Slavenska-Franklin Ballet in Montreal in October 1952, and by the Ballet Theatre in October 1954. For reviews, see John Martin, "Ballet Company Stages 'Streetcar,'" *New York Times*, 9 December 1952; Douglas Watt, "Back to New Orleans," *New Yorker*, 20 December 1952.

4. North made the Piano Sequence arrangements at the urging of the Motion Picture Holding Corporation when they realized that they were in danger of losing the music's copyright. In North's agreement with the MPHC, clause 6 stated that if no music from the score is published within a year, then copyright of the score would revert to North (Agreement with MPHC, dated 11 December 1950). The MPHC persuaded North to extend this period to eighteen months, during which time the Sequences were published by Witmark. *Streetcar*, Folder 1507, WBA USC. A recording of the piano suite can be heard on the album *American Piano*, Volume 1 (Premier Recordings B00000205L), played by Alan Mandel.

5. *Great Movie Themes*, The Norman Luboff Choir (RCA Victor LP–2895).

6. These may be found in *Streetcar*, Folder 19–267, AMPAS.

7. For a detailed examination of Kazan's role in the "naming of names," see Victor Navasky, *Naming Names* (New York: Viking Press, 1980).

8. The episode is the second of the fourth season, and first aired on the Fox network on 1 October 1992 in the United States.

9. The play became a musical for the show because, although the *The Simpsons*' producers were not authorized to use much of Williams's dialogue, their lawyer argued that songs based on the play *would* be allowed.

10. It premiered at the *San Francisco Opera* on 19 September 1998.

11. Previn cited in Barry Paris, "A Knight at the Opera," *Vanity Fair* (September 1998), 226.

12. I am not alone in the view that this oft-cited quotation from Previn is disingenuous towards arguably the most musical and lyrical

of Williams's plays. See, for example, Alan Rich, "Opera: 'Streetcar Named Desire,'" *Variety* (28 September–4 October 1998): 191, also cited in Philip C. Kolin, *Williams:* A Streetcar Named Desire *(Plays in Production)*, (Cambridge: Cambridge University Press, 2000), 167. Rich sees "so much music implicit in the melancholy prose of . . . *Streetcar* that the notion of adding more, by turning the play into an actual opera, becomes an exercise in redundancy."

13. Previn in Jesse Hamlin, "Taking *Streetcar* to the Opera," *San Francisco Chronicle*, "Datebook," 6 September 1998, also cited in Kolin, *Williams:* A Streetcar Named Desire, 168. I agree wholeheartedly with Previn's sentiment here, though I am a little surprised by his apparent naivete, given that he worked as a musical director, composer, and arranger in Hollywood for many years.

14. Leff, "And Transfer to Cemetery."

APPENDIX

A comparison of the soundtrack album releases of North's score for *A Streetcar Named Desire* for Capitol and Varese Sarabande.

Capitol Records CAP L289 (1951), conducted by Ray Heindorf

Track Listing	Cue name and Reel/Part number (from Warner Bros. cue sheet)
1. Streetcar	Belle Reve (Main Title), 17 bars
2. Four Deuces	Stan and Stella (R5: P3), (10 bars) then Stan (R2: P3) from b. 3
3. Belle Reve	Soliloquy (R7: P1)
4. Blanche	Blanche and Mitch (R5: P4) and (R8: P2) and (R7: P1a)
5. Della Robia Blue	Birthday Party (R10: P2) and Blanche's Solitude (R10: P3)
6. Flores para los Muertos	Revelation (R11: P1)
7. Mania	Scherzo (R11: P2 and R12: P1)
8. Lust	Stan Meets Blanche (R3: P1) and Seduction (R13: P1)
9. Soliloquy	Doctor (R14: P1)
10. Redemption	Affirmation (R14: P2)

Varese Sarabande LC6083 (1995), conducted by Jerry Goldsmith

Track Listing	Cue name and Reel/Part number (name given only when different)
1. A Streetcar Named Desire (Main Title)	Belle Reve (Main Title)
2. New Orleans Street	New Orleans Street (R1: P3—not used in film)
3. Belle Reve Reflections	(R2: P2)
4. Stan Meets Blanche	(R3: P1)
5. Blanche and Mitch	(R8: P2)
6. Stan and Stella	(R5: P3) as per original/restored
7. Blanche	Blanche and Mitch (R4: P1b)
8. Belle Reve	Soliloquy (R7: P1)
9. Birthday Party	(R10: P2)
10. Revelation	(R11: P1)
11. Mania	Scherzo (R11: P2 and R12: P1)
12. Soliloquy	Collector (R7: P2)
13. Seduction	(R13: P1)
14. Della Robia Blue	Soliloquy (R13: P2)
15. The Doctor/Affirmation	(R14: P1 and R14: P2)

BIBLIOGRAPHY

Adler, Thomas P. *A Streetcar Named Desire: The Moth and the Lantern*. Boston: Twayne, 1990.

Alexander, William. "Frontier Films, 1936–1941: The Aesthetics of Impact." *Cinema Journal* 15, no. 1 (Autumn 1975): 16–28.

Atkinson, Brooks. "*Death of a Salesman:* Arthur Miller's Tragedy of an Ordinary Man." *New York Times*, 20 February 1949.

Atkinson, Brooks. "*The Innocents:* A Ghost Story from Henry James' *The Turn of the Screw*." *New York Times*, 2 February 1950.

Bak, John S. "Criticism on *A Streetcar Named Desire*: A Bibliographic Survey, 1947–2003." *Cercles* 10 (2004): 3–32.

[n.a.] *Ball-room Dancing Without a Master, and Complete Guide to the Etiquette, Toilet, Dress and Management of the Ball-room; With All the Principal Dances in Popular Use*. New York: Hurst and Co., c. 1872. Extracts of the book are viewable online as part of the Library of Congress *American Memory* project, An American Ballroom Companion: Dance Instruction Manuals memory.loc.gov /ammem/dihtml/dihome.html (6 July 2006).

Bazelon, Irwin. *Knowing the Score: Notes on Film Music*. New York: Van Nostrand Reinhold Co., 1975.

Behlmer, Rudy. "Alex North on *A Streetcar Named Desire*." *The Cue Sheet* 3, no. 3 (September 1986): 36–38.

Behlmer, Rudy, ed. *Inside Warner Brothers (1935–1951)*. London: Weidenfield and Nicolson, 1986.

"Bernstein Leads Three Premieres," *New York Times*, 19 November 1946, 40. H.T.

Bigsby, C.W.E. *A Critical Introduction to Twentieth-Century American Drama, Vol. 2. Tennessee Williams, Arthur Miller, Edward Albee*. Cambridge: Cambridge University Press, 1984.

Black, Gregory D. *The Catholic Crusade Against the Movies, 1940–1975*. Cambridge: Cambridge University Press, 1998.

Braun, Edward. *Meyerhold: A Revolution in Theatre* [2nd revised edition]. London: Methuen, 1995.

Brown, Maurice J. E. "Varsovienne (Fr.; It. varsoviana)," *Grove Music Online*, ed. L. Macy, www.grovemusic.com (5 July 2006).

Brown, Royal S. *Overtones and Undertones: Reading Film Music*. Berkeley: University of California Press, 1984.

Burt, George. *The Art of Film Music: Special Emphasis on Hugo Friedhofer, Alex North, David Raksin, Leonard Rosenman*. Boston: Northeastern University Press, 1994.

Butler, David. *Jazz Noir: Listening to Music from* Phantom Lady *to* The Last Seduction. Westport, CT: Praeger, 2002.

Cahir, Linda Costanzo. "The Artful Rerouting of *A Streetcar Named Desire*." *Literature/Film Quarterly* 22, no. 2 (1994): 72–77.

Care, Ross. "Hot Spell: Alex North's Film Score for *A Streetcar Named Desire*." *Performing Arts Annual* (1989): 4–23.

Casey, Betty. *Dancing Across Texas*. Austin: University of Texas Press, 1985.

Chesler, Alan S. "*A Streetcar Named Desire*: Twenty-Five Years of Criticism." *Notes on Mississippi Writers* 7 (1973): 44–53.

Ciment, Michael, ed. *Kazan on Kazan*. New York: Viking Press, 1974.

"C.I.O. Chorus: Alex North's *Morning Star* Featured in Concert." *New York Herald Tribune*, 26 May 1947, 17. A.V.B.

Cloud, David, and Leslie Zador. "Alex North Interview: The Missing Score for '2001.'" *Los Angeles Free Press* 7, no. 48 (November 27, 1970): 39, 42.

Clum, John. *Acting Gay: Male Homosexuality in American Drama*. New York: Columbia University Press, 1992.

Cohn, Ruby. *Dialogue in American Drama*. Bloomington: Indiana University Press, 1971.

Cooke, Mervyn. *A History of Film Music*. Cambridge: Cambridge University Press, 2008.

Cooke, Mervyn. "Anatomy of a Movie: Duke Ellington and 1950s Film Scoring." In *Thriving on a Riff: Jazz and Blues Influences in African American Literature and Film*, edited by Graham Lock and David Murray. New York: Oxford University Press, 2009.

Copland, Aaron, and Vivian Perlis. *Copland: Since 1943*. New York: St. Martin's Press, 1989.

Corrigan, Mary Ann. "Realism and Theatricalism." 49–60 in *Modern Critical Interpretations: Tennessee Williams's* A Streetcar Named

Desire, edited by Harold Bloom. New York and Philadelphia: Chelsea House Publishers, 1988.

Crist, Elizabeth B. *Music for the Common Man: Aaron Copland During the Depression and War.* New York: Oxford University Press, 2005.

Daubney, Kate. *Max Steiner's* Now, Voyager: *A Film Score Guide.* Westport, CT: Greenwood Press, 2000.

Dickson, Vivienne. "*A Streetcar Named Desire*: Its Development Through the Manuscripts." 154–171 in *Tennessee Williams: A Tribute*, edited by Jac Tharpe. Jackson: University Press of Mississippi, 1977.

Dowling, Ellen. "The Derailment of *A Streetcar Named Desire.*" *Literature/Film Quarterly* 9, no. 4 (1981): 233–240.

Downing, Robert. "Streetcar Conductor: Some Notes from Backstage." *Theatre Annual* 8 (1950): 25–33.

Dyer, Richard. *White: Essays on Race and Culture.* London: Routledge, 1997.

Farber, Stephen. "Alex North and His Oscar Make Musical Movie History." *New York Times*, 30 March 1986: 17.

Farfan, Penny. "Music." 156–158 in *The Tennessee Williams Encyclopedia*, edited by Philip C. Kolin. Westport, CT, and London: Greenwood Press, 2004.

Ferrero, Edward. *The Art of Dancing, Historically Illustrated.* New York: Edward Ferrero, 1859.

Flinn, Caryl. *Strains of Utopia: Gender, Nostalgia, and Hollywood Film Music.* Princeton, NJ: Princeton University Press, 1992.

Frith, Simon. *Performing Rites: On the Value of Popular Music.* Oxford: Oxford University Press, 1996.

Gann, Kyle (with Kurt Stone). "Henry Brant." *Grove Music Online*, edited by L. Macy, www.grovemusic.com (12 December 2006).

Geraghty, Christine. *Now a Major Motion Picture: Film Adaptations of Literature and Drama.* Lanham, MD: Rowman & Littlefield, 2008.

Gloag, Kenneth. "Russian Rites: *Petrushka, The Rite of Spring*, and *Les Noces.*" 79–97 in *The Cambridge Companion to Stravinsky*, edited by Jonathan Cross. Cambridge: Cambridge University Press, 2003.

Hanks, Pamela Ann. "Must We Acknowledge What We Mean? The Viewer's Role in Filmed Versions of *A Streetcar Named Desire.*" *Journal of Popular Film and Television* 14, no. 3 (Fall 1986): 114–122.

Hastings, Chris. "Da Vinci Code Music—Not the Killing—Is Too Scary for Children, Say Censors." *Telegraph Online*, www

.telegraph.co.uk/news/main.jhtml?xml=/news/2006/05/07/ncode07 .xml (2 January 2007).

Hatch, Kristen. "Movies and the New Faces of Masculinity." 43–64 in *American Cinema of the 1950s: Themes and Variations*, edited by Murray Pomerance. Oxford: Berg, 2005.

Henderson, Sanya Shoilevska. *Alex North: Film Composer*. Jefferson, NC, and London: McFarland & Co., 2003.

Hirsch, Foster. *A Method to Their Madness: The History of the Actors Studio*. New York and London: W. W. Norton and Co., 1984.

Huffman, Nicole. "New Frontiers in American Documentary Film." Unpublished master's thesis, American Studies, University of Virginia, 2001. See also http://xroads.virginia.edu/~MA01/Huffman /Frontier/frontier.html (17 November 2006).

"Joan Slessinger Heard in Town Hall." *New York Sun*, 22 September 1947. H.C.S.

Johns, Sarah Boyd. "Williams' Journey to 'Streetcar': An Analysis of Pre-Production Manuscripts of 'A Streetcar Named Desire.'" PhD thesis, University of South Carolina, 1980.

Kazan, Elia. "Pressure Problem: Director Discusses Cuts Compelled in *A Streetcar Named Desire*." *New York Times*, 21 October 1951.

Kazan, Elia. "Notebook for *A Streetcar Named Desire*." 364–379 in *Directors on Directing: A Source Book of the Modern Theatre*, edited by Toby Cole and Helen Krich Chinoy. London: Peter Owen, 1973.

Kazan, Elia. *A Life*. London: André Deutsch, 1988.

Kendall, Raymond. "Saga of Hollywood Music: North Composes for Stage, Screen." *Mirror News* (Los Angeles), 12 October 1959. P2: 5.

Kolin, Philip C. "The First Critical Assessments of *A Streetcar Named Desire*: The *Streetcar* Tryouts and the Reviewers." *Journal of Dramatic Theory and Criticism* 6, no. 1 (Fall 1991): 45–68.

Kolin, Philip C. *Williams: A Streetcar Named Desire (Plays in Production)*. Cambridge: Cambridge University Press, 2000.

Kolin, Philip C., ed. *Confronting Tennessee Williams's A Streetcar Named Desire: Essays in Critical Pluralism*. Westport, CT, and London: Greenwood Press, 1993.

Kolin, Philip C., ed. *Tennessee Williams: A Guide to Research and Performance*. Westport, CT: Greenwood Press, 1998.

Kolin, Philip C., ed. *The Tennessee Williams Encyclopedia*. Westport, CT, and London: Greenwood Press, 2004.

Kozlenko, William. "Soviet Music and Musicians." *Musical Quarterly* 23, no. 3 (July 1937): 295–305.

Kraft, David. "A Conversation with Alex North." *Soundtrack! The Collector's Quarterly* 4, no. 13 (March 1985): 3–8.

Kuntz, Andrew. *The Fiddler's Companion: A Descriptive Index of North American and British Isles Music for the Folk Violin and Other Instruments.* An online resource available via http://ibiblio .org/fiddlers/index.html (5 July 2006).

Law, Alma H., and Mel Gordon. *Meyerhold, Eisenstein and Biomechanics: Actor Training in Revolutionary Russia.* Jefferson, NC, and London: McFarland & Co., 1996.

Leff, Leonard J. "And Transfer to Cemetery: The Streetcars Named Desire." *Film Quarterly* 55, no. 3 (Spring 2002): 29–37.

Leff, Leonard J., and Jerrold Simmons. *The Dame in the Kimono: Hollywood Censorship, and the Production Code.* Revised edition. Lexington: University Press of Kentucky, 2001.

Lewin, Frank. *"A Street Car Named Desire." Film Music* 11, no. 3 (January–February 1952): 13–20.

Lloyd, Norman. [untitled introduction], *Film Music* 15, no. 2 (Winter 1955): 3.

Londré, Felicia Hardison. "A *Streetcar* Running Fifty Years." 45–66 in *The Cambridge Companion to Tennessee Williams,* edited by Matthew C. Roudané. Cambridge: Cambridge University Press, 1997.

Maltby, Richard. "More Sinned Against Than Sinning: The Fabrications of 'Pre-Code Cinema.'" *Senses of Cinema* Issue 29 (November–December 2003), www.sensesofcinema.com/contents/03/29 /pre_code_cinema.html (6 February 2007).

Martin, John. "The Dance: New Blood." *New York Times,* 29 August 1937.

Martin, John. "Dance Debut Here by Anna Sokolow." *New York Times,* 15 November 1937.

Martin, John. "Ballet Company Stages 'Streetcar.'" *New York Times,* 9 December 1952.

McCall, Martin. "American Ballad Singers and Young Composer Heard in Excellent Programs." *Daily Worker* [New York], 22 February 1940, 7.

McCraw, Harry W. "Tennessee Williams, Film, Music, Alex North: An Interview with Luigi Zaninelli." *Mississippi Quarterly: The Journal of Southern Culture* 48, no. 4 (1995): 763–775.

McDonagh, Michael. "North by North's Wife." *21st Century Music* 7, no. 4 (April 2000): 1–5.

McMurry, William J., Jr. "Music in Selected Works of Tennessee Williams." EdD dissertation, East Texas State University, 1982.

Mehegan, John. *Tonal and Rhythmic Principles* (Series on Jazz Improvisation). New York: Watson-Guptill Publications, 1959.

Miller, Arthur. "Introduction." ix–xiv in Tennessee Williams, *A Streetcar Named Desire*. New York: New Directions, 1947/2004.

Miller, Jordan Yale, ed. *Twentieth Century Interpretations of* A Streetcar Named Desire: *A Collection of Critical Essays*. Englewood Cliffs, NJ: Prentice-Hall, 1971.

Moschovakis, Nick. "Tennessee Williams's American Blues: From the Early Manuscripts through *Menagerie*." *Tennessee Williams Annual Review* 7 (2005). Available online at www.tennesseewilliams studies.org/archives/2005/02moschovakis.htm (27 April 2007).

Murphy, Brenda. *Tennessee Williams and Elia Kazan: A Collaboration in Theatre*. Cambridge: Cambridge University Press, 1992.

Navasky, Victor. *Naming Names*. New York: Viking Press, 1980.

North, Alex. "Composer Sends Message from Camp." *Hartford Times*, 12 April 1943.

North, Alex. "Notes on the Score of *The Rose Tattoo*." *Film Music* 15, no. 2 (Winter 1955): 3–15.

North, Alex. "Notes on *The Rainmaker*." *Film and TV Music* 16, no. 3 (Spring 1957): 3–16.

Palmer, Christopher. "Film Music Profile: Alex North." *Crescendo International* (April 1975): 28–29, 32.

Palmer, R. Barton. "Hollywood in Crisis: Tennessee Williams and the Evolution of the Adult Film." 204–231 in *The Cambridge Companion to Tennessee Williams*, edited by Matthew C. Roudané. Cambridge: Cambridge University Press, 1997.

Paris, Barry. "A Knight at the Opera." *Vanity Fair* (September 1998): 222–234.

"Philharmonic Performs for Children Under Nine." *New York Herald Tribune*, 19 October 1947. J.S.H.

Phillips, Gene D. *The Films of Tennessee Williams*. Philadelphia: Art Alliance Press; London and Toronto: Associated University Presses, 1980.

Phillips, Gene D. "*A Streetcar Named Desire*: Play and Film." 223–235 in *Confronting Tennessee Williams's* A Streetcar Named Desire: *Essays in Critical Pluralism*, edited by Philip C. Kolin. Westport, CT, and London: Greenwood Press, 1993.

Raksin, David. "The Subject Is Film Music." An interview with Alex North as a part of the Yale University oral history program (American Music Series). Transcription by Fred Karlin.

Reisner, Joel, and Bruce Kane. "An Interview with Alex North." *Cinema* 5, no. 4 (December 1969): 42–45.

Roudané, Matthew C., ed. *The Cambridge Companion to Tennessee Williams*. Cambridge: Cambridge University Press, 1997.

Schatz, Thomas. *The Genius of the System: Hollywood Filmmaking in the Studio Era*. New York: Pantheon Books, 1988.

Schatz, Thomas. *Boom and Bust: The American Cinema in the 1940s*. Volume 6 of *History of the American Cinema*, Charles Harpole, general editor. New York: Charles Scribner's Sons, 1997.

Schuller, Gunther. *The Swing Era: The Development of Jazz, 1930–1945*. New York: Oxford University Press, 1991.

Schuller, Gunther. "Arrangement." *Grove Music Online*, ed. L. Macy, www.grovemusic.com (19 June 2008).

Schumach, Murray. "Play's Tunes Piped from Padded Cell." *New York Times*, 16 March 1949, XI.

Schumach, Murray. *The Face on the Cutting Room Floor: The Story of Movie and Television Censorship*. New York: William Morrow, 1964.

Shapiro, Anne Dhu. "Melodrama," *Grove Music Online*, ed. L. Macy, www.grovemusic.com (18 June 2008).

Sherk, Warren. "Welcome to Hollywood: Alex North's Unused Score for *Distant Drums* (1951)." *The Cue Sheet* 16, no. 2 (April 2000): 21–30.

Shipton, Alyn. *A New History of Jazz*. London and New York: Continuum, 2001.

Siegmeister, Elie, ed. *The Music Lover's Handbook*. New York: William Morrow and Company, 1943.

Stanford, Thomas, and A. Chamorro. "Mexico." *Grove Music Online*, ed. L. Macy, www.grovemusic.com (16 February 2007).

Strong, Barbara. "Theatre: Not So Incidental." *Concerto* (February 1950), 5–6.

Sutak, Ken. "The Return of 'A Streetcar Named Desire.'" (1/3) *Pro Musica Sana* 3, no. 1 (Spring 1974): 4–10; (2/3) *Pro Musica Sana* 3, no. 4 (Winter 1974/75: 9–15; (3/3) *Pro Musica Sana* 4, no. 3 (1976): 13–18.

Tagg, Philip, and Bob Clarida. *Ten Little Title Tunes: Towards a Musicology of the Mass Media*. New York and Montreal: Mass Media Music Scholars' Press, 2003.

Taubman, Howard. "Plays with Music Between the Lines." *New York Times*, 27 March 1949.

Tharpe, Jac, ed. *Tennessee Williams: A Tribute*. Jackson: University Press of Mississippi, 1977.

Thomas, Tony. *Music for the Movies*. London: Tantivy Press, 1973.

Thomas, Tony, ed. *Film Score: The View from the Podium.* London: Thomas Yoseloff Ltd., 1979.

Tischler, Nancy. *Tennessee Williams: Rebellious Puritan.* New York: Citadel Press, 1961.

Van Duyvenbode, Rachel. "Darkness Made Visible: Miscegenation, Masquerade and the Signified Racial Other in Tennessee Williams' *Baby Doll* and *A Streetcar Named Desire.*" *Journal of American Studies* 35, no. 2 (2001), 203–215.

Vlasopolos, Anca. "Authorizing History: Victimization in *A Streetcar Named Desire.*" *Theatre Journal* 38 (October 1986): 322–338.

Walsh, Frank. *Sin and Censorship: The Catholic Church and the Motion Picture Industry.* New Haven, CT, and London: Yale University Press, 1996.

Warren, Larry. *Anna Sokolow: The Rebellious Spirit.* Amsterdam: Harwood Academic Publishers, 1998.

Watt, Douglas. "Back to New Orleans." *New Yorker,* 20 December 1952.

Williams, Tennessee. *A Streetcar Named Desire* [Reading Version]. New York: New Directions Publishing Corporation, 1947/2004.

Williams, Tennessee. *The Glass Menagerie* [Acting Version]. New York: Dramatists Play Service, 1948.

Winters, Ben. *Erich Wolfgang Korngold's* The Adventures of Robin Hood: *A Film Score Guide.* Lanham, MD: Scarecrow Press, 2007.

Wood, Audrey, with Max Wilk. *Represented by Audrey Wood.* Garden City, NY: Doubleday, 1981.

Yacowar, Maurice. *Tennessee Williams and Film.* New York: Ungar, 1977.

INDEX

ABOUT THE AUTHOR

Annette Davison completed her doctorate on film music theory and analysis at the University of Sheffield. She taught at the University of Leeds for several years and joined Music at the University of Edinburgh in 2004. Her first monograph, *Hollywood Theory, Non-Hollywood Practice: Cinema Soundtracks in the 1980s and 1990s*, was published by Ashgate in 2004. She co-edited a collection of essays (with Erica Sheen), *American Dreams, Nightmare Visions: The Cinema of David Lynch*, which was published by Wallflower in 2004. Dr. Davison has also contributed essays to a number of books and journals.